IN ACTION

Measuring Return on Investment

VOLUME 3

ELEVEN

CASE STUDIES

FROM THE

REAL WORLD

OF TRAINING

JACK J. PHILLIPS

SERIES EDITOR

PATRICIA PULLIAM PHILLIPS

EDITOR

D0763449

Ordering information: Books published by ASTD can be ordered by calling 800.628.2783 or 703.683.8100, or via the Website at www.astd.org.

Library of Congress Catalog Card Number: 2001087840

ISBN: 1-56286-288-X

Table of Contents

Introduction to the
In Action Series

Like most professionals, the people involved in human resource development (HRD) are eager to see practical applications of models, techniques, theories, strategies, and issues relevant to their field. In recent years, practitioners have developed an intense desire to learn about the firsthand experiences of organizations implementing HRD programs. To fill this critical void, the Publishing Review Committee of the American Society for Training & Development established the *In Action* casebook series. Covering a variety of topics in HRD, the series significantly adds to the current literature in the field.

The *In Action* series objectives are:

- *To provide real-world examples of HRD program application and implementation.* Each case describes significant issues, events, actions, and activities. When possible, actual names of organizations and individuals are used. Where names are disguised, the events are factual.

- *To focus on challenging and difficult issues confronting the HRD field.* These cases explore areas where it is difficult to find information or where processes or techniques are not standardized or fully developed. Emerging issues critical to success are also explored.

- *To recognize the work of professionals in the HRD field by presenting best practices.* Each casebook represents the most effective examples available. Issue editors are experienced professionals, and topics are carefully selected to ensure that they represent important and timely issues. Cases are written by highly respected HRD practitioners, authors, researchers, and consultants. The authors focus on many high-profile organizations—names you will quickly recognize.

- *To serve as a self-teaching tool for people learning about the HRD field.* As a stand-alone reference, each volume is a practical learning tool that fully explores numerous topics and issues.

- *To present a medium for teaching groups about the practical aspects of HRD.* Each book is a useful supplement to general and specialized

HRD textbooks and serves as a discussion guide to enhance learning in formal and informal settings.

These cases will challenge and motivate you. The new insights you gain will serve as an impetus for positive change in your organization. If you have a case that might serve the same purpose for other HRD professionals, please contact me. New casebooks are being developed. If you have suggestions on ways to improve the *In Action* series, your input is welcomed.

Jack J. Phillips
Series Editor
Box 380637
Birmingham, AL 35238-0637

Preface

Since the publication of *Measuring Return on Investment,* volume 1, the interest in measuring the return on investment (ROI) in training and performance improvement continues to grow. Volume 1 filled an important void in the training literature. Published in 1994, it remains one of ASTD's all-time best-sellers. Volume 2, published in 1997, demonstrated further progress with measuring the return on investment in a variety of programs.

We hope to repeat the success of the first two volumes with the case studies in volume 3. *Measuring Return on Investment,* volume 3, incorporates case studies from a variety of industries including telecommunications, computer and technology, retail stores, automotive, and the government sector. The authors of these case studies are diligently pursuing accountability in training and performance improvement programs. Through their writing, they share their experiences with a process that continues to be at the forefront of measurement and evaluation.

Target Audience

The book should interest anyone involved in training, human resource development, human resources, and performance improvement. The primary audience is practitioners who are struggling to determine the value of programs and to show how programs contribute to the strategic goals of the organization. They are the ones who request more real-word examples. This same group also expresses concern that there are too many models, methods, strategies, and theories, and too few examples to show if any of them has really made a difference. This publication should satisfy practitioners' needs, by providing successful examples of the implementation of comprehensive evaluation processes.

The second audience comprises instructors and professors. Whether they choose this book for students in university classes who are pursuing degrees in HRD, internal workshops for professional HRD staff members, or public seminars on HRD implementation, the casebook will be a valuable reference. It can be used as a supplement to a standard HRD textbook. In our workshops on ROI in training and performance improvement, we use casebooks as supplements to the textbook *Handbook of Training Evaluation and Measurement Methods,* by Jack Phillips, published in 1997. This combination of text and casebooks offers the technical details of the measurement and evaluation process along with examples of practical applications, which together show participants that the measurement and evaluation process makes a difference.

A third audience is composed of the researchers and consultants who are seeking ways to document results from programs. This book provides additional insight into how to satisfy the client with impressive results. It shows the application of a wide range of models and techniques, some of which are based on sound theory and logical assumptions and others of which may not fare well under close examination. Unfortunately, the HRD measurement and evaluation process does not have a prescribed set of standards and techniques, although the case studies in this volume represent steps and methodologies that are becoming routine practices.

The last audience is made up of managers who must work with HRD on a peripheral basis—managers who are participants in HRD programs to develop their own management skills, managers who send other employees to participate in HRD programs, and managers who occasionally lead or conduct sessions of HRD programs. In these roles, managers must understand the process and appreciate the value of HRD. This casebook should provide evidence of this value.

Each audience should find the casebook entertaining and engaging reading. Questions are placed at the end of each case to stimulate additional thought and discussion. One of the most effective ways to maximize the usefulness of this book is through group discussions, using the questions to develop and dissect the issues, techniques, methodologies, and results.

The Cases

The most difficult part of developing this book was to identify case authors who were implementing a credible and practical process to measure the ROI of training and performance improvement programs and were willing to share their experience. The author sent letters soliciting cases to approximately 13,000 people who have expressed interest in measurement and evaluation, including 1,500 abroad, in order to tap the global market. We were pleased with the number of responses and have selected 11 case studies to be presented in this volume.

The case studies we selected met very specific guidelines. Each case study includes data that can be converted to a monetary value so that ROI can be calculated. This fifth level of Donald Kirkpatrick's four-level evaluation framework, created by Jack Phillips, aligns the return on the training and performance improvement investment with that of other operational investments in organizations. (A description of Kirkpatrick's evaluation framework appears in his book *Evaluating Training Programs,* published in 1998. Further information on the fifth level is available in Phillips' article "The Search for Best Practices" in the February 1996 issue of *Training & Development.)* The selected case studies also provide a method of isolating the effects of the training and performance improvement program. The isolation step is imperative in showing the true value of a program. Although volumes 1 and 2 did not require this step, volume 3 recognizes its importance and required that all case studies include some method to isolate the effects of the program. Methodologies included in the case studies presented in this book are control groups, trend-line analysis, forecasting, and participant and manager estimates.

Although there was some attempt to structure cases similarly, they are not identical in style and content. It is important for the reader to experience the programs as they were developed and identify the issues pertinent to each particular setting and situation. The result is a variety of presentations with a variety of styles. Some cases are brief and to the point, outlining precisely what happened and what was achieved. Others provide more detailed background information, including how the need for the program was determined, the personalities involved, and how their backgrounds and biases created a unique situation.

In some cases, the name of the organization is identified, as are the individuals who were involved. In others, the organization's name is disguised at the request of either the organization or the case author. In today's competitive world and in situations where there is an attempt to explore new territory, it is understandable why an organization would choose not to be identified. Identification should not be a critical issue, however. Though some cases are lightly modified, they are based on real-world situations faced by real people.

Case Authors

It would be difficult to find a more impressive group of contributors than those for this casebook. For such a difficult topic, we expected to find the best, and we were not disappointed. If we had to describe the group, we would say they are experienced, professional, knowledgeable, and on the leading edge of HRD. Collectively, they represent practitioners, consultants, researchers, and professors. Individually, they represent a cross section of HRD. Most are experts, and some are well known in the field. A few are high-profile authors who have made a tremendous contribution to HRD and have taken the opportunity to provide an example of their top-quality work. Others have made their mark quietly and have achieved success for their organizations.

Best Practices?

In our search for cases, we contacted the most respected and well-known organizations in the world, leading experts in the field, key executives in HRD, and prominent authors and researchers. We were seeking examples that represent best practices in measurement and evaluation. Whether they have been delivered, we will never know. What we do know is that if these are not best practices, no other publication can claim to have them either. Many of the experts producing these cases characterize them as the best examples of measurement and evaluation in the field.

Suggestions

We welcome your input. If you have ideas or recommendations regarding presentation, case selection, or case quality, please send them to me. You can contact me with your comments and suggestions at The Chelsea Group, PO Box 380637, Birmingham, AL 30543, or email me at thechelseagroup@aol.com.

Acknowledgments

Although this casebook is a collective work of many individuals, the first acknowledgment must go to all the case authors. They are appreciated not only for their commitment to developing their case studies, but also for their interest in furthering the development and implementation of ROI evaluation in their organization. We also want to acknowledge the organizations that have allowed us to use their names and programs for publication. We realize this action is not without risk. We trust the final product has portrayed them as progressive organizations interested in results and willing to try new processes and techniques.

I would also like to thank Katherine Sanner and Jaime Beard who have provided support in developing this casebook. Their help in soliciting case studies, working with case authors, and assisting me throughout the process is greatly appreciated.

Many thanks go to Kelly Perkins who provided assistance in developing case guidelines and in the initial stages of producing the casebook. Also, great appreciation goes to Joyce Alff who provided editorial assistance and managed the casebook process to ensure a smooth transition from case author to ASTD.

Many thanks goes to Nancy Olson, ASTD's vice president of publications, and Ruth Stadius, ASTD's manager of book publishing. Nancy and Ruth are always supportive and willing to help to ensure the success of each publication. They have a sincere interest in providing quality and meaningful publications to HRD professionals.

Finally, many, many thanks go to my husband, Jack Phillips, for his support, encouragement, and assistance through the development of this book. Through his work and the development of the ROI process, Jack has provided the industry with an opportunity to show the value that training and performance improvement programs bring to an organization. I appreciate the opportunity to work with him in such an exciting and important field.

Patricia Pulliam Phillips
Birmingham, Alabama
April 2001

How to Use This Casebook

These cases present a variety of approaches to evaluating training and performance improvement programs in HRD. Most of the cases focus on evaluation at the ultimate level—return on investment (ROI). Collectively, the cases offer a wide range of settings, methods, techniques, strategies, and approaches and represent manufacturing, service, and governmental organizations. Target groups for the programs vary from all employees to managers to technical specialists. Although most of the programs focus on training and development, others include organization development and performance management. As a group, these cases represent a rich source of information about the strategies of some of the best practitioners, consultants, and researchers in the field.

Each case does not necessarily represent the ideal approach for the specific situation. In every case it is possible to identify areas that could benefit from refinement and improvement. That is part of the learning process—to build on the work of other people. Although the implementation processes are contextual, the methods and techniques can be used in other organizations.

Table 1 represents basic descriptions of the cases in the order in which they appear in the book. This table can serve as a quick reference for readers who want to examine the implementation approach for a particular type of program, audience, or industry.

Using the Cases

There are several ways to use this book. It will be helpful to anyone who wants to see real-life examples of the return on investment of training and performance improvement. Specifically, the author recommends the following four uses:

- This book will be useful to HRD professionals as a basic reference of practical applications of measurement and evaluation. A reader can analyze and dissect each of the cases to develop an understanding of the issues, approaches, and, most of all, possible refinements or improvements.

Table 1. Overview of case studies.

Case	Industry	HRD Program	Target Audience
Cracker Box, Inc.	Restaurant	Performance management training	Managers, manager trainees
Apple Computer	Computer manufacturing	Process improvement	Training and development consultants, executives, and operations managers
Hewlett-Packard Company	Computer support services	Sales training	Inside sales management team, inside sales representatives
First Union National Bank	Financial services	Sales training	Sales representatives, sales managers
Focus Corporation	Computer manufacturing	Process improvement	Production managers, production employees
Verizon Communications	Telecommunications	Customer service skills training	Training practitioners, customer service managers
Global Automotive Corporation	Automotive manufacturing	Sales launch training	Sales representatives, all employees
Slick Manufacturing	Manufacturing	Computer training	Managers
Nassau County Police Department	Police department	Interpersonal skills training	Officer manager, police officers
Miami VA Medical Center	Health care	Self-mastery training	All employees
Retail Merchandise Company	Retail stores	Interactive selling skills training	Sales associates, sales managers

- This book will be useful in group discussions in which interested individuals can react to the material, offer different perspectives, and draw conclusions about approaches and techniques. The questions at the end of each case can serve as a beginning point for lively and entertaining discussions.
- This book will serve as a supplement to other training and performance improvement or evaluation textbooks. It provides the extra dimensions of real-life cases that show the outcomes of training and performance improvement.
- Finally, this book will be extremely valuable for managers who do not have primary training and performance improvement responsibility. These managers provide support and assistance to the HRD staff, and it is helpful for them to understand the results that HRD programs can yield.

It is important to remember that each organization and its program implementation are unique. What works well for one may not work for another, even if they are in similar settings. The book offers a variety of approaches and provides an arsenal of tools from which to choose in the evaluation process.

Follow-Up

Space limitations necessitated that some cases be shorter than the author and editor would have liked. Some information concerning background, assumptions, strategies, and results had to be omitted. If additional information on a case is needed, the lead author can be contacted directly. The lead authors' addresses are listed at the end of each case.

The ROI Process:
Trends and Issues

Patricia Pulliam Phillips

The trend to evaluate the business impact of training and performance improvement programs is continuing as increasing numbers of organizations worldwide undertake these evaluations. Executives and managers want to see the economic contributions—including return on investment (ROI)—that training and performance improvement programs bring to their organizations. Globally, interest in measurement and evaluation is spreading, and many learning opportunities are focused on them. Consulting organizations throughout the United States, Canada, Europe, the United Kingdom, and the Asia-Pacific region are promoting and implementing measurement processes and ROI.

An increased number of resources are available that address ROI. Whether through newsletters, articles, books, Websites, listservs, or online chat rooms, a variety of audiences in a variety of industries are discussing the topic. One process—the ROI process—is being used by hundreds of organizations in 31 countries (Phillips, 1997). This unique process provides a balanced view of training and performance improvement effectiveness by developing six types of measures that provide a complete picture of their contribution to the organization.

The Status of Measurement and Evaluation

There are 10 specific measurement and evaluation trends. They are:
1. Evaluation is an integral part of the instructional system design process, a part of every model.
2. Evaluation is shifting from a reactive to proactive approach within the training and performance improvement function.

3. Measurement and evaluation processes are systematic and methodical, often built into the training and performance improvement process.
4. Technology is significantly enhancing the measurement and evaluation process.
5. Evaluation planning is becoming a critical part of the measurement and evaluation cycle.
6. The implementation of a comprehensive measurement and evaluation process usually leads to increased emphasis on the front-end analysis.
7. Organizations without comprehensive measurement and evaluation have reduced or eliminated their training and performance budgets.
8. Organizations with comprehensive measurement and evaluation have enhanced their training and performance budgets.
9. There are many successful examples of comprehensive measurement and evaluation applications.
10. A comprehensive measurement and evaluation process can be implemented for about 4 percent or 5 percent of the direct training and performance improvement budget.

Along with these trends are significant drivers for moving evaluation of training and performance improvement to the same level as that of other business processes. For centuries, the concept of ROI has been used to place a value on the payoff of capital investments. Businesses have long used the classical definition of *ROI*, earnings divided by investment, to show the contribution of plant and equipment to the organization. Now, they are using this same concept to place a value on the contribution of other processes such as quality, technology, human resources, and training and performance improvement.

The first and foremost reason for this growing interest in ROI is that an estimated $500 billion is spent on training and performance improvement. Over $15 billion is spent on global executive education alone. The average operating budget for 175 organizations with corporate universities is $15 million. These large expenditures and huge budgets demand increased accountability.

The second reason for the interest in ROI is the heightened awareness of, and increased attention to, measurement throughout organizations. This new focus on measurement places increased pressure on the training and performance improvement function to develop measures of success.

Other reasons for the interest in ROI include the following:
• organization restructuring and reengineering initiatives
• lack of alignment between training and business needs

- competitive pressures on costs and productivity
- the business management mindset of today's training and performance improvement managers
- the persistent trend of accountability in organizations all over the globe.

ROI's success has been phenomenal. The number of organizations and individuals implementing the ROI process underscores the magnitude of ROI implementation, as these figures show.
- The ROI process has been refined over a 20-year period.
- Thousands of studies have been developed using the ROI process.
- One hundred case studies are published on the ROI process.
- Seven hundred individuals are certified to implement the ROI process.
- Organizations in 31 countries have implemented the ROI process.
- Twelve books have been developed to support the process.
- A 400-member professional network has been formed to share information.
- The ROI process has been adopted by hundreds of organizations in manufacturing, service, nonprofit, and government settings.

With this much evidence of the growing interest, the ROI process is becoming a standard tool for evaluation.

Building the Process

The building of a comprehensive measurement and evaluation process is much more involved than the implementation of a statistical process. It includes significant components and is best represented as a puzzle in which the pieces are developed and put in place over time. Figure 1 depicts this puzzle and the individual pieces. The first piece is the selection of an evaluation framework, which is a categorization of data.

The recommended framework for the process is a modification of Kirkpatrick's (1998) four levels to include a fifth level, ROI. The concept of different levels of evaluation is both helpful and instructive in understanding how 0ROI is calculated. Table 1 shows a modified version of Kirkpatrick's four-level framework with the fifth level added to include a cost-benefit comparison.

Next, an ROI process model must be developed showing how data is collected, processed, analyzed, and reported to various target audiences. This process model ensures that appropriate techniques and procedures are consistently used to address almost any measurement issue. Also, there must be consistency as the process is implemented. A description of the ROI process model appears in more detail later.

Figure 1. The pieces of the puzzle.

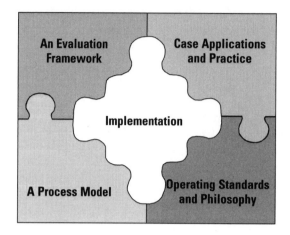

The third piece of the puzzle is the development of operating standards, which provide rules for processing data. Also, these standards help ensure that the results of the study are stable and that the person conducting the study does not overly influence the study. Replication is critical for the credibility of an evaluation process, and operating

Table 1. Five levels of evaluation.

Level	Measurement Focus
1 Reaction, satisfaction, and planned action	Measures participants' reaction to, and satisfaction with, the program and captures planned actions
2 Learning	Measures changes in knowledge, skills, and attitudes
3 Application and implementation	Measures changes in on-the-job behavior and progress with planned actions
4 Business impact	Measures changes in business impact variables
5 Return on investment	Compares program monetary benefits to the costs of the program

standards in the form of guiding principles allow for replication. The following guiding principles have a conservative approach:

- When an evaluation is planned for a higher level, the previous level does not have to be comprehensive.
- When a higher level evaluation is conducted, data must be collected at lower levels.
- When collecting and analyzing data, use the most credible sources.
- When analyzing data, choose the most conservative approach among alternatives.
- At least one method must be used to isolate the effects of the program or initiative.
- If no improvement data is available for a population or from a specific source, it is assumed that little or no improvement occurred.
- Estimates of improvement should be adjusted for the potential error of the estimate.
- Extreme data items and unsupported claims should not be used in ROI calculations.
- The first year of benefits (annual) should be used in the ROI analysis of short-term programs.
- Program costs should be fully loaded for ROI analysis.

Next, appropriate attention must be given to implementation as the ROI process becomes a routine part of the training and performance improvement function. Several issues must be addressed involving skills, communication, roles, responsibilities, plans, and strategies. Implementation was the focus of an earlier *In Action* casebook (Phillips, 1998).

Finally, there must be successful case studies that describe the implementation of the process within an organization, the value that a comprehensive measurement and evaluation process brings to the organization, and the impact specific programs evaluated have on the organization. Although it is helpful to refer to case studies from other organizations, such as those in this casebook, it is more useful and convincing to have a collection of studies developed by the training and performance improvement function within the organization.

The ROI Process

The ROI process is a balanced approach to measuring the impact of training and performance improvement. The process develops a scorecard of six measures (the five in table 1 plus intangible measures). It also includes at least one technique to isolate the effects of the program from other influences. The ROI process model, shown in figure 2, provides a systematic approach to ROI calculations. It shows

Figure 2. The ROI process model.

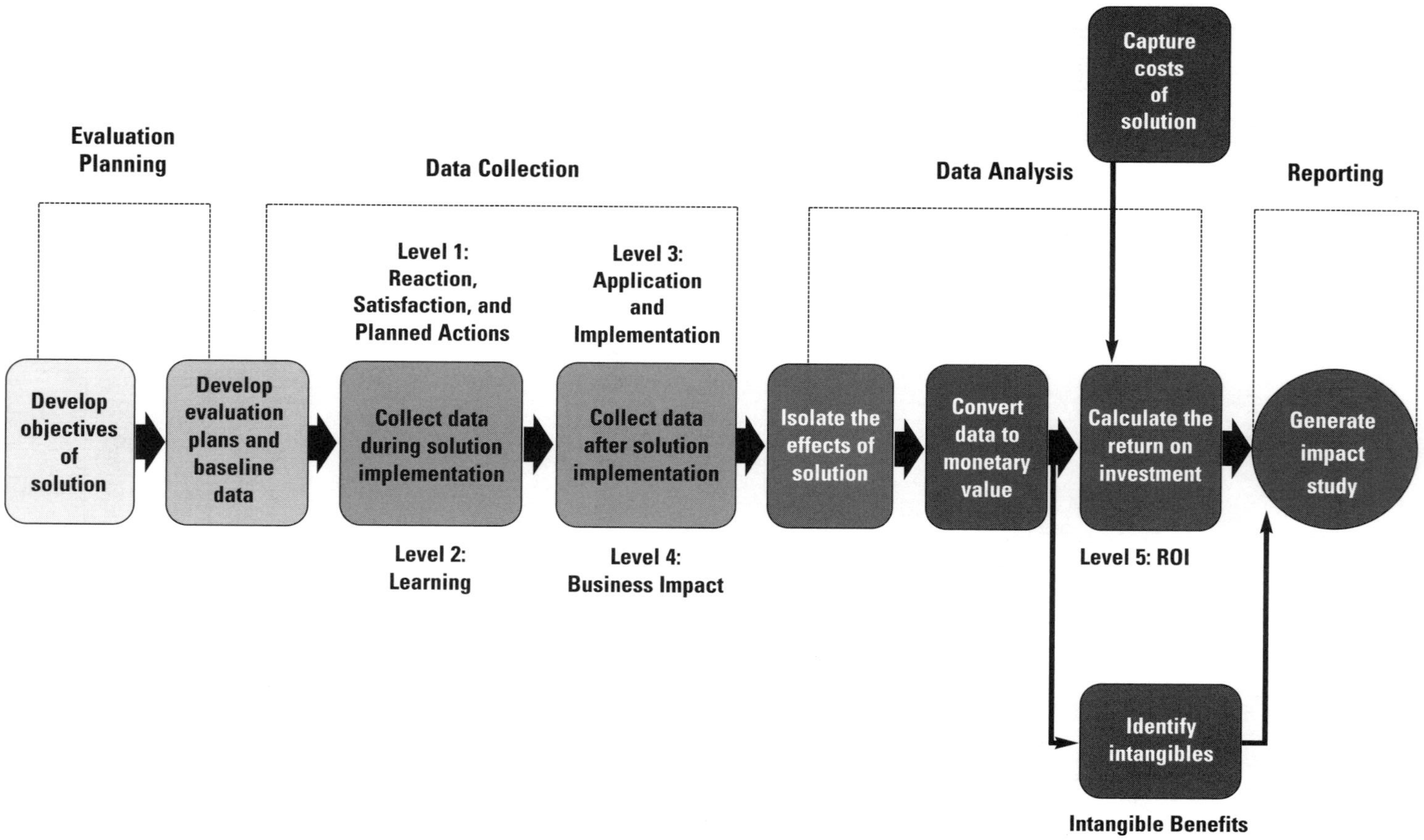

the steps involved in calculating the return on investment of a business performance solution. A step-by-step approach helps keep the process manageable so that practitioners can address one issue at a time. Application of the model provides a consistent methodology from ROI calculation to ROI calculation. Following is a brief description of each step of the model.

Planning the Evaluation

One of the most important and cost-saving phases in the ROI process is the planning of the evaluation because a comprehensive evaluation plan provides a step-by-step guide to completing the evaluation. A first step in the planning process is to develop specific objectives at different levels, sometimes including all five levels described in table 1. Objectives for application, impact, and ROI are necessary to generate the business contribution of training and performance improvement.

Data collection is necessary for a comprehensive evaluation, and a data collection plan outlines in detail the steps involved. When selecting the data collection methods and developing the plan, people should consider four elements—evaluation purposes, instruments, levels, and timing. Typical items in a plan include the following:

- Broad areas for objectives are initially identified; more specific program objectives are developed later.
- Specific measures or data descriptions are indicated when they are necessary to explain the measures linked to the objectives.
- Specific data collection methodologies for each objective are listed.
- Sources of data such as participants, team leaders, and company records are identified.
- The time frame in which to collect the data is noted for each data collection method.
- Responsibility for collecting data is assigned.

The ROI analysis plan is a continuation of the data collection plan. This planning document captures information on several issues that are key to development of the ROI calculation. These issues include

- significant data items, usually Level 4, business impact measures, but in some cases could include Level 3 data
- the method for isolating the effects of the program
- the method for converting data to monetary values
- the cost categories, noting how certain costs should be prorated
- the anticipated intangible benefits

- the communication targets—those to receive the information
- other issues or events that might influence program implementation.

These two planning documents are necessary to successfully implement and manage the ROI process.

Collecting Data

Following the planning process, implementation begins. Data collection is central to the ROI process. It includes both hard data, representing output, quality, costs, and time, and soft data, including work habits, work climate, and attitudes. Data is usually collected during two time frames: the training and performance improvement process, for Levels 1 and 2; and following the program, for Levels 3 and 4. A variety of methods are available for collecting the postprogram data to be used in the ROI evaluation. Figure 3 lists these data collection techniques.

The important challenge is to match the data collection method or methods with the setting and the specific program, within the time and budget constraints of the organization.

Isolating the Effects of the Program

The most critical step in the evaluation process is one that organizations often overlook: isolation of the effects of the training and performance improvement program. In this step of the ROI process, organizations explore specific strategies that determine the amount of output performance directly related to the program. The specific

Figure 3. Postprogram data collection techniques.

	Level 3	Level 4
• Follow-up surveys	√	√
• Follow-up questionnaires	√	√
• Observation on the job	√	√
• Interview with participants	√	√
• Follow-up focus groups	√	√
• Program assignments	√	√
• Action planning	√	√
• Performance contracting	√	√
• Program follow-up sessions	√	√
• Performance monitoring		√

techniques of this step will pinpoint the amount of improvement directly related to the program. The result is increased accuracy and credibility of the ROI calculation. Organizations have used the following techniques to address this important issue:

- use of a control group arrangement
- trend line analysis of performance data
- use of forecasting methods of performance data
- participant's estimate of program impact (percent)
- supervisor's estimate of program impact (percent)
- management's estimate of program impact (percent)
- use of previous studies
- subordinate's report of other factors
- calculating or estimating the impact of other factors
- use of customer input.

Collectively, these 10 techniques provide a comprehensive set of tools to isolate the effects of training and performance improvement programs.

Converting Data to Monetary Values

To calculate the ROI, organizations convert data collected at Level 4 to monetary values so they can compare them with program costs. This step requires that a value be placed on each unit of data connected with the program. Ten approaches are available to convert data to monetary values where the specific technique selected usually depends on the type of data and the situation. These approaches are as follows:

- converting output to contribution—standard value
- converting the cost of quality—standard value
- converting employee's time
- using historical costs
- using internal and external reports
- using data from external reports
- using data from external databases
- linking with other measures
- using participants' estimates
- using supervisors' and managers' estimates
- using staff estimates.

This step is absolutely necessary for determining the monetary benefits from training and performance improvement programs. This is a challenging step, particularly with soft data, but can be methodically accomplished using one or more of the above techniques.

Tabulating Program Costs

Tabulation of program costs involves monitoring or developing all of the related costs of the program targeted for the ROI calculation. Among the cost components that should be included are the following:

- the cost to design and develop the program, possibly prorated over the expected life of the program
- the cost of all program materials provided to each participant
- the cost of the instructor or facilitator, including preparation and delivery times
- the cost of the facilities
- travel, lodging, and meal costs for the participants, if applicable
- salaries plus employee benefits of the participants for the time they attend the program
- administrative and overhead costs of the training and performance improvement function allocated in some convenient way to the program.

Organizations should also include appropriate costs related to the front-end analysis and evaluation. The conservative approach is to include all of these costs so that the total is fully loaded.

Calculating the ROI

The ROI is calculated using the program benefits and costs. The benefit-cost ratio (BCR) is the program benefits divided by cost. In formula form, it is as follows:

$$BCR = \frac{\text{Program Benefits}}{\text{Program Costs}}$$

The ROI uses the net benefits divided by program costs. The net benefits are the program benefits minus the costs. In formula form, the ROI becomes:

$$ROI\ (\%) = \frac{\text{Net Benefits}}{\text{Program Costs}} \times 100$$

This is the same basic formula used in evaluating other investments where the ROI is traditionally reported as earnings divided by investment. The ROI from some programs may be high. For example, in sales, supervisory, leadership, and managerial training, the ROI is frequently over 100 percent, whereas the ROI value for technical and operator training may be lower.

Identifying Intangible Benefits

In addition to tangible, monetary benefits, most training and performance improvement programs have intangible nonmonetary benefits. Organizations should consider those data items not converted to monetary values as intangible benefits. Although organizations could convert many of these items to monetary values, they often do not do so because the conversion process is too subjective and the resulting value loses credibility through the process. These intangible benefits are the sixth measure reported in the ROI impact study report and may include

- increased job satisfaction
- increased organizational commitment
- improved teamwork
- improved customer service
- reduced complaints
- reduced conflicts.

For some programs, these intangible, nonmonetary benefits are extremely valuable, often carrying as much influence as the hard data items.

Implementing the ROI Process

Successful implementation of the ROI process takes time and a concerted effort by those involved in the evaluation process as well as those supporting the evaluation effort to integrate the pieces of the evaluation puzzle, shown in figure 1, into the training and performance improvement function. The ROI process is not a quick fix to proving a program's worth. It is a comprehensive process that, when implemented to its fullest, can help position the training and performance improvement function as a strategic player in the organization. Initial strategies that will assist in ensuring successful implementation of the ROI process include the following:

- **Planning and discipline:** A great deal of planning and a disciplined approach will keep the process on track. Elements this strategy requires are implementation schedules, evaluation targets, data collection plans, measurement and evaluation policies, and follow-up schedules.
- **Assigning responsibilities:** There are two key areas of responsibilities: one for all members of the training and performance improvement staff and one for the group that handles measurement and evaluation. The entire training and performance improvement staff, regardless of the members' individually assigned responsibilities, is responsible

for measurement and evaluation. These responsibilities include ensuring training and performance improvement needs include business impact measures, developing appropriate program objectives to include Level 3 (application and implementation) and Level 4 (business impact) objectives, focusing content to relate to the desired objectives, designing appropriate data collection instruments, and communicating processes and evaluation results. The second area of responsibility is for the group specifically involved with measurement and evaluation. Those members' responsibilities include designing data collection instruments, providing assistance for developing an evaluation strategy, analyzing data, interpreting results, developing the evaluation report or case study, and providing technical assistance with the ROI process.

- **Developing staff skills:** Many training and performance improvement staff members do not understand ROI or have the basic skills necessary to apply the process within their scope of responsibilities. The typical program does not focus on business results; it focuses more on learning outcomes. Consequently, staff skills must be developed to utilize the results-based approach.
- **Improving front-end analysis:** Organizations often undertake the ROI process to improve the evaluation of existing programs. This process often uncovers inadequate front-end analysis. Organizations should only implement programs that they need and that are aligned properly with their business needs. By uncovering flawed front-end analyses, the ROI process results in positive contributions to organizations' bottom lines.
- **Communicating progress:** Training and performance improvement groups that communicate their efforts to address strategic needs to the appropriate audience ensure that their work gets recognized. It is also important for them to show the impact the programs have on the organization. Usually, training and performance improvement functions also generate routine reports.

Conclusion

Hundreds of organizations develop ROI calculations to meet the demands of influential stakeholders. The ROI process described in this chapter is the most recognized process for bringing balance and credibility to measurement and evaluation. The trend to develop a comprehensive measurement process is likely to continue as organizations become more streamlined, yet have greater global reach. Through careful planning, methodical procedures, and logical and practical analysis, ROI calculations can be developed reliably and accurately for any type of training and performance improvement program, in any organization, in any part of the world. Examples of the successful application of ROI evaluation appear throughout this book.

References

Kirkpatrick, Donald L. (1998). *Evaluating Training Programs* (2d edition). San Francisco: Berrett-Koehler.

Phillips, Jack J. (1997). *Return on Investment in Training and Performance Improvement Programs*. Boston: Gulf Publishing.

Phillips, Jack J. (Ed.). (1998). *Implementing Evaluation Systems and Processes*. Alexandria, VA: ASTD.

Performance Management Training

Cracker Box, Inc.

Jack J. Phillips and Patricia Pulliam Phillips

This case study describes how one organization—a restaurant chain—built evaluation into the learning process and positioned it as an application tool. This approach is a powerful one that uses action plans, which participants develop during the training program to drive application, impact, and return-on-investment (ROI) data. This training program adds significant value to the restaurant store chain in this case study and shows how the evaluation process can be accomplished with minimum resources. The keys to success are planning for the evaluation, building it into the learning process, and using the data to help future participants.

Background
Situation

Cracker Box is a large, fast-growing restaurant chain located along major interstates and thoroughfares. In the past 10 years, Cracker Box has grown steadily and now has over 400 stores with plans for continued growth. Each store has a restaurant and a gift shop. A store manager is responsible for both profit units. The turnover of store managers is approximately 25 percent, lower than the industry average of 35 percent, but still excessive. Because of the store's growth and the turnover, the organization needs to develop almost 150 new store managers per year.

Store managers operate autonomously and are held accountable for store performance. Working with the members of the store team,

This case was prepared to serve as a basis for discussion rather than to illustrate either effective or ineffective administrative and management practices. All names, dates, places, and organizations have been disguised at the request of the authors or organization.

managers control expenses, monitor operating results, and take actions as needed to improve store performance. Each store records dozens of performance measures in a monthly operating report and other measures weekly.

Stores recruit managers both internally and externally and require that they have restaurant experience. Many of them have college degrees. The training program for new managers usually lasts nine months. When selected, a store manager trainee reports directly to a store manager who serves as a mentor. Trainees are usually assigned to a specific store location for the duration of manager training. During the training period, the entire store team reports to the store manager trainee as the store manager coaches the trainee. As part of formal training and development, each store manager trainee attends at least three one-week programs at the company's Corporate University, including the Performance Management Program.

Performance Management Program

The Performance Management Program teaches new store managers how to improve store performance. Program participants learn how to establish measurable goals for employees, provide performance feedback, measure progress toward goals, and take action to ensure that goals are met. The program focuses on using the store team to solve problems and improve performance and also covers problem analysis and counseling skills. The one-week program is residential and often includes evening assignments. Corporate University staff and operation managers teach the program, and they integrate skill practice sessions throughout the instruction. Program sessions take place at the location of the Corporate University near the company's headquarters.

Needs Assessment

The overall needs assessment for this process was in two parts. First, there was a macrolevel needs assessment for the store manager position. The Corporate University's performance consultants identified specific training needs for new managers, particularly with issues involving policy, practice, performance, and leadership. This needs assessment was the basis for developing the three programs for each new manager trainee. The second part of the assessment was built into this program as the individual manager trainees provided input for a microlevel or store-level needs assessment.

The program facilitator asked participants to provide limited needs assessment data prior to the program. Each participant was asked to meet with the store manager (that is, his or her mentor) and identify at least three operating measures that, if improved, should enhance store performance. Each measure was to focus on changes that both the store manager and manager trainee thought should be made. These business impact measures could be productivity, absenteeism, turnover, customer complaints, revenues, inventory control, accidents, or any other measure that could improve performance. It would be possible for each participant in a specific manager trainee group to have different measures.

To ensure that the job performance needs are met, each participant was asked to review the detailed objectives of the program and select only measures that could be improved by the efforts of the team and skills taught in the program. The important point in this step is to avoid selecting measures that cannot be enhanced through the use of the input of the team and the skills covered in the program.

As participants register for the program, they are reminded of the requirement to complete an action plan as part of the application of the process. This requirement is presented as an integral part of the program and not as an add-on data collection tool. Action planning is necessary for participants to see the improvements generated from the entire group of program participants. Credit is not granted until the action planning process is completed.

Measurement Requirements
Why Evaluate This Program?

The decision to conduct an ROI analysis for this program was reached through a methodical and planned approach. A Corporate University team decided at the outset that data would be collected from this program. Therefore, the team built the evaluation into the program. This decision was based on the following reasons:

- This program is designed to add value at the store level and the outcome is expressed in store-level measures that are well-known and respected by the management team. The evaluation should show the actual value of improvement.
- This evaluation positions the data collection process from an evaluation perspective to an application process. The manager trainees did not necessarily perceive that the information they provided was for the purpose of evaluation, but saw it as more of an application tool to show the impact of their training.
- The application data enables the team to make improvements and adjustments. The data also helps the team gain respect for the program from the operating executives as well as the store managers.

The ROI Process

The Corporate University staff used a comprehensive evaluation process in many of its programs. This approach, called the ROI process, generates the following six types of data:
- reaction and satisfaction
- learning
- application and implementation
- business impact
- ROI
- intangible measures.

To determine the contribution the training program makes to the changes in business impact measures, a technique to isolate the effects of the program is included in the process.

Figure 1 shows the ROI process model. It begins with detailed objectives for learning, application, and impact. It shows development of data collection plans and ROI analysis plans before data collection actually begins. Four different levels of data are collected, namely, the first four types of data listed above. The process includes a method to isolate the effects of a program and techniques to convert data to monetary value. The ROI is calculated when comparing the monetary benefits to the cost of the program. The intangible measures, the sixth type of data, are those measures not converted to monetary value. This comprehensive model allows the organization to follow a consistent standardized approach each time it is applied to evaluate training and development programs.

Planning for Evaluation

Planning for the evaluation is critical to saving costs and improving the quality and quantity of data collection. It also provides an opportunity to clarify expectations and responsibilities and shows the client group—in this case, the senior operating team—exactly how this program is evaluated. Two documents are created: the data collection plan and the ROI analysis plan.

Data Collection Plan

Figure 2 shows the data collection plan for this program. Broad objectives are detailed along the five levels of evaluation, which represent the first five types of data collected for programs. As the figure illustrates, the typical reaction and satisfaction data is collected at the end of the program by the facilitator. Learning objectives focus on the five major areas of the program: establishing employee goals, providing feedback and motivating employees, measuring employee

Figure 1. The ROI process model.

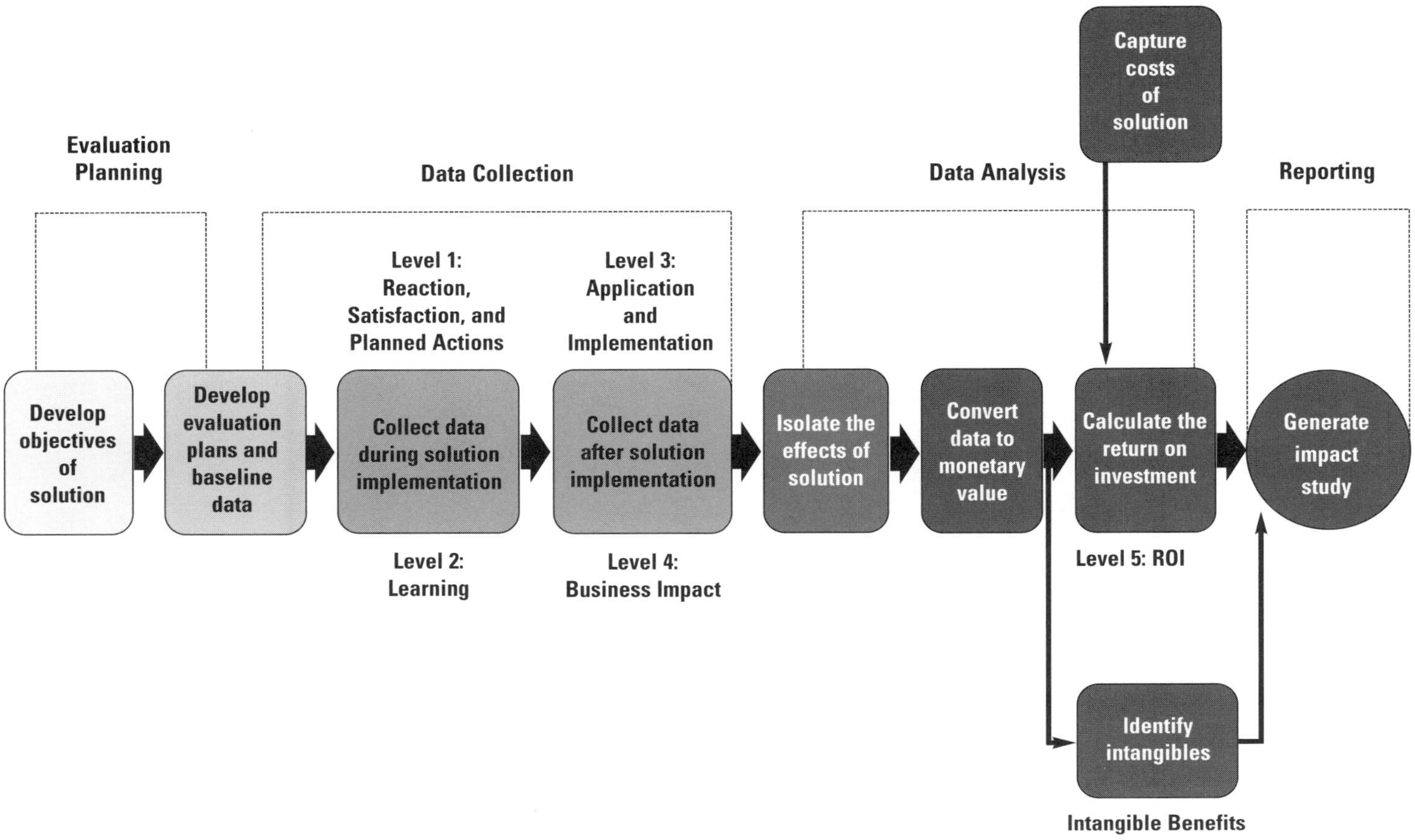

Figure 2. Data collection plan.

Program: Performance Management Program   **Responsibility:**   **Date:**

Level	Objective(s)	Measures and Data	Data Collection Method	Data Sources	Timing	Responsibilities
1	**Reaction and satisfaction** • Obtain positive reaction to program and materials • Identify planned actions	• Average rating of 4.0 out of 5.0 on quality, quantity, and usefulness of material • 100% submit planned actions	• Standard feedback questionnaire	• Participant	• End of program	• Facilitator
2	**Learning** • Establishing employee goals • Providing feedback and motivating employees • Measuring employee performance • Solving problems • Counseling employees	• Be able to identify 100% of steps necessary to establish, monitor, and achieve goals • Demonstrate ability to provide employee feedback, solve problems	• Skill practice • Facilitator assessment • Participant assessment	• Participant	• During program	• Facilitator

	Broad program objectives	Measures	Data collection method		Timing	Responsibilities
3	**Application and implementation** • Apply skills in appropriate situations • Complete all steps of action plan	• Ratings on questions • The number of steps completed on action plan	• Follow-up questionnaire • Action plan	• Participant • Participant	• Three months after program • Six months after program	• Corporate University staff
4	**Business impact** • Identify three measures that need improvement	• Varies	• Action plan	• Participant	• Six months after program	• Corporate University staff
5	**ROI** • 25%					

Comments:

performance, solving problems, and counseling employees. Learning measures are obtained through observations from the facilitator as participants practice the various skills.

Through application and implementation, participants focused on two primary broad areas. The first was to apply the skills in appropriate situations, and the second was to complete all steps in their action plan. In terms of skill application, the evaluation team developed a follow-up questionnaire to measure the use of the skills along with certain other related issues. This was planned for three months after the program. Six months after the program, the action plan data is provided to show the actual improvement in the measures planned.

Business impact objectives vary with the individual because each store manager trainee identifies at least three measures needing improvement. These measures appear on the action plan and serve as the basic documents for the Corporate University staff to tabulate the overall improvement.

The overall ROI objective is 25 percent, which was the standard established for internal programs at Cracker Box. This was slightly above the internal rate of return expected from other investments such as the construction of a new restaurant and gift shop.

ROI Analysis

The ROI analysis plan, which appears in figure 3, shows how the organization processes and reports data. Business impact data is listed and forms the basis for the rest of the analysis. The method for isolating the effects of the program at Cracker Box was participant estimation. The method to convert data to monetary values relied on three techniques: standard values (when they were available), expert input, or participant's estimate. Cost categories represent a fully loaded profile of costs, anticipated intangibles are detailed, and the communication targets are outlined. The ROI analysis plan basically represents the approach to process business impact data to develop the ROI analysis and to capture the intangible data. Collectively, these two planning documents outline the approach for evaluating this program.

Action Planning: A Key to ROI Analysis

Figure 4 shows the sequence of activities from introduction of the action planning process through reinforcement during the program. The requirement for the action plan was communicated prior to the program along with the request for needs assessment information. On the first day of training, Monday, the program facilitator described the action planning process in a 15-minute discussion. At Cracker Box,

Figure 3. ROI analysis plan.

Program: _Performance Management Program_   **Responsibility:** _____   **Date:** _____

Data Items (Usually Level 4)	Methods for Isolating the Effects of the Program and Process	Methods of Converting Data to Monetary Values	Cost Categories	Intangible Benefits	Communication Targets for Final Report	Other Influences and Issues During Application	Comments
• Three measures identified by manager trainee and manager	• Participant estimation	• Standard values • Expert input • Participant estimation	• Needs assessment • Program development • Program material • Travel and lodging • Facilitation and coordination • Participant salaries plus benefits • Training overhead • Evaluation	• Achievement • Confidence • Job satisfaction • Permanent store assignment	• Store managers • Participants • Corporate University staff • Regional operating executives • VP store operations • Senior VP human resources		

Client Signature: _____   Date: _____

participants received specially prepared notepads on which to capture specific action items throughout the program. They were instructed to make notes when they learned a technique or skill that could be useful in improving one of the measures on their list of three. In essence, this notepad became a rough draft of the action plan.

The action planning process was discussed in greater detail in a one-hour session on Thursday afternoon. This discussion included three parts:
- actual forms
- guidelines for developing action plans and SMART (*s*pecific, *m*easurable, *a*chievable, *r*ealistic, and *t*ime based) requirements
- examples to illustrate what a complete action plan should look like.

The program facilitator distributed the action planning forms in a booklet containing instructions, five blank action plans (only three are required, one for each measure), and the examples of completed action plans. On Thursday evening, participants completed the booklets in a facilitated session that lasted approximately one and a half hours. Participants worked in teams to complete all three action plans. Each plan took about 20 to 30 minutes to complete. Figure 5 shows a blank action plan. During the session, participants completed the top portion, the left column on which they list the action steps,

Figure 4. Sequence of activities for action planning.

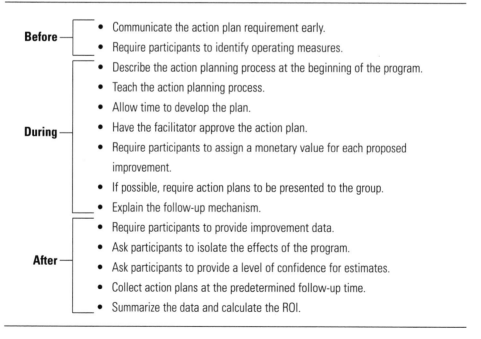

Before
- Communicate the action plan requirement early.
- Require participants to identify operating measures.

During
- Describe the action planning process at the beginning of the program.
- Teach the action planning process.
- Allow time to develop the plan.
- Have the facilitator approve the action plan.
- Require participants to assign a monetary value for each proposed improvement.
- If possible, require action plans to be presented to the group.
- Explain the follow-up mechanism.

After
- Require participants to provide improvement data.
- Ask participants to isolate the effects of the program.
- Ask participants to provide a level of confidence for estimates.
- Collect action plans at the predetermined follow-up time.
- Summarize the data and calculate the ROI.

Figure 5. Action plan form.

Name:	**Instructor Signature:** _____ **Follow-Up Date:** _____
Objective: _____	**Evaluation Period:** _____ **to** _____
Improvement Measure: _____	**Current Performance:** _____ **Target Performance:** _____

Action Steps

1. _____

2. _____

3. _____

4. _____

5. _____

6. _____

7. _____

Analysis

A. What is the unit of measure? _____

B. What is the value (cost) of one unit? $ _____

C. How did you arrive at this value? _____

_____

_____

_____

_____

D. How much did the measure change during the evaluation period? _____
(monthly value)

E. What percent of this change was actually caused by this program? _____
_____ %

F. What level of confidence do you place on the above information?
(100% = certainty and 0% = no confidence)
_____ %

Intangible Benefits: _____

Comments: _____

and parts A, B, and C in the right column. They completed the remainder of the form—parts D, E, and F as well as intangible benefits and comments—in a six-month follow-up. The senior facilitator monitored most of these sessions and sometimes an operations executive was also present. The involvement of the operations executive provided an additional benefit of keeping the participants focused on the task. Also, this involvement usually impressed operating executives with the focus of the program and the quality of the action planning documents.

The action plan could focus on any specific steps as long as they were consistent with the skills required in the program and were related to the business improvement measures. The most difficult part of developing the plan was to convert the measure to a monetary value. Three approaches were offered to the participants. First, standard values were used when they were available. Fortunately, for Cracker Box, standard values are available for most of the operating measures. Operations managers had previously assigned a cost (or value) to a particular measure for use in controlling costs and to develop an appreciation for the impact of different measures. Second, when a standard value was not available, the participants were encouraged to use expert input. This option involved contacting someone in the organization who might know the value of a particular item. The program facilitator encouraged participants to call the expert on Friday morning and include the value in the action plan. Third, when a standard value or expert input was not available, participants were asked to estimate the cost or value using all of the knowledge and resources available to them. Fortunately, the measure was a concern to the trainee and the store manager so there was some appreciation for the actual value. An estimation was possible in every case when standard values and expert input were not available. It was important to require that this value be developed during the program or at least soon after completion of the program.

The next day, Friday, the participants briefly reviewed the action planning process with the group. Each action plan took about five minutes. To save time, each group chose one action plan to present to the entire group to underscore the quality of the action planning process. The program facilitator explained the follow-up steps to the group. Staff of the Corporate University and operation managers recommended that the manager trainee and the store manager discuss the document before they send a copy to the university staff. They should include contact information in case a staff member has a question about the data.

Results

Staff of the Corporate University and operation managers reported the results in all six categories developed by the ROI process, beginning with reaction and moving through ROI and the intangibles. Following are the results in each category together with additional explanation about how some of the data was processed.

Reaction and Learning

Reaction data is collected at the end of the program using a standard questionnaire, which focuses on issues such as relevance of the material, the amount of new information, and intention to use the skills. The content, delivery, and facilitation are also evaluated. Table 1 shows a summary of the reaction data on a rating scale in which one is unsatisfactory and five is exceptional.

Learning improvement is measured at the end of the program using a self-assessment and a facilitator assessment. Although these measures are subjective, they provide an indication of improvements in learning. Typical programs usually report significant improvements in both the self-assessments and facilitator-assessments. In this study, the facilitator-assessment data reported that all participants had acquired the skills at a satisfactory level.

Application and Implementation

To determine the extent to which the skills are being used and to check progress of the action plan, participants received a questionnaire three months after the program. This two-page, user-friendly questionnaire covered the following areas:
- skill usage
- skill frequencies
- linkage to store measures

Table 1. Reaction of program participants.

Topic	Rating
Relevance of material	4.3
Amount of new information	3.8
Intention to use skills	4.6
Content of the program	3.7
Delivery of the program	4.1
Facilitation of the program	4.2

- barriers to implementation
- enablers for implementation
- progress with the action plan
- quality of the support from the manager
- additional intangible benefits
- recommendations for program improvements.

Participants reported progress in each of the areas and indicated that they had significant use of the skills even beyond the projects involving action plans. Also, the store manager trainees indicated linkage of this program with many store measures beyond the three measures selected for action planning. Typical barriers of implementation that they reported included lack of time, understaffing, changing culture, and lack of input from the staff. Typical enablers were the support from the store manager and early success with the application of the action plan. This follow-up questionnaire allowed manager trainees an opportunity to summarize the progress with the action plan. In essence, this served as a reminder to continue with the plan as well as a process check to see if there were issues that should be explored. The manager trainees also gave the store managers high marks in terms of support provided to the program. Participants suggested several improvements, all minor, and store managers implemented those that added value. Explanations of some intangible benefits that participants identified appear later.

Business Impact

Participants collected business impact data that were specific to the manager trainees. Although the action plan contains some Level 3 application data (the left side of the form), the primary value of the action plan was business impact data obtained from the planning documents.

In the six-month follow-up the participants were required to furnish the following five items:

1. The actual change in the measure on a monthly basis is included in part D of the action plan. This value is used to develop an annual (first year) improvement.

2. The only feasible way to isolate the effects of the program is to obtain an estimate directly from the participants. As they monitor the business measures and observe their improvement, the participants probably know the actual influences driving a particular measure, at least the portion of the improvement related directly to their actions, which are detailed on the action plan. Realizing that other factors could have

influenced the improvement, the manager trainees were asked to estimate the percent of improvement resulting from the application of the skills required in the training program (the action steps on the action plan). Each manager trainee was asked to be conservative with the estimate and express it as a percentage (part E on the action plan).

3. Recognizing that the above value is an estimate, the manager trainees were asked to indicate the level of confidence in their allocation of the contribution to this program. This is included in part F on the action plan, using 100 percent for certainty and 0 percent for no confidence. This number reflects the degree of uncertainty in the value and actually frames an error range for the estimate.

4. The participants were asked to provide input on intangible measures observed or monitored during the six months that were directly linked to this program.

5. Participants were asked to provide additional comments including explanations.

Figure 6 shows the completed action plan. The example focuses directly on absenteeism from participant number three. This participant has a weekly absenteeism rate of 8 percent and a goal to reduce it to 5 percent. Specific action steps appear on the left side of the form. The actual value is $41 per absence, an amount that represents a standard value. The actual change on a monthly basis is 2.5 percent, slightly below the target. The participant estimated that 65 percent of the change is directly attributable to this program and that he is 80 percent confident in this estimate. The confidence estimate frames a range of error for the 65 percent allocation, allowing for a possible 20 percent plus or minus adjustment in the estimate. The estimate is conservative, adjusted to the low side, bringing the contribution rate of this program to absenteeism reduction to 52 percent:

$$65\% \times 80\% = 52\%$$

This particular location, which is known because of the identity of the store manager trainee, has 40 employees. Also, employees work an average 220 days. The actual improvement value for this example can be calculated as follows:

$$40 \text{ employees} \times 220 \text{ days} \times 2.5\% \times \$41 = \$9,020$$

This is a total first-year improvement before the adjustments. Table 2 shows the annual improvement values on the first measure only for

Figure 6. Action plan.

Name:	John Mathews	Instructor Signature:		Follow-Up Date: 1 September
Objective:	Reduce weekly absenteeism rate for team	Evaluation Period:	March to April	
Improvement Measure:	Absenteeism rate	**Current Performance:** 8%		**Target Performance:** 5%

Action Steps

1. Meet with team to discuss reasons for absenteeism—using problem-solving skills   _10 March_

2. Review absenteeism records for each employee—look for trends and patterns   _20 March_

3. Counsel with "problem employees" to correct habits and explore opportunities for improvement

4. Conduct a brief "performance discussion" with an employee returning to work after an unplanned absence

5. Provide recognition to employees who have perfect attendance

6. Follow up with each discussion and discuss improvement or lack of improvement and plan other action   _31 March_

7. Monitor improvement and provide recognition when appropriate

Intangible Benefits:

Less stress, greater job satisfaction

Analysis

A. What is the unit of measure? _One absence_

B. What is the value (cost) of one unit? $ _41.00_

C. How did you arrive at this value?
Standard value

D. How much did the measure change during the evaluation period?
(monthly value) _2.5%_

E. What percent of this change was actually caused by this program?
_65_ %

F. What level of confidence do you place on the above information?
(100% = certainty and 0% = no confidence)
_80_ %

Comments: _Great program—it kept me on track with this problem._

the 14 participants in this group. (Note that participant number five did not return the action plan so that person's data was omitted from the analysis.) A similar table is generated for the second and third measures. The values are adjusted by the contribution estimate and the confidence estimate. In the absenteeism example, the $9,020 is adjusted by 65 percent and 80 percent to yield $4,690. This same adjustment is made for each of the values, with a total first-year adjusted value for the first measure of $68,240. The same process is followed for the second and third measures for the group, yielding totals of $61,525 and $58,713, respectively. The total first-year monetary benefit for this group is the sum of these three values.

Program Cost

Table 3 details the program costs for a fully loaded cost profile. The cost of the needs assessment is prorated over the life of the program, which is estimated to be three years with 10 sessions per year. The program development cost is prorated over the life of the program as well. The program materials and lodging costs are direct costs. Facilitation and coordination costs were estimated. Time away from work represents lost opportunity and is calculated by multiplying five days times daily salary costs adjusted for 30 percent employee benefits factor (that is, the costs for employee benefits). Training and education overhead costs were estimated. Actual direct costs for the evaluation are included. These total costs of $47,242 represent a conservative approach to cost accumulation.

ROI Analysis

The total monetary benefits are calculated by adding the values of the three measures, totaling $188,478. This leaves a benefits-to-cost ratio (BCR) and ROI as follows:

$$\text{BCR} = \$188,478 / \$47,242 = 3.98$$
$$\text{ROI} = (\$188,478 - \$47,242) / \$47,242 = 298\%$$

This ROI value of almost 300 percent greatly exceeds the 25 percent target value. The target audience considered the ROI value credible, although it is extremely high. Its credibility rests on the following principles on which the study was based:
1. The data comes directly from the participants in concert with their store manager.

Table 2. Business impact data.

Participant	Improvement ($ Values)	Measure	Contribution Estimate From Manager Trainees	Confidence Estimate	Adjusted $ Value
1	5,500	Labor savings	60%	80%	2,640
2	15,000	Turnover	50%	80%	6,000
3	9,020	Absenteeism	65%	80%	4,690
4	2,100	Shortages	90%	90%	1,701
5	0	—	—	—	—
6	29,000	Turnover	40%	75%	8,700
7	2,241	Inventory	70%	95%	1,490
8	3,621	Procedures	100%	80%	2,897
9	21,000	Turnover	75%	80%	12,600
10	1,500	Food spoilage	100%	100%	1,500
11	15,000	Labor savings	80%	85%	10,200
12	6,310	Accidents	70%	100%	4,417
13	14,500	Absenteeism	80%	70%	8,120
14	3,650	Productivity	100%	90%	3,285

Total annual benefit for first measure is $68,240.
Total annual benefit for second measure is $61,525.
Total annual benefit for third measure is $58,713.

Table 3. Program cost summary.

Items	Cost ($)
Needs Assessment (prorated over 30 sessions)	1,500
Program Development (prorated over 30 sessions)	1,700
Program Materials, 14 @ $40	560
Travel and Lodging, 14 @ $900	12,600
Facilitation and Coordination	8,000
Facilities and Refreshments, 5 days @ $350	1,750
Participants' Salaries Plus Benefits, 14 @ 521 $\times$ 1.3	9,482
Training and Education Overhead (Allocated)	900
ROI Evaluation	10,750
	47,242

2. Most of the data could be audited to see if the changes were actually taking place.

3. To be conservative, the data includes only the first year of improvements. With the changes reported in the action plans, there should be some second- and third-year value that has been omitted from the calculation.

4. The monetary improvement has been discounted for the effect of other influences. In essence, the participants take credit only for the part of the improvement related to the program.

5. This estimate of contribution to the program is adjusted for the error of the estimate, adding to the conservative approach.

6. The costs are fully loaded to include both direct and indirect costs.

7. The data is for only those individuals who completed and returned the action plans. No data appeared for participant five in table 2 because that person did not return an action plan.

8. The business impact does not include value obtained from using the skills to address other problems or to influence other measures. Only the values from three measures taken from the action planning projects were used in the analysis.

The ROI process develops convincing data connected directly to store operations. From the viewpoint of the chief financial officer, the data can be audited and monitored. It should be reflected as actual improvement in the stores. Overall, the senior management team considered the results credible and fully supported them.

Intangible Data

As a final part of the complete profile of data, the intangible benefits were itemized. The participants provided input on intangible measures at two time frames. The follow-up questionnaire provided an opportunity for trainees to indicate intangible measures they perceived to represent a benefit directly linked to this program. Also, the action plan had an opportunity for trainees to add additional intangible benefits. Collectively, each of the following benefits were listed by at least two individuals:

- a sense of achievement
- increased confidence
- improved job satisfaction
- promotion to store manager
- stress reduction
- improved teamwork.

To some executives these intangible measures are just as important as the monetary payoff.

The Payoff: Balanced Data

This program drives six types of data items: satisfaction, learning, application, business impact, ROI, and intangible benefits. Collectively these six types of data provide a balanced, credible viewpoint of the success of the program.

Communication Strategy

Table 4 shows the communication strategy for communicating results from the study. All key stakeholders received the information. The communications were routine and convincing. The information to store managers and regional managers helped to build confidence in the program. The data provided to future participants was motivating and helped them to select measures for action plans.

Lessons Learned

It was critical to build evaluation into the program, positioning the action plan as an application tool instead of a data collection tool. This approach helped secure commitment and ownership for the process. It also shifted much of the responsibility for evaluation to the participants as they collected data, isolated the effects of the program, and converted the data to monetary values, the three most critical steps in the ROI process. The costs were easy to capture, and the report was easily generated and sent to the various target audiences.

Table 4. Communication strategy.

Timing	Communication Medium	Target Audience
Within one month of follow-up	Detailed impact study (125 pages)	Program participants; Corporate University staff • responsible for this program in some way • involved in evaluation
Within one month of follow-up	Executive summary • including business impact data	Corporate and regional operation executives
Within one month of follow-up	Report of results (1 page) • in-store manager magazine	Store managers
After registration	Report of results (1 page) • in prework material	Future participants

This approach has the additional advantage of evaluating programs where a variety of measures are influenced. This situation is typical of leadership, team building, and communication programs. The application can vary considerably, and the actual business measure driven can vary with each participant. The improvements are integrated after they are converted to monetary value. Thus, the common value among measures is the monetary value representing the value of the improvement.

Discussion Questions

1. Is this approach credible? Explain.
2. Is the ROI value realistic?
3. How should the results be presented to the senior team?
4. What can be done to ease the challenge of converting data to monetary values?
5. How can the action planning process be positioned as an application tool?
6. What types of programs would be appropriate for this approach?

The Authors

Jack J. Phillips is with the Jack Phillips Center for Research, a division of the FranklinCovey Company. Phillips developed and pioneered the utilization of the ROI process and has provided consulting services to some of the world's largest organizations. He has written over 10 books on the subject. Phillips can be reached at roiresearch@mindspring.com.

Patricia Pulliam Phillips is chairman and CEO of The Chelsea Group, an international consulting company focused on the implementation of the ROI process. She has provided consulting services and support for the ROI process for several years and has served as co-author on the topic in several publications. She can be reached at thechelseagroup@aol.com.

Program Process Improvement Teams

Apple Computer

Holly Burkett

This case describes an impact study measuring the return on investment (ROI) of a pilot process improvement team deployed as a strategy for increased operational efficiency in a dynamic manufacturing environment. Solution implementation and evaluation planning efforts were significantly challenged by accelerating business changes and the attrition of key stakeholders. This study was awarded a select International Society for Performance Improvement (ISPI) research grant and was conducted in accordance with ISPI guidelines for human performance technology research.

Organizational Profile

Since its inception as a two-person operation to a global company employing more than 8,000 employees worldwide, Apple Computer has been a leader of technological innovation in the microcomputer industry. Apple ignited the personal computer revolution in the 1970s with the Apple II, and reinvented the personal computer in the 1980s with the Macintosh. It was the first in color graphics, sound, mass production, expandability, disk data storage, Pascal, bitmapped graphics, and integrated software since its incorporation as a business in 1977. Since Steve Job's return in 1997 and the launch of the hot-selling iMac in 1998, Apple has been committed to its original mission—to bring the best personal computing products and support to students, educators, designers, scientists, engineers, business persons, and consumers in over 140 countries around the world.

This case was prepared to serve as a basis for discussion rather than to illustrate either effective or ineffective administrative and management practices.

Apple owns manufacturing facilities in the United States, Ireland, and Singapore. Its distribution facilities are in the United States, Europe, Canada, Australia, Singapore, and Japan. The Sacramento Operations Center, with over 1,200 employees currently, is the sole Apple-owned production facility for all desktop Apple computers sold in North and South America.

Background and Business Need

The Continuous Improvement Team (CIT) initiative began as a performance improvement strategy to support the operational goal of improving factory capacity to ensure Sacramento's viability as a world class configured-to-order (CTO) factory for Apple Manufacturing. Senior management had communicated an Apple 2000 vision in which an Apple customer, anywhere in the world, would have the ability to receive a customized, configured-to-order system on his or her desktop five days after placing an order (including shipping time). The intent was to place greater emphasis on partnering with customers to create business solutions that would provide more commercial products and services.

From a manufacturing perspective, CTO processes present unique reengineering challenges. For example, a configured build demands special attention to the detail of the customer order and the individual parts or components specified within that order. In standard build-to-replenishment (BTR) assembly, there are predictable like numbers and types of parts for every unit coming down the line. With a configured order, an operator must determine which of five possible drives the customer is requesting, determine the location of that drive in the material bin, verify the part number, and assemble not only to the correct specifications of that particular part but also to the factory standards for labor efficiency and units per person per hour. CTO lines also require unique material storage and material placement designs, given the wide array of components available to meet customer demands.

Needs Assessment

Engineering staff had determined that the current state of the factory (at the time of this study) was not conducive to the desired state of increased CTO performance, with the exception of one line specifically targeted for that purpose. Specifically, most lines were geared for batch or replenishment building, that is, building like units with like parts. Increased CTO capacity required a different type of material flow and line design so that the multitude of parts operators needed could be properly identified and available for assembly.

The site's senior training and development consultant initiated further assessment of individual job performers' needs and skill gaps with respect to the critical knowledge, skills, and abilities required by the process improvement team to support new business processes associated with increased CTO capacity. Needs assessment approaches included the following: job and task analysis, select focus groups with targeted management and employee groups, on-the-job performance observations, and analysis of extant data with assistance from subject matter experts. Table 1 summarizes these assessments.

Due to needs assessment results, the training consultant also determined that additional resources were needed to supplement program and evaluation expenses. To that end, the consultant submitted a research proposal to ISPI, describing the company's business need and the human performance technology intervention planned to address that need. Subsequently, the ISPI Research Committee awarded Apple one of six grants, from 24 proposals, to support "use of an appropriate methodology . . . relevant to the goal and mission of ISPI . . . and the field of human performance technology." The grant stipend provided added credibility and authority to the consultant's evaluation plan and generated supplemental funds, in a resource-constrained environment, for program intervention materials.

Program Description

On the basis of information collected during the assessment process, the consultant developed a customized performance improvement strategy that included a 40-hour, six-week experiential process improvement training curriculum, with a corresponding qualification, action plan, and ROI evaluation plan. This solution focused on meeting the needs of senior management, defining customer and job performer requirements in a CTO environment, and improving CTO work-processes for increased productivity and organizational readiness in meeting CTO demands. Because of previous fluctuations in Apple's business health, quality improvement training had not been in place for a considerable amount of time. Accelerated changes in areas of factory capacity, temporary head-count volume, and new product developments gave preeminence to core skills in process flow mapping, root cause analysis, and problem solving.

Program Design

The curriculum design focused on providing a cross-functional team of 12 with fundamental process improvement tools for immediate application to their designated process improvement opportunity.

Table 1. Performance analysis and interventions.

	Gap	Cause	Intervention
Organization	**Desired:** CTO capacity 100% BTR capacity **Undesired:** CTO below 100% BTR capacity	Lack of data, environmental design not conducive to new business processes	Reengineering of factory design, culture change, resource management
Process	**Desired:** Seamless material flow of multiple components **Undesired:** Bottlenecks in material flow of multiple components	Inefficient cell and conveyer designs impacting material flow and run rate; inconsistencies in process management	Process reengineering and management; education and training; CIT to identify value chain, process goals, and road map of flow process in its current and desired state
Performer and Job	**Desired:** Labor efficiency at 1.0 or above **Undesired:** Labor efficiency below 1.0	Excessive head count to support desired CTO process cycle time; poor link between job outputs and process standards; lack of equipment support; lack of task support; ambiguous process goals	Job and work design and management; task support; equipment resource support; education and training; performance specifications; performance feedback; structured on-the-job training; coaching

Individual training modules consisted of six weekly sessions covering such topics as: foundations of continuous improvement; value-added flow analysis; root cause analysis; the Plan, Do, Check, Act model; team problem solving and decision making; and action planning, including how to measure the effectiveness of improvement efforts through quality indicators.

Training Transfer

The consultant custom designed the course to support full transfer of skills to the workplace through the following:
- high levels of participant interaction
- peer coaching and feedback skill practices
- classroom application of tools and principles to an immediate, real-world improvement opportunity
- regular reference to individual and group action planning, along with tangible business impact, as targeted training outcomes.

The consultant presented the action plan, shown in figure 1, as a useful tool to keep employees focused in a dynamic, ever-changing work setting with a steady influx of temporary, untrained employees. In addition, the project sponsor and production management staff were on hand to launch the program and communicate the importance of the team's work to desired business results. Management also emphasized the expectation that participants were to demonstrate successful completion of the process improvement qualification and requisite action plans. Various management staff also attended portions of individual training modules along with a summary segment during the closing session. Following the six-week program, participants met with the senior training consultant for a one-hour, individual action planning session. During this time, trainees were audited on successful completion of the qualification and asked to initiate their individual 30-day action plan. The focus of the action plan was each participant's identification of two to three specific skills learned at the continuous improvement training program that the participant would apply to his or her own team project action planning within the next 30 days.

Communication Process

Both the training consultant and the engineering manager, as project sponsor, presented the proposed performance improvement strategy during a communications briefing with site operational staff. This senior management group represented functional areas of finance, new product development, production, supply chain management and

Figure 1. Action plan for Continuous Improvement Training program.

Name:

Instructor Signature:

Follow-up Date:

Objective: To apply skills and knowledge from continuous improvement program

Evaluation Period: _____ to _____

Improvement Measures: (productivity, labor efficiency and downtime, PPA failures, rework, customer response, communication, cycle time, other)

Action Steps	Analysis
As a result of what you have learned in this program, what specific actions will you apply: Specify frequency (for example, weekly, daily). 1. _____ _____ _____ 2. _____ _____ 3. _____ _____ 4. _____ _____ _____	What specific unit of measure will change as a result of your actions? 1. _____ _____ 2. _____ _____ 3. As a result of the anticipated changes in the above, please estimate the monetary benefits to your department over a one-month period. $ _____ 4. What is the basis of your estimate? _____ _____ 5. What level of confidence, expressed as a percentage, do you place on the above estimate? (100% = certainty and 0% = no confidence) _____ % 6. What other factors, besides training, may contribute to process improvements or changes you make? _____ 7. What barriers, if any, may prevent you from using skills or knowledge gained from this program? _____

Intangible Benefits: _____

Source: Phillips, Jack J. (1997). *Return on Investment.* Houston, TX: Gulf Publishing Company

planning, human resources, and logistics. At that time, the engineering manager and project sponsor described the purpose of the program by explaining the following:

> The goal of this process improvement activity is twofold. First, by involving production manufacturing in the line layout process, engineering hopes to develop a more streamlined cell with the appropriate hardware, software, processes, and assembly tools. Second, the gain to the corporation as a whole is increased labor efficiency, which gives us a higher run rate and [unit per person per hour]. The improvements resulting from this training exercise will be proliferated across the CTO lines and incorporated into future line layouts. This ensures Sacramento's viability as a world-class CTO factory for Apple Manufacturing.... The end result will be a flexible manufacturing system capable of supporting both BTO [build to order] and CTO production.

The intent of the briefing was to generate operational support for the planned intervention and to solicit project support in the form of an executive steering committee. Specifically, both the senior training consultant and the project sponsor recommended that select operations staff serve as steering committee members, with the project sponsor as chair and the training consultant as a technical resource, for the duration of the project. This was approved by operational staff, with steering committee roles and responsibilities defined as follows:

- communicate purpose and importance of the process improvement effort
- provide coaching, feedback, and subject matter expertise
- monitor the process improvement effort through steering committee meeting attendance, as required
- assist in removing barriers to the team's implementation of process improvement action plan
- assist in evaluation planning upon request (that is, establishment of performance objectives, leverage of resources for data collection, conversion of data to monetary value)
- evaluate project deliverables and elicit and provide feedback to the improvement team about lessons learned from the project experience.

After receiving senior management's approval, the training consultant and the project sponsor communicated the following objectives and expectations to the hand-selected, prescreened process improvement team:

- *business objective:* to increase operational capacity in meeting factory 2000 strategic goals

- *performance objectives:* to analyze a designated CTO work process using process improvement tools; to initiate a common language for communicating about process issues; to apply participatory problem-solving and decision-making skills toward continuous improvement efforts in increasing CTO capacity; to identify the information, skills, and resources needed to carry out team tasks; and to demonstrate increased individual and team readiness to meet CTO requirements
- *research objective:* to evaluate the impact of process improvement teams as a performance improvement strategy.

Program Deliverables

During the participant briefing, the consultant and project sponsor also conveyed the program deliverables expected of team members. These deliverables were initiated by the engineering sponsors and approved by the steering committee. Specifically, these included
- schematic of new cell layout using one point of material flow integration
- cell conveyer job aids showing revised material flow
- road map drawing of the revised cell layout (with dimensions) identifying all shelving, lighting, tools (and their locations)
- preliminary unit per person per hour (UPPH) and labor efficiency data to measure impact of cell-to-main-line integration point
- customized process improvement training product with practical, real-time improvement scenarios
- a core team of qualified process improvement champions for future cross training and knowledge management
- impact study (internal and external for ISPI grant sponsors) and executive report of findings.

Program Design Parameters

Similarly, engineering sponsors established project scope and design parameters that were also communicated to the process improvement team at their initial briefing session. These included
- The cell must have only one point of integration into the main line.
- The operators must not preassemble parts and must think about raw material storage, consumption, and material flow through the cell.
- Cell design must include conveyors with no benches.
- The existing cell head count (that is, the number of employees required) must be maintained or reduced.
- Design must not incur capital equipment expenses.
- Design implementation should not interrupt or have an impact on existing production.

Process Improvement Validation

Following receipt of the team's deliverables, engineering sponsors assumed responsibility for coordinating, with production control, the pilot reengineering plan and documenting necessary process deviations for the line. The steering committee assigned production the responsibility for selecting the team and collecting UPPH and labor efficiency data during the pilot. The training consultant collected all documents related to project deliverables and provided them to the project sponsor and steering committee. These also included data collection validation sheets.

Evaluation Methodology
Purpose of Evaluation

The training consultant recommended the program for ROI evaluation based upon the following criteria:
- the criticality of the business need the program was meant to address
- the high-profile nature of the pilot process improvement team's assignment
- the interest of senior management to track operational results, including ROI of the team's training and action planning time.

ROI data from the pilot team was also considered a factor for senior management in assessing the value of deploying future process improvement teams as a strategy toward increased operational efficiency.

Finally, another reason the site performed an ROI was that it had an opportunity to apply for research grant funds from ISPI.

Model

Phillips's (1997) ROI model, as shown in figure 2, provided the framework for calculating the project's ROI. Key elements of this model included data collection selection, isolating the effects of training, converting data to monetary values, and identifying intangible benefits linked to the performance improvement solution but not converted to monetary value.

Data Collection Methods

The data collection process included objectives and methodologies for each level of evaluation targeted, as shown in table 2. These included the following targets, by objective:
- *Reaction:* Data collection included participant feedback at the end of the training program to judge reaction to the relevance and effectiveness of the training. The consultant solicited participant reaction during distribution of the 30-day impact questionnaire, as shown

Figure 2. ROI process model.

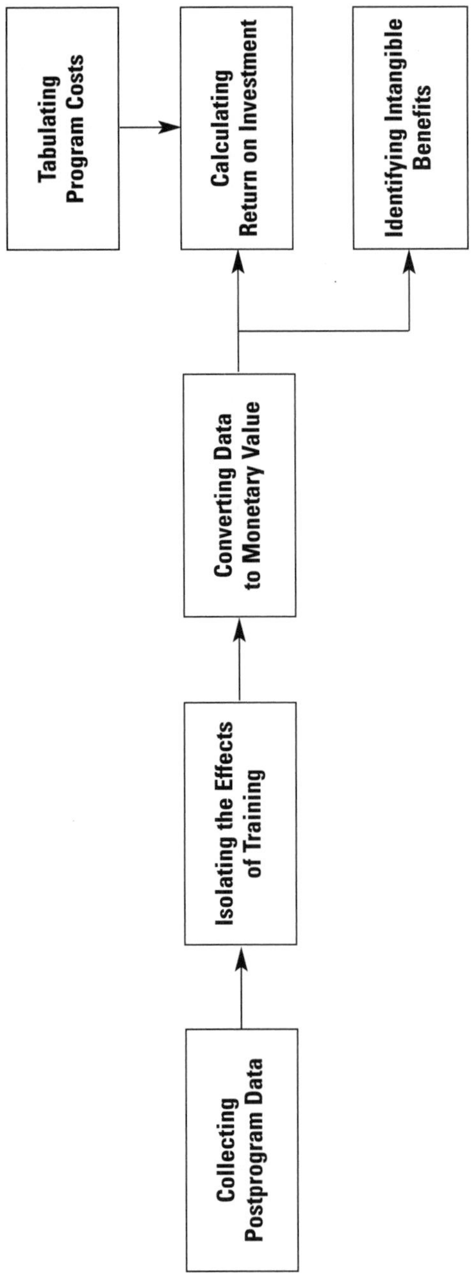

in figure 3. Project sponsor and steering committee reaction was collected through an impact questionnaire at the end of the project.

- *Learning:* Pre- and post-self-assessments and observed behaviors during skill practice and review activities were used to evaluate learning. In addition, a corresponding qualification or competency instrument was used to measure learning gains during and after the program. The qualification itemized critical knowledge or skill sets, or both, associated with core performance objectives and served as a training job aid and source of interactive, peer teach-back, and learning review throughout the training program itself, as figure 4 shows.
- *Job application:* On-the-job behavior change was monitored and measured through action plan implementation (table 2). The action plan shows a series of questions designed to capture data about the frequency of applied behaviors that were linked to process improvement learning and performance objectives.
- *Business impact:* In the action plan, participants estimated the potential cost benefits of their applied behaviors over a 30-day period after training. A 30-day follow-up questionnaire determined the extent to which participants used their action plan or experienced barriers in their planned application of skills and knowledge. For example, questions included
  — What specific unit of measure will change as a result of your actions?
  — As a result of anticipated changes in the above, please estimate the monetary benefits to your department over a one-month period.
  — What is the basis of your estimate?
  — What level of confidence do you place on the above information (where 100 percent equals certainty and 0 percent equals no confidence)?
  A sample of participants' responses includes

1. unit of measure—productivity: based upon downtime, rework, yield or attainment rates

2. unit of measure—quality: based upon rework, material loss, process errors

3. unit of measure—labor efficiency: based upon training time, units per person per hour, teamwork, confidence, morale.

A 30- and 60-day impact questionnaire was also used to collect data about applied skills and knowledge and their perceived business impact. Key areas addressed in the questionnaire included the following:
  — success of training objectives
  — relevance to job
  — usefulness of the training
  — knowledge and skills increase

Table 2. Data collection plan for Process Improvement Team.

Evaluation Level	Objective(s)	Data Collection Method	Data Sources	Timing	Responsibilities
1	**Reaction and Satisfaction** • To measure participant satisfaction with process improvement training • To identify recommendations for improvement in instructional design	Reaction questionnaire Impact questionnaire	Participants Managers, supervisors Steering committee	After each session During session 30, 60 days	Training and development consultant
2	**Learning** • To measure participants' learning gains with process improvement learning objectives	Skill practice exercises, simulations Qualification instrument	Participants	During session Before and during One week after	Participants Training and development consultant
3	**Job Application** • To measure participants' application of process improvement skills and knowledge • To measure frequency and relevance of use • To identify barriers in applying learned skills and knowledge	Individual action plans Team project Follow-up sessions	Participants Steering committee Supervisors Line personnel affected by project actions	During action plan implementation Two months after program	Training and development consultant Project sponsor Steering committee Participants Participants' supervisors

4	**Business Impact** • To measure extent to which applied skills and knowledge had an impact on strategic goal of increasing CTO capacity	Performance monitoring of line Impact questionnaire UPPH and labor-efficiency data	Steering committee Production recorder data Participants	Two months after action plan implementation	Training and development consultant Subject matter experts
5	**ROI** • To measure return on investment with performance improvement strategy • To measure benefits to cost ratio	Cost-benefit analysis Impact questionnaire UPPH and labor-efficiency data	Participants Production data	Two months after action plan completion Three months after program	Training and development consultant Subject matter experts

Source: Phillips, Jack J. (1997). *Return on Investment*. Houston, TX: Gulf Publishing Company

Figure 3. Continuous Improvement Team impact questionnaire (sample questions).

1. Listed below are the performance objectives from the continuous improvement training project. After reflecting on this training one month later, please use the following scale to show the degree to which your skills and knowledge have been enhanced as a result of this training.

   5   Completely Enhanced
   4   Very Much Enhanced
   3   Moderately Enhanced
   2   Somewhat Enhanced
   1   No Change
   NA = No Opportunity to Use Skill

Objective

a) Apply a common language for communicating about process issues	1	2	3	4	5	NA
b) Define customer requirements in a work process	1	2	3	4	5	NA
c) Analyze a work process, using continuous improvement tools provided	1	2	3	4	5	NA
d) Identify weak links or bottlenecks in a work process	1	2	3	4	5	NA
e) Demonstrate consensus-building skills in problem solving and decision making	1	2	3	4	5	NA
f) Increase capability to meet BTO/CTO requirements	1	2	3	4	5	NA

2. Did you implement an on-the-job action plan for this project?

   Yes ____ No ____

   If not, please explain why.

3. *Approximately* how many hours a week did you devote to action plan meetings with your team? Include additional hours spent individually on team tasks. Briefly, list action planing tasks that you completed, on your own or with the team.

   Weekly team meeting hours (beginning week of May 10,1999)   _____
   Average weekly hours on individual tasks   _____
   Action planning tasks:

4. List behaviors, training materials, job aids, or skills gained from the continuous improvement training series that you've used on the job as a result of this program.

5. Use the following checklist to ***assess your actions as a Continuous Improvement Team member*** during the past month. Answer as you think others on your team would describe your actions.

5 Almost Always
4 Usually
3 Sometimes
2 Seldom
1 Almost Never
NA = No Opportunity to Use Skill

As a Team Member, I:

a) Show appreciation for other team members' ideas	1	2	3	4	5	NA
b) Willingly assume a leadership role when needed	1	2	3	4	5	NA
c) Volunteer for all types of tasks, including the hard ones	1	2	3	4	5	NA
d) Help organize and run effective meetings	1	2	3	4	5	NA
e) Help examine the way we're doing as a team and seek ways to continuously improve the way we work together	1	2	3	4	5	NA
f) Ensure that the team includes people in the decision-making process	1	2	3	4	5	NA
g) Clearly state my concerns about team issues or problems	1	2	3	4	5	NA
h) Search for common ground when team members have different views	1	2	3	4	5	NA
i) Actively support team decisions	1	2	3	4	5	NA
j) Help identify the information, skills, and resources needed to carry out team tasks	1	2	3	4	5	NA
k) Encourage others on the team to state their views	1	2	3	4	5	NA
l) Give specific, timely, and constructive feedback to others	1	2	3	4	5	NA

Use the following checklist to ***assess other members' team actions as a Continuous Improvement Team member*** during the past month:

5 Almost Always
4 Usually
3 Sometimes
2 Seldom
1 Almost Never
NA = No Opportunity to Use Skill

As a whole, team members:

a) Show appreciation for other team members' ideas	1	2	3	4	5	NA
b) Willingly assume a leadership role when needed	1	2	3	4	5	NA
c) Volunteer for all types of tasks, including the hard ones	1	2	3	4	5	NA
d) Help organize and run effective meetings	1	2	3	4	5	NA
e) Help examine the way we're doing as a team and seek ways to continuously improve the way we work together	1	2	3	4	5	NA
f) Ensure that the team includes people in the decision-making process	1	2	3	4	5	NA

(continued on page 52)

Figure 3. Continuous Improvement Team impact questionnaire (sample questions) (continued).

g) Clearly state concerns about team issues or
problems   1   2   3   4   5   NA

h) Search for common ground when team members have
different views   1   2   3   4   5   NA

i) Actively support team decisions   1   2   3   4   5   NA

j) Help identify the information, skills, and resources
needed to carry out team tasks   1   2   3   4   5   NA

k) Encourage others on the team to state their views   1   2   3   4   5   NA

l) Give specific, timely, and constructive feedback
to others   1   2   3   4   5   NA

6. Please rate the extent to which this program has positively influenced each of the following measures of your work unit.

> 5   Completely Influenced
> 4   Very Much Influenced
> 3   Moderate or Average Influence
> 2   Some Influence
> 1   No Influence
> NA = No Opportunity to Influence

Improvement Measure

a) Productivity   1   2   3   4   5   NA

b) Labor Efficiency   1   2   3   4   5   NA

c) Process-Induced Failures   1   2   3   4   5   NA

d) Quality   1   2   3   4   5   NA

e) Communications   1   2   3   4   5   NA

f) Other (please name)   1   2   3   4   5   NA

7. What, if anything, has changed about your daily work as a result of this program?

8. Please identify any accomplishments or improvements you've made personally—to your department or your job performance—that you would link directly to this program (specific behavior change, action items, new projects, etc.).

9. What potential cost benefit, in dollars, would you attach to the above improvements *over a one-month period?*

$: _____
Basis of estimate (rework, downtime, labor efficiency, etc.):

10. ***Your degree of confidence*** with the above estimate, based on a percentage.

____%
(0% = no confidence and 100% = full confidence)

11. Other factors, besides training, may have influenced your improvements. Please list any other factors (e.g., change in management, attention to the program) that might have influenced you and estimate the percentage of its influence.

Other factor (specify): _____%
Other factor (specify): _____%

12. Please indicate the percent of your improvements or accomplishments that you consider **directly related** to the continuous improvement training project?

_____%

NOTE: The total percentage for items 11 and 12 cannot exceed 100%.

13. Do you think the continuous improvement training project represented a good investment for Apple?

Yes ___ No ___

Please explain.

14. What barriers, if any, have you encountered in trying to apply skills or knowledge gained in the continuous improvement training? List all that apply. Please be specific.

15. How would you describe management support of this project, based upon your experience?

16. One month later, what suggestions do you have that would improve continuous improvement training or team projects going forward? Please be specific.

Other comments:

Figure 4. Sample areas in the process improvement qualification.

Qualification Scope

Procedures, job aids, manuals, classes, or other resources for the scope of this qualification.

Continuous Process Improvement Training Program   Date Completed_____
Preassessment   Date Completed_____
Postassessment   Date Completed_____
Process Improvement Qualification   Date Completed_____
Action Plan(s) Completion   Date Completed_____

1. Foundations of Continuous Process Improvement
    ____ a. Identify the customer requirements for your designated process improvement project with completion of the Input-Process-Output (IPO) Model.
    Skill Practice exercise, date completed _____.

2. Value-Added Flow Analysis
    ____ a. Three steps to performing a Value-Added Flow Analysis include: _____ the process; identifying _____ activities; and calculating the _____ spent on value-adding activities.
    ____ b. Name three criteria for identifying whether a step adds value.
    ____ c. Complete a Value-Added Flow Analysis for your designated process improvement project.
    Skill Practice exercise, date completed _____.

3. Cause and Effect Analysis
    ____ a. Name three tests of a good problem statement
    ____ b. Create a problem statement for your designated process improvement project.
    Skill Practice exercise, date completed _____.
    ____ c. Describe two ways that fixed thinking hinders continuous improvement.

4. Plan, Do, Check, Act (PDCA) Model
    ____ a. Match the correct step in the PDCA process with its proper definition.
    ____ b. Complete a force-field analysis for your designated process improvement project.
    Skill Practice exercise, date completed _____.

5. Problem Solving and Decision Making
    ____ a. Demonstrate one way to reframe assumptions or mindsets about a problem.
    Skill Practice exercise, date completed _____.
    ____ b. Describe the purpose of the divergent zone in group problem solving and decision making.
    ____ c. Complete a consensus-building exercise for your process improvement project plan.
    Skill Practice exercise, date completed _____.

6. Action Planning
   ___ a. Complete a group action plan according to defined design parameters and project deliverables.
   ___ b. Complete a 30-day action plan to improve your effectiveness in select areas.
   Date Completed_____.

Signatures:
Employee Qualified _____Date _____
Qualifier_____Date _____
Database Entry _____

— actions taken
— accomplishments linked to training
— barriers to implementation
— supervisor support
— business measures linked to training
— recommended changes.

The 30- and 60-day questionnaires were administered during a 90-minute follow-up session, scheduled one month and two months, respectively, after the initial training and co-facilitated by production management. Line management ensured a strong response rate by expecting employees to attend and paying them on company time.

Finally, business impact was evaluated by comparing line performance measures of UPPH and labor efficiency indexes for the 60 days prior to implementation of the process improvement action plan with those 60 days following implementation.

Data Analysis and Results
Reaction

Participants' reactions to the training program and process improvement project experience were overwhelmingly positive. On a five-point scale, the average response for all 15 items was 4.8. The highest rankings were for "relevance to daily work" with the lowest ranking for "immediate supervisor support." Steering committee responses, on the same five-point scale, averaged 4.1.

Learning

On a learning level of evaluation, participant self-assessments showed an average overall gain of 76 percent between pre- and postlearning objectives. In addition, all participants completed the process improvement qualification with 100 percent accuracy.

Job Application

Data from individual action plans and the 30- and 60-day questionnaires was analyzed to assess the degree to which targeted performance objectives were met. As figure 5 shows, performance areas showing the most degree of influence include "demonstrating problem-solving skills" and "defining customer requirements."

Business Impact

Through the 30- and 60-day impact questionnaires, business impact was evaluated by analyzing participants' estimates of the impact of their applied behaviors upon daily work measures. As shown in figure 6, participants reported that applied behavioral changes most influenced daily communication processes, whereas business areas of postprocess audit failures, labor efficiency, productivity, and quality were very much influenced.

Figure 5. Perceived success with targeted performance objectives by percentage.

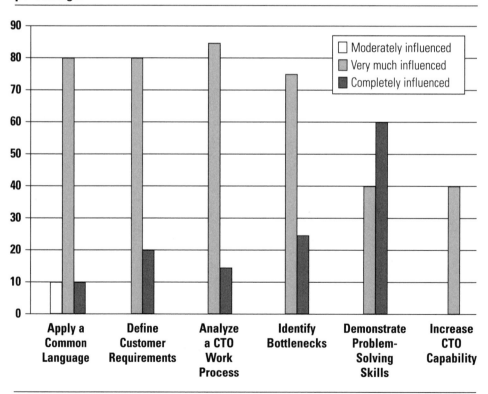

Figure 6. Perceived influence on daily work measures by percentage.

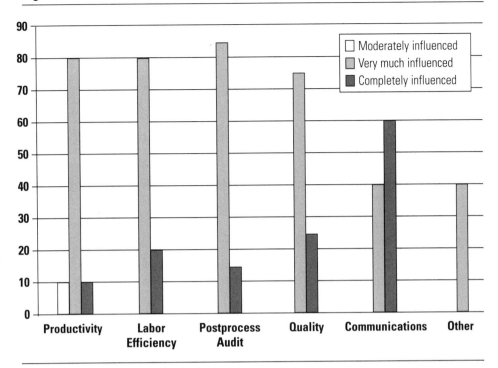

Finally, the consultant and subject matter experts collaboratively analyzed business impact by comparing line performance measures of UPPH and labor efficiency indexes for the 60 days prior with those measures for the 60 days following the process improvement intervention implemented by the pilot team. Figure 7 shows that the UPPH increased from 4.27 to 4.48 and that the labor efficiency increased from 1.14 to 1.20 (5 percent), for the targeted line during the process validation time period.

UPPH increases indicate that more of a product is being built per hour without adding more people to build it. Labor efficiency indexes of 1.0 or above indicate that the increase in shippable goods is occurring at the right cycle time with the appropriate staffing of people. In other words, you can produce a high volume of product, or show a high run rate, but incur high labor costs by having excess head count to produce that volume. Therefore, the product factory capacity model (often referred to as the UPPH model), developed by the Manufacturing Engineering department stipulated a formula for assessing the correct head count to produce the desired quantity of product in

Figure 7. Line performance before and after process improvement intervention.

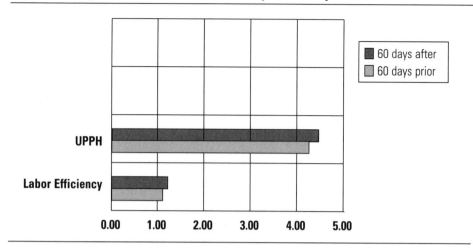

the right amount of cycle time. This formula, when applied properly, sets a labor efficiency standard of 1.0 or above.

Isolation Methodology

Isolation methods used in evaluation included the following:
- end user or performer's estimate of the impact (expressed as a percent)
- use of experts.

Based upon participants' estimates, other factors contributing to the improvement results of increased UPPH and increased labor efficiency included the following: engineering support, steering committee support, production support, and training support. In response to the question, "Please indicate the percent of your improvements or accomplishments that you consider *directly related* to the continuous improvement training program," however, participants estimated the total averaged percent of improvement directly linked to the training intervention at 85 percent. It's significant to note, however, that the other factors attributed to project success were, in actuality, components of the improvement initiative itself and not necessarily external factors.

Data Conversion Methodology

Expert opinion, participants' estimates, and historical costs and savings were the primary methods of converting line performance data to monetary value. As previously noted, line performance of the targeted line was tracked for the 60 days before and after the improvement team's action plan implementation. This occurred during a validation phase using the UPPH model developed by the Manufacturing Engineering department.

Costs

A conservative approach to tabulating program costs was used. In calculating the ROI, these costs were fully loaded and included all analysis costs, personnel costs, program development costs, implementation costs, and evaluation costs. While the stipend from the ISPI research grant offset some material and evaluation expenses, this reimbursement was not included in the analysis to ensure that the costs were fully loaded. Cost components included the following:

- training solution research, needs assessment, $2,000
- solution design, development, $7,000
- cost of materials for the solution and project, $4,000
- facilitator salary and benefits, $11,000
- end user and performer's salaries and benefits, $22,000 (for 40 hours of training and eight weeks of action planning and implementation, at an average of 15 hours per week per person)
- steering committee salaries and benefits, $3,500 (excluding training consultant, factored above)
- evaluation costs, $3,500
- total, $53,000.

The evaluation costs, in particular, included all costs to conduct the impact study data collection and analysis and the development of the management report. Employees completed the questionnaires and action plan on company time, and the estimate reflects this cost.

Barriers

Participants reported on their experience with implementation barriers during the action planning process, the 30- and 60-day questionnaire data collection process, and the final feedback session with the steering committee. During these reports, common themes emerged regarding lack of support from some immediate line supervisors. Other primary concerns were noted regarding overall resistance to change from both assemblers on the targeted improvement line and some equipment support staff asked to support cell conveyer and material flow design changes. Other barriers included loss of two members of the steering committee. The most notable departure was that of the original project sponsor who left to pursue other career opportunities during the initiative, although another engineering manager immediately stepped up to the plate as a project champion. There was also turnover in the process improvement team itself, with one original member being promoted to another part of the organization following completion of training, and another member requiring medical leave during the action planning phase.

Finally, the dynamic nature of the manufacturing business and the need for production lines to support rapid product changeovers caused a delay in launching the initial project. The delay made it necessary to request an extension of the timeline for the research grant. During the project itself, dynamic business changes created several starts and stops in the team's action plan implementation and its data collection process with the targeted line. These starts and stops required that the team extend its improvement plan implementation and 60-day measurement cycle, which in turn contributed to complaints from supervisors about the amount of time team members were away from their normal work duties. Accelerating business changes also caused a last-minute shift in the selection of the production line targeted for the performance improvement exercise.

As a result, key individuals representing that line were not part of the original project briefings and, therefore, showed varying degrees of resistance to the performance improvement team's data collection, data analysis, and performance intervention throughout the project. While it was the original intent of the team and its sponsors to implement an improvement plan with minimal disruption to the line, in actuality, there was substantial disruption to line operation due to extensive cell and conveyer changes. These disruptions tended to reinforce negativity from some operators, supervisors, and select steering committee members. At one point when the team was three-quarters of the way through implementation and measurement of the action plan, a steering committee member called an emergency meeting to recommend pulling the plug on the entire project because of concerns with production deviations and perceived line stoppages.

Surmounting such obstacles in operational support was a challenge met only by the sheer tenacity and credibility of the engineering project champion; key allies among the steering committee group; and the impressive flexibility, conviction, and perseverance of the pilot team in demonstrating the bottom-line value of their improvement design. It is significant that results from the self-assessments and other assessments of applied team competencies show that "assuming a leader role," "seeking common ground," and "active support of team decisions" were among the performance measures that the training intervention very much or completely influenced.

Intangible Benefits

Participants reported the following intangible benefits directly linked to the program but not converted to monetary values:

- It's a good investment because it provides a common language and tools to work on any kind of project . . . for example, the IPO model helps identify your customer and supplier needs.
- Gives the opportunity to work with a variety of groups toward a common solution.
- Easier to see whole picture now. . . .
- I think out of the box more often.
- Provided tools to work on all kinds of projects (for example, identifying the customer; mapping the process; fishbone diagram; plan, do, check, act).
- Quick fixing of ideas is no good—I like "dolphin" (that is, creative, free flowing) thinking.
- Consensus played an important part—we had to really respect and evaluate other points of view.
- I look for solutions now instead of problems.
- I'm more aware of value-adding steps in a process.
- Good investment for Apple—helps us all work smarter, not harder.
- Outstanding experience!
- It gave us all a better picture of the cost associated with production and how we can help.

ROI Calculation

The ROI calculation for this study was calculated by using the following formula:

$$\text{ROI (\%)} = \frac{\text{Net Program Benefits}}{\text{Program Costs}} \times 100$$

To calculate the cost benefit of a 5 percent increase in units per person per hour, the labor cost of $7.42 per unit was multiplied by 5 percent, resulting in a .37 labor cost benefit per person per unit, as the equation shows. This improvement was in turn annualized for an approximate 21.5-week pay period to take into account factory estimated product life cycles. Subject matter experts determined that obtained business results could be sustained throughout an annual product life cycle.

Labor cost benefit per person per unit	Average units per week	Average product life cycle		
= .37	× 10,000	= $3,700	× 21.5 weeks	= $79,550

In addition, both participants and sponsors estimated and annualized the cost benefit of increased labor efficiency, along with other noted process improvements, during the final review of findings, with extreme values being discarded in the process.

For example, participants responded to the question, "What potential cost benefit, in dollars, would you attach to the above improvements over a product life cycle period?"

The consultant then adjusted this data to reflect participants' confidence levels, expressed as a percentage. Specifically, "Your confidence level for this estimate, on a scale of 0 percent for No Confidence and 100 percent for Full Confidence." Next, participants' response to the question, ". . . the percentage of improvement directly related to the training" was multiplied by their individual estimated dollar value of the improvement. These two adjustments yielded a mean total of $140,116. Due to concerns about participants' overinflation of cost benefits, the steering committee then assigned a second, "executive" confidence level of 50 percent to that sum, so that this figure became $70,058 (that is, $140,116 × .50 = $70,058).

The combined cost benefit of improved UPPH and labor efficiency indexes was obtained by adding the figures $70,058 and $79,550 (assumed to be 100 percent accurate), thus totaling $149,608.

Subsequently, the final, sanctioned ROI calculation for the impact study was as follows:

$$ROI = \frac{149,608 - 53,000 \text{ (Program Costs)}}{53,000} = 1.82 \times 100 = 182\%$$

Lessons Learned

Overall, project success was defined by tangible business results that showed more CTO products being produced in desired and improved amounts of time, with a positive return on the training investment. It was uniformly felt that this increased CTO capacity was directly linked to the cell and material flow design implemented by the performance improvement team and that this process improvement could be replicated on other lines with similar results.

Given the many bumps in the road toward achieving such results, however, both participants and sponsors learned several valuable lessons. One lesson involved the need to better anticipate the resource requirements for assigned process improvement opportunities, since it was unanimously agreed that the scope of this particular project was much larger than originally envisioned.

Sensitivity to the intrusive and threatening nature of a change effort was also an area identified as critical to future process improvement planning. Finally, the reengineering project did much to highlight the importance of management support and consistent communication from management to employees during the process of any operational initiative.

In summary, specific recommendations include

- Clarify the effort. Be clear about your purpose and begin with the end in mind.
- Solicit executive, operational support from the beginning.
- Have an evaluation plan for every intervention.
- Build internal capabilities in evaluation skill sets (starting with your *own* capabilities).
- Develop a culture for the use of estimates in calculating ROI.
- Ensure the credibility and commitment of your project champion.
- Share responsibilities for major steps.
- Rely heavily on existing data.
- Start small. Build credibility with manageable projects or BETA groups.
- Remember that systematic evaluation is a change effort that might be perceived as invasive, intrusive, or threatening.

Questions for Discussion

1. What implication does the small sample size of this pilot group have for your interpretation of the results?
2. How would the executive staff in your organization critique the results of this study?
3. What additions or revisions would you make to the evaluation strategies provided?
4. How have you successfully handled barriers in operational support to your own planned performance improvement interventions?
5. What steps would you take to ensure the success of future process improvement teams in this type of environment?

The Author

Holly Burkett has over 18 years of progressive achievement in performance improvement. As an internal training and HRD consultant with Apple Computer (Sacramento Operations), she designs, manages, and evaluates diverse operational initiatives in such areas as leadership development, OJT, and career pathing. A senior professional in human resources (SPHR) and a certified ROI professional, she is a board member of the ROI Network and has frequently been selected as a conference presenter on evaluation best practices. Her publications include a case study featured in ASTD's *In Action: Measuring Learning and Performance,* published in 1999; the ASTD *Info-line* "ROI on a Shoestring," of which she is co-author; and featured profiles in *Training & Development* and the Japanese *HRM and Training* magazine. She earned her B.A. degree in social work from Ohio University and her M.A. degree in human resources and organization development from the University of San Francisco. She can be reached at Apple Computer, Inc., 2911 Laguna Blvd., MS 204 B-11, Elk Grove, CA 95758, email: burkett@apple.com.

References

Phillips, Jack J. (1997). *Return on Investment in Training and Performance Improvement Programs.* Houston: Gulf.

Mission Possible: Selling Complex Services Over the Phone

Hewlett-Packard Company

Theresa L. Seagraves

Many businesses, such as Internet service providers, banks, hospitals, and stock exchanges, have critical computing systems and networks that cannot afford to be down. In some cases, it can truly be life or death stakes. These systems must be always on, or what is also known as "highly available." In 1997, common knowledge at Hewlett-Packard was that telephone-based sales representatives (reps) would never be able to proactively sell customized, complex, and relatively more highly priced high-availability computing system support services to their customer base. This case study will show how an innovative, multistep sales skill intervention completely rewrote the book on what was possible for telephone-based sales. The key components of this intervention were a custom-developed sales skill workshop based on role modeling and skill practice, a reinforcing yearlong sales contest to motivate behavior change, and ongoing peer-to-peer and district manager coaching. The return-on-investment (ROI) analysis focuses on evaluating the most visible and controversial cost investment, the custom workshop.

Background
Organizational Profile and Program Background

Traditional sales models maintain that the more critical a service is to a customer and the greater the complexity of the service to be sold, the more the customer will demand a face-to-face relationship with a skilled and trusted sales representative before he or she will purchase the service. Sales reps who work face-to-face with

This case was prepared to serve as a basis for discussion rather than to illustrate either effective or ineffective administrative and management practices.

customers are expensive, however, and slower than reps who sell using the telephone as their primary communication vehicle. The reps that Hewlett-Packard (HP) charters to use the telephone to make proactive outbound sales calls are known as inside sales reps, or ISRs.

Hewlett-Packard originally targeted high-availability services for the large enterprise customer in a face-to-face selling environment. HP's worldwide services marketing departments believed that the price point, complexity, customization to the customer's situation, longer sales cycle time, and face-to-face sales model made high-availability computing support services impossible to sell to the smaller commercial customer and over the phone to any customer. HP was not alone. This view was held widely across the computing services industry.

When the North American Service and Support Inside Sales organization decided to perform this intervention, the organization was less than a year old. Since Inside Sales had been formed to work with a high number of customers and an extremely low funding model, the management team knew that for reps to survive and thrive they had to grow their sales skills to handle increasingly complex and larger deals. As their field development representative, the author was considered a full member of the North American Inside Sales management team. In the fall of 1997, the team set an aggressive goal to ensure that Inside Sales had the capability to find and close custom high-availability computer-support service business.

Need Assessment

In September 1997, the Inside Sales management team had just received the results from a comprehensive organizational knowledge and skill assessment for all service and support sales reps in North America. Since many inside reps were new to the sales role, the top sales skill development needs that came up for the Inside Sales organization were the basic sales skills of objection handling, sales planning and territory analysis, product value propositions, sales and business writing, and qualification skills. The term *qualification skills* means the ability to determine whether a particular type of sale is likely with a particular customer.

Of the needs identified, the Inside Sales management team believed that the most critical skills were the ones that helped their reps learn to find and focus on the highest value opportunities. The average ISR had been assigned to many, many more customers than their traditional face-to-face sales counterparts. The customers they were assigned to spent, on the average, far fewer dollars per order. Since the goal was to find a less expensive sales model for HP, the Inside

Sales organization had been given less discretionary funds to cover the costs of bringing in their orders. Inside Sales people had to be highly disciplined and precise in where they spent their time. All of these factors led the Inside Sales management team to consider sales planning, territory analysis, and qualification skills as the keys to success or failure. The team determined that the quickest, most efficient and effective way to raise the organization's skill level was to hold an off-site training meeting in December 1997.

The training meeting had three completely custom sales workshops for reps to attend. The high-availability workshop contained a knowledge presentation, success stories from two inside reps who had managed to sell custom high-availability services on their own, and qualification role plays tailored to a telephone selling environment. After the training, sales management planned to continue its focus with monthly reviews of potential sales deals, one-on-one coaching, peer coaching, and special Inside Sales contest incentives.

For the Inside Sales management team to hold a separate and completely customized training meeting was a bold and controversial move for three reasons. First, conventional wisdom continued to state that the Inside Sales team could not sell custom high-availability services. Why waste precious organizational resources? Second, expenses in this new organization were to be kept to the absolute bare minimum. ISRs were not centralized, but spread all over the United States and Canada. Travel was supposed to be almost nonexistent, so why allow Inside Sales to spend the time and money to hold a customized training meeting? Third, another training meeting was going to be held one month later for the traditional face-to-face sales reps. It was to cover high-availability services as well, though not with the same intense focus on qualification, best practice modeling, and roles plays for telephone sales situations. But if it was to offer high-availability training, why create another workshop for Inside Sales? How could Inside Sales management and the Field Development department justify this effort?

Purpose of the Evaluation

The intervention was so successful that the Inside Sales team sold over half of all North American custom high-availability computer support service deals in 1998. The Inside Sales team had more than doubled its 1998 deals by the third quarter of 1999.

The Inside Sales management team had not originally planned to create an ROI evaluation. For the Inside Sales management team, *not* holding the training was never an option. As the sales results appeared, the team did not think an ROI report was necessary. The results were self-evident. The Inside Sales team was sold on tailored training and annual training meetings.

When it came time for the next year's training meeting, however, controversy arose again. Other sales and marketing departments, head-quarter divisions, and even very senior level sales managers raised questions about the need for customized training and the timing of the cost outlay. The ROI evaluation became an opportunity to help HP's extended sales and marketing management community gain confidence in supporting Inside Sales annual training meetings.

Evaluation Methodology
Model

This intervention and evaluation were completed in three phases, as figure 1 shows.

Phase one started with the review of the needs assessment and completed with the delivery of the custom sales skill workshop for

Figure 1. Timeline of events.

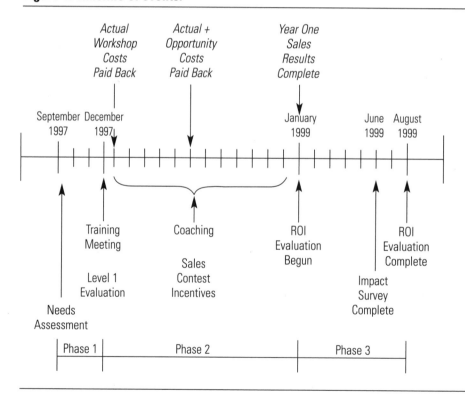

high-availability services. Phase two consisted of coaching and sales contest incentives. Phase three was evaluation activities. It took two years to complete all phases for this intervention and evaluation.

Data Collection Methodology
Level 1 Data Collection

It is mandatory at HP to collect Level 1 reaction data after sales training classes in North America. Instructors distributed a standard evaluation form to all participants and stood by the doors as they left to ensure everyone turned one in. Norms have shown that no matter how badly done the course is, North American sales training Level 1 evaluations rarely average below a four and above a 4.5 on a five-point scale, where five means "strongly agree with the question" or "excellent."

For this workshop, the average score for the standard Level 1 quantitative questions was a 4.54. It is interesting to note that three-quarters of the qualitative written responses regarding what the reps liked most about the workshop were about role-playing. The reps declared the role-playing and practice the most valuable portion of the workshop. The single most consistent comment about what the reps liked least was that there was not enough time for role-playing and practice!

Level 2 and Level 3 Data Collection

Since the ROI evaluation was not planned from the beginning of the intervention, Level 2 (learning) and Level 3 (implementation) data was not statistically collected. Anecdotal evidence of learning and implementation were, however, readily available within the organization. Each month in their staff meetings, the management team discussed the number of high-availability deals in the funnel (that is, the number of deals sales reps in their districts were trying to close with their customers). They also discussed any difficulties reps were consistently experiencing in closing these deals and what could be done to remove them. The district managers discussed how to coach their people on what they could do to close more deals and how to use the most successful sales reps as role models and adjunct coaches within their teams.

Level 4 Data Collection

The final part of the planned intervention was an ongoing sales contest, open only to ISRs. While the structure of the contest remained the same, the management team changed the rules for the types of service deals to be rewarded every three months. Different combinations of services were eligible depending on the organization's focus during the quarter. The organization considered custom high-availability services so important that it rewarded these types of deals for over two years after the initial training workshop.

Since the Inside Sales team already had this contest structure in place, it was easy to collect Level 4 (business impact) data. The administrative coordinator for the North American Inside Sales manager kept a spreadsheet with the name of the rep, the customer, the services sold, the amount of the deal, and the date closed for all sales contest submissions. By the time the evaluation was undertaken, it was not feasible to go back and get data from HP's sales compensation systems, so the contest records became the critical link to trace sales results back to the participants in the training workshop.

Isolation Methodology

When the Inside Sales management team undertook this intervention, common knowledge said it could not be done. This limited the author's options to isolate cause and effect. There were no expert projections and no forecasts on which to base any calculations. There were no preexisting trend lines or studies. The customer base had not had a consistent sales methodology focus in the past and could not be approached for comparisons. Control groups were not an option because the skill level had to be raised across the whole organization simultaneously. As was later verified by leading computer industry analysts, none of HP's competitors had an outbound, telephone-based sales organization selling the equivalent level of complex services, so there was no way to benchmark results externally to HP. This was the cutting-edge group.

Estimation was left as the only feasible alternative for isolating the impact of the intervention. The three types of estimates were as follows:
- participating sales rep estimates of personal impact
- sales management estimation of organizational impact
- estimation of impact of other variables.

As the first step in isolating the impact of the training workshop from other variables, the author conducted an Inside Sales impact survey in June 1999, one and a half years after completion of the initial workshop. It was recognized that while the workshop, coaching, and the sales contest were planned parts of the intervention, other variables could also have helped the sales reps perform so well. The author asked ISRs to estimate the impact of the following five variables on their ability to sell custom high-availability services:

1. training programs (workshop)
2. coaching (peer-to-peer and manager)
3. special incentive programs (sales contest)
4. information resources (desktop reference guide and Websites)
5. marketing programs (lead campaigns).

Each variable was scored on a five-point scale. The responses were charted for two levels of reps that by 1999 had been organized into distinct job functions. One set, territory reps, had fewer customer accounts assigned to them, and their managers expected them to regularly bring in higher dollar amount deals. The other set, account reps, had a much higher number of customer accounts and were expected to occasionally bring in higher dollar amount deals. The territory reps rated the impact of their training and information resources higher than the account reps. While both territory reps and account reps rated peer-to-peer coaching as important, for the account reps it was easily the most critical element of their success. Account reps relied heavily on the territory reps to continue to model best practices and help them learn to be more effective. From the reps' perspective, manager coaching and sales contests had a moderate impact on their success. Marketing programs had a low impact.

The second step in the isolation process was to discuss the survey results with the North American Inside Sales regional manager. The regional manager considered the training workshop a turning point for the organization. However, the need to be conservative and recognize other factors was key. The objective for the evaluation was to convince HP sales management that the ROI in the training meeting was justified. Too high an estimate of impact would jeopardize credibility and waste the Inside Sales management team's and the Field Development department's efforts. Too low an estimate would understate the criticality of the workshop in starting the chain of success. This would then call into question the original need to have held the workshop. The author and the North American Inside Sales regional manager agreed, based on the survey results, that assigning 25 percent of the first year's custom high-availability sales results to the training workshop was appropriate.

Data Conversion Methodology

Several other restrictions on the accounting for results were as follows:
- Only sales that closed within one year after the workshop would be counted.

- For those support contracts that covered a multiple-year period, only the first year's value was counted.
- While peer-to-peer coaching of nonparticipants by workshop participants may have been important, only deals sold by people who participated in the workshop were counted.
- No high-availability sales made throughout the year by the two reps who had each sold one deal at the time of the workshop were counted.

The most conservative estimate of sales results was used as the numerator in the benefit-to-cost ratio (BCR), payback, and ROI calculations. On the basis of these data conversion rules, for the sales period of January 1998 to January 1999, 25 percent of the sales impact came to $3,296,977.

Costs

The author divided program costs into four phases: analysis, development, delivery, and postworkshop evaluation. Every direct and indirect cost was calculated and tracked, regardless of whether the Inside Sales, Field Development, headquarters division, field marketing, or other organization incurred them. Actual costs and opportunity costs were included in the calculation, as shown in table 1. For the calculation of the fully loaded overhead costs of sales managers and other staff time used in each phase, a supporting spreadsheet of standard costing definitions was created, as shown in table 2. The standard costing definition included not just salary and benefits but also a loaded cost per person that HP uses to allocate costs of floor space, computing time, telephone charges, and other indirect expenses of maintaining an employee. Costs were tracked by pay level of employee, so that the higher the level of the employee involved, the more costs were allocated to the project.

The only prorated costs were for travel for developers, management staff, participants, and other observers. Only one-quarter of the total training meeting time was devoted to this workshop. Therefore, only one-quarter of the travel time incurred in any phase was allocated to this workshop.

Table 1. Cost summary.

Actual Direct and Indirect Costs	$58,599
Opportunity Costs	$1,057,692
Total Costs	**$1,116,291**

Table 2. Details of program costs.

	Item Cost
Analysis Costs	
Salaries and employee benefits—Training and Inside staff	$3,918
Teleconference charges	100
General Training Department overhead allocation	481
Total Analysis Costs	**$4,499**
Development Costs	
Salaries and employee benefits—Training and Inside staff	$11,125
Meals, travel, and incidental expenses	750
Teleconference charges	300
Program materials and supplies—overhead transparencies	200
Printing and reproduction	50
Outside services	3,125
General Training Department overhead allocation	1,154
Total Development Costs	**$16,704**
Delivery Costs	
Participant Costs	
Salaries and employee benefits	$12,019
Meals, travel, and accommodations	6,250
Program materials and supplies	1,000
Opportunity cost	1,057,692
Observer Costs	
Salaries and employee benefits	2,692
Meals, travel, and accommodations	500
Instructor Costs	
Salaries and employee benefits	3,135
Meals, travel, and accommodations	1,000
Outside services	4,500
Facility Costs	
Facilities rental	3,000
General Training Department overhead allocation	96
Total Delivery Costs	**$1,091,885**
Evaluation Costs (Level 1 and Training Meeting Report)	
Salaries and employee benefits—Training staff	$2,178
Teleconference charges	50
Office supplies and expense	15
Training Management System records	576
General Training Department overhead allocation	385
Total Evaluation Costs	**$3,204**
TOTAL PROGRAM COSTS	**$1,116,291**

Intangible Benefits

The intangible benefits from this intervention were very high. Although by definition intangible benefits do not have a monetary value assigned to them, the Inside Sales management team's belief is that the intangible benefits were worth the effort alone. The first intangible benefits to appear were the following:

- There was a quick and sustained rise in personal sales confidence and self-esteem among ISRs, leading to willingness to take risks on other new, complex, or difficult programs.
- Teamwork and esprit de corps were reinforced through group achievement of what was considered an unachievable goal. People inside and outside the organization repeatedly commented on the high morale and attitude. Success is attractive and contagious.
- A high retention rate of ISRs, compared with industry averages, and attraction of top candidates for new sales positions were evident. Candidates valued the personal impact that an excellent training program could have on their career growth.

Following were the next set of intangible benefits to appear:

1. recognition by two leading industry analyst companies as being the number one computing support services Inside Sales team in late 1998 based in large part on being the only team currently selling high-availability services in the industry

2. encouragement for Inside Sales teams in Europe, Latin America, and Asia Pacific to increase high-availability sales efforts

3. reevaluation of market potential by headquarter divisions and the North American marketing center.

Finally, two other intangible benefits appeared:

1. increased sales capacity allowing more business to be moved from the more expensive face-to-face sales model to a proactive outbound telephone-based sales model

2. ability to replicate learning success; based on the success of the high-availability services workshop and similar interventions, Inside Sales has learned much about how to create a learning organization that generates a true competitive advantage and how to institutionalize learning across many reps instead of relying on a select few.

ROI Calculation

The author calculated the benefit-to-cost ratio, ROI percentage, and payback time period for this case study. The Inside Sales management team and the Field Development department were both actively involved in the evaluation and review process. The two teams used a conservative accounting of actual deals sold and costs incurred. No annualized data was used, since this could have given some individuals an opportunity to discount what they did not want to believe.

Benefit-to-Cost Ratio

For the sales period of January 1998 to January 1999, Inside Sales returned almost three dollars for every one spent on the training workshop. Based on the conservative 25 percent sales impact and a fully loaded cost structure, the benefit-to-cost ratio (BCR) is

$$\text{Program benefits} / \text{program costs} = \text{BCR}$$
$$\$3,296,977 / \$1,116,291 = 2.95$$

ROI Percentage

The training workshop had an almost 200 percent ROI within one year. Once again, this is based on the conservative 25 percent sales impact and a fully loaded cost structure. The ROI calculation is

$$(\text{Net program benefits} / \text{program costs}) \times 100 = \text{ROI percentage}$$
$$\$2,180,616 / \$1,116,291 \times 100 = 195\%$$

ROI based solely on real costs would be 3,721 percent for the 25 percent of total impacted sales attributed to the training event. These numbers are *not* realistic and should not be used in evaluating the success of the program. All sales training investments must account for the opportunity cost of time that could have been used to retire real quota and realize actual gain to the corporation.

Payback time is also a key number for sales managers. Sales turnover is often high, and sales managers are frequently measured on a year-to-year basis. Payback periods of one year or less are highly desired.

For the training workshop, the payback periods were even better:
- for actual direct and indirect costs, one month
- for actual and opportunity costs, six months.

Communication Process

The high-availability ROI evaluation was one of three case studies the author prepared as part of an Inside Sales training and development ROI project. Each case study evaluated a different training method or training topic with positive but varying levels of results. All three case studies were prepared simultaneously and were released together as a package within Hewlett-Packard.

Several business opportunities provided a forum for a presentation of the case studies. The first, and most important, was the inclusion of the case studies in the North American Service and Support Inside Sales' submission package for HP's President's Quality Award. The highest award that HP gives, it goes to model organizations hand-selected by HP's CEO. The requirements for the award are stringent and include a minimum of three years of outstanding results against a number of criteria. Inside Sales won the award after its first three years of existence. The North American Inside Sales regional manager was asked to present the success formula to HP sales and marketing organizations around the world. Several of his audiences asked him what his single most important success factor was, and he always cited the organization's training program and its results.

Other opportunities included an annual service and support marketing department review and the formal distribution of the case studies to the North American and Worldwide Service and Support Sales vice presidents. Although information is already widespread about these case studies within HP's Service and Support organizations, new Inside Sales organizations are continually being formed in other areas of HP. As these organizations plan their training and development, the same case studies and their supporting sales results and cost estimation spreadsheets are always provided. The response to the information is consistently positive.

Lessons Learned
Importance of Sales Ownership of Training and Program Design

Nothing is more critical than to step back from the ROI evaluation and look at the factors that made the success possible. This was a true team accomplishment for Inside Sales. The management staff "owned" its training program and focused time and attention on it every day. This was reflected in three elements of the design process and the final program.

First, the training program was not done for the Inside Sales management team, but designed closely with the team. Management commitment to the design of the training program cannot be underestimated as a critical success factor. Though the timeline for the project was extremely tight, **all forward progress was halted until all district managers were completely comfortable with the direction set by the training for their reps.**

Second, the training program relied heavily on testimonials and real-world role plays. Over two-thirds of the time was spent in these activities. While key to the reps understanding of the services, less than one-third of the time was spent on a slide show explaining the components of the services. The importance of this design feature is validated in the June 1999 Inside Sales Training Impact Survey.

Third, the training was not a stand-alone event. It was built to support an Inside Sales management initiative, and the Inside Sales management team vigorously reinforced it for the remainder of the year through funnel reviews, coaching, incentives, and team motivation.

Trust and teamwork enabled the intervention and the ROI evaluation. Establishing this environment with any sales organization is a prerequisite to any ROI project proposal. No ROI project should be attempted until this environment is established.

Value of Conservative Sales Result and Cost Estimation

When this ROI evaluation was first proposed, it was met with skepticism by senior sales management. The most common objections were that it was not possible to account for the gray areas of people costs, and the numbers would not be valid unless the opportunity cost of taking reps out of the field was included. Like the high-availability sale by an ISR, ROI evaluations for training and development were something that common knowledge said could not be done.

The conservative claims to sales results, the systematic, comprehensive documentation of costs, the standard costing worksheet, and the inclusion of all opportunity costs were critical to the acceptance of the ROI evaluation within HP. While it would be possible to nitpick at the sales results or the costing, the documentation methodology made it clear that we were harder on ourselves than anyone else would have been. This was a well-thought-through analysis. It passed senior management's approval and has since made it easier to do the right thing for our reps.

It is interesting to note that when it was time for the third Inside Sales annual training meeting, the controversy that gave rise to the ROI evaluation process did not recur. Recently, when a new Inside Sales manager objected to taking reps away from their desks even for a day, the numbers were presented and the objection stopped. With conservative, irrefutable numbers, people stop looking at why they shouldn't do something and start figuring out how to make it happen.

Organizational Learning

The learning organization is a huge business topic. One of the central activities to creating a learning organization is to have key contributors step back and look at what they are doing to be successful. The ROI evaluation process helped us articulate our success factors, listen even more closely to our reps, and standardize best practices. The teamwork, business knowledge, and discipline introduced by the ROI evaluation is now helping us build competitive advantage on a broader scale. We have learned how to learn about ourselves. We are recommending the process to each new Inside Sales organization.

Plan Early for Data Collection

Planning for the ROI analysis would have helped us in two areas. As a retrospective evaluation, we found that we could not re-create statistical data for the Level 2 (learning) and Level 3 (behavior) stages. By not having this data, we missed the opportunities to further improve our ROI as sales were being made. We also missed the opportunity to document the factors for success and their timing so that we could replicate the process even more quickly in other situations.

The other way that early planning would have helped us was in shortening the cycle time to complete the evaluation. The ROI evaluation process was several months long for this case study. This could have been much shorter had we planned for the evaluation from the beginning. We could have avoided some of the controversy surrounding our second training meeting if we had numbers available earlier to show our results. Since most business situations call for a faster analysis cycle, it is recommended that the ROI evaluation be planned from the beginning of any highly visible or controversial intervention.

Questions for Discussion

1. The author states that no ROI evaluation should be attempted without the trust and teamwork of the managers who oversee the participants in the intervention, in this case the sales reps. Do you agree or disagree?

2. Many factors could have contributed to this success. Some were measured in an impact survey, but some may not have been. Was the decision to calculate ROI based on 25 percent of the custom high-availability sales a valid one?

3. Several potential sources of additional sales results were not counted in the evaluation. Some reviewers may see this as *too* conservative in establishing the value of training and development interventions. Should additional work have been done to include annualized sales results for more than one year? Should the cascading effect of participants coaching nonparticipants have been estimated?

4. A strong statement is made regarding the importance of including sales opportunity costs. Do you agree or disagree with the author's position?

5. Levels 2 and 3 were not specifically measured. What impact does this have on the validity of the evaluation? Does it have any?

6. With hindsight it is easy to pick a winner. Do retrospective ROI evaluations have the same credibility as an evaluation process that is chartered before the results are obvious? Why or why not?

The Author

Theresa L. Seagraves joined Hewlett-Packard in 1983. During her career, she has worked in the areas of information technology, research and development, quality programs, direct marketing, and sales training and development. In addition to her involvement in her career and family, Seagraves is an active volunteer for her company and professional communities. She has been a leader in HP's women's diversity networks and has facilitated general manager programs to understand the impact of diversity within organizations. Most recently, she has worked with the International Society of Performance Improvement's Executive Development Task Force. Her current assignment in HP is to lead the implementation of customer relationship management (CRM) systems in HP's worldwide Inside Sales organizations. She can be reached at Hewlett-Packard Co., 10000 Geddes Avenue, Englewood, CO 80112; phone: 303.649.5724; email: theresa_seagraves@hp.com.

Partnering to Achieve Measurable Business Results in the New Economy

First Union National Bank

Debra Wallace

In today's competitive financial services industry, it is more important than ever that a company performs as Wall Street expects. The new economy demands accountability for results rather than activities. When senior leaders have concerns about a company's performance, they investigate its financial goals. They need a team of professionals to partner with them to assess performance goals, identify performance issues, recommend viable and targeted solutions, implement the appropriate solution, provide data that facilitates inspection of progress, and demonstrate business impact. This case depicts this type of challenge and describes the process from performance assessment through the final stages of inspection and reporting to ensure success.

Background

First Union is the nation's sixth largest bank holding company, and it serves more than 16 million customers. It has the third largest branch network and a footprint that spans from Connecticut to Miami. With more than 1 million online banking customers, the nation's sixth largest brokerage firm, and 70,000 plus employees, the company is always competing to be better by providing higher levels of customer service and improving shareholder value through increased revenue and income.

This case began when the president of a multistate region within First Union received his budget goals for the coming year. First Union's president expected him to nearly double revenue and income

This case was prepared to serve as a basis for discussion rather than to illustrate either effective or ineffective administrative and management practices.

in the Capital Management Group (CMG) products area over that year's performance. Based on historical data and his own experience with the sales force (known as relationship managers [RMs]), he knew this goal was unattainable without some intervention. He feared that the sales force was not prepared to properly prospect or to position these products with clients.

In a meeting with his direct reports and supporting leaders, he discussed the coming year's goals and challenges. Priority number one from this meeting was to quickly assess the sales team's ability to prospect and sell CMG products, and to propose a solution that would ensure they were prepared to meet revenue and income goals for the coming year.

Assessment

The first step in the process involved conducting an assessment to identify the cause of the human performance issue. In this case, the leader knew his sales team had never performed at the level they were expected to in the coming year. As is often the case, he and his leaders felt training was the solution, but was that really what was needed to ensure performance?

The First University client partner for this region conducted a performance analysis that included interviews and written self-assessments with product specialists, sales managers, and both average and top-performing RMs. First University is the bank's training and development division. The client partner is responsible for partnering with senior wholesale bank leaders in the region to address human performance issues. This analysis revealed the following performance issues:

- RMs knew very little about CMG product features and benefits. While they were somewhat familiar with products such as 401(k) and personal trust, they could not identify the basic features and benefits of most other CMG products and services. Furthermore, there was very little difference between average and top-performing RMs' basic knowledge of CMG product features and benefits or in their experience level in prospecting for these products.
- RMs were generally unfamiliar with the process for qualifying and referring prospects to CMG product specialists. They were also unable to name their CMG product specialist over 90 percent of the time when asked.
- RMs could not describe the incentive for selling CMG products and services, and didn't know what was in it for them financially. They

also reported very little if any emphasis on CMG sales goals historically and admitted that no inspection or coaching had occurred.

- Managers' observations of RMs during sales calls resulted in disturbing results regarding their effectiveness in positioning CMG products and services. One manager reported an incident in which an RM introduced personal trust products to a valued client by saying, "Well, Jo, you know you're going to die one day, so don't you think we'd better talk about estate planning?"

Performance Improvement Proposal

As a result of this analysis, the client partner made the following recommendations to the senior management team:

- provide training in a two-staged approach that includes (1) self-directed learning to transfer basic knowledge of CMG product features and benefits, preparing RMs to profile ideal clients for CMG products, and preparing RMs to match CMG products to client needs; and (2) classroom learning to prepare RMs to utilize a needs-based sales approach with CMG prospects and clients, to transfer the process for referring CMG prospects, and to provide practice opportunities to master the skills learned
- arrange for CMG product specialists to attend sales meetings after the classroom training to ensure that RMs know whom to work with on these deals, and to ensure that collaboration and communication occurred
- effectively communicate the personal financial impact to RMs for selling CMG products by opening the classroom experience with a focus on it from the president of this regional area and by providing written handouts in sales meetings to RMs from product specialists
- create a tracking and reporting process to facilitate effective capture of referral and closed transaction data at the individual RM level
- develop tools and a process to facilitate after-training coaching on behaviors taught to ensure transfer of new skill and knowledge to the job
- implement a measurement and evaluation strategy that will (1) allow RMs to exempt part or all of the self-directed learning experience, (2) ensure knowledge transfer from the self-directed learning, (3) provide for consistent feedback both during and after classroom training on performance during prospect calls, (4) provide forecast data to senior managers for CMG products and services both

at a state and an individual level, and (5) determine the impact of the training to the business unit.

The senior leader team accepted this proposal, and work began immediately to implement the plan.

Evaluation and Data Collection Plan

Based on the proposal, the client partner developed the following evaluation plan for each phase of the project:

Self-Directed Learning Phase

In order to allow RMs to exempt part or all of this phase, the program designer developed a multiple choice pretest based on program learning objectives. The test was broken into four parts representing the four modules in the program. Learners who scored 80 percent on any module were exempt from completing that one. Otherwise, they were directed to the specific section of the self-directed learning guide to complete the training. When learners had completed all required modules, they took a required posttest. They needed a minimum score of 80 percent on all modules to register for the classroom phase.

Sales managers (SMs) participated in this phase by using a tool for scoring posttests for RMs on their team. This tool included information that SMs could use as discussion points on topics still not clear to RMs after they had completed the self-directed learning guide. This feedback ensured that learners were prepared to move to the next phase of training.

First University also captured participant reaction data for this phase.

Classroom Learning Phase

This phase of the training required RMs to use the product knowledge they gained in the previous phase, and it introduced them to a needs-based selling model. Using a combination of case studies and role plays, participants had many opportunities to practice their new skills. At the end of this program, the facilitator solicited participant reaction data as well as observation data based on a final role play. A checklist based on the program's learning objectives was used by the facilitator and subject matter experts present to determine the extent to which the RMs had learned the material presented.

The action planning method of forecasting addressed senior leaders' need to gather data that would indicate how much revenue and income participants felt they would generate from CMG products and services.

Each RM completed an action plan describing the actions he or she planned to take and the expected outcome if the plan was successful. These outcomes were both quantitative and qualitative, including helpful data on barriers and enablers for implementing their plans.

Follow-Up Phase

The client partner conducted intensive follow-up for 90 days following phase two. This follow-up included:

- joint calls with RMs and their product specialists or SMs to both support and observe RM performance on the call and provide coaching and feedback after the call
- tracking and reporting of all referrals and closed transactions during this period
- biweekly meetings of RMs and their SM to discuss progress to date with the goals established using action plan data gathered at the end of phase two
- product specialists attending each of the SM's sales meetings at least once a month to answer questions and share success stories and progress to date, and to address any concerns about gaps in the process
- inspection by the president of this region in his weekly meeting with his senior leaders to discuss progress to date and how barriers are being removed or minimized.

At the end of this phase, the client partner asked RMs to provide estimates using the same action plan as that at the end of phase two to indicate the actual results during this follow-up period. Table 1 shows the data collection plan for all phases of this program.

Postprogram Data Analysis

First University requires that all programs evaluated at Level 1 use a standard questionnaire designed to gather this feedback. The questionnaire used a scale in which one was strongly disagree; two, disagree; three, neutral; four, agree; and five, strongly agree. We focused on specific results from this questionnaire, described in table 2, for this program.

Participants had a more favorable overall reaction to the classroom phase of this learning experience than they did to the self-directed learning phase. This is common both for programs developed by First University and in the industry. (Similar evaluations throughout the

Table 1. Data collection plan.

Level	Method	Measure	Timing
Reaction and Planned Action	End of program questionnaire	• New information • Intent to use • Relevance to job needs • Overall satisfaction • Planned actions and results (behavioral)	Phase one: collected after completion of all required modules and used to award course credit Phase two: end of class
	Action plan	• Planned actions and results (quantitative) • Barriers • Enablers	Action plans collected at end of phase two class
Learning	Pre- and posttests Observation checklists with role play	• % correctly answered questions • % behaviors, skill, and knowledge successfully applied	Phase one: before and after self-directed learning Phase two: end of class
Job Application	Action plan	• Actual actions and results (behavioral) • Barriers • Enablers	90 days after phase two classroom training
Business Impact	Action plan Performance monitoring	• Actual actions and results (quantitative estimates) • Increased revenue and income by RM • Increased referral volume by RM	90 days after phase two classroom training

Table 2. Reaction data.

Variable	Phase One Results		Phase Two Results	
	Rating	% Responses	Rating	% Responses
The course provided me with new information.	4.25	83	4.57	73
This course was clearly related to my job.	3.62	83	3.91	73
I will apply what I learned back on my job.	3.94	83	4.17	73
Overall, I was satisfied with this course.	3.40	83	4.04	73

industry receive the same type of response from participants.) Most participants indicated that they prefer having the opportunity to practice and receive feedback, therefore preferring the classroom method to most forms of distributed learning. Most participants indicated strongly that the information presented was new, validating the performance assessment work done previously.

Open-ended comments from this questionnaire provided exceptional feedback to facilitate improvements to the course. In addition, the comments unveiled the unhealthy reality that, in many cases, CMG product specialists were "competing for shelf space" with RMs. These comments enabled senior leaders to effectively confront and resolve this problem.

Open-ended comments also showed that some participants resented having to participate in phase one of this program because of their perceived knowledge of CMG product features and benefits. Although they felt they were "seasoned commercial bankers" who "already knew this information," on the basis of their results on the pretest, a majority of them were not able to be exempt from the program. Table 3 describes results from the pre- and posttests for phase one, which shows a 40 percent improvement from pretest to test mean scores.

Participants' low scores on the pretest were another validation point for the assessment work done. Their significant improvement on posttest scores (40 percent) over pretest scores also indicated that the content of the program was appropriate for the target audience.

Forecast Performance Improvement

Participants completed an action plan at the end of the program. This data would be used to describe the behavioral actions they planned to take to transfer the training they received to their job performance. They were also asked to quantify the impact of their plan if they were successful in implementing it. Additionally, they provided feedback on things they felt would prevent them from successfully implementing their plan (barriers) as well as ideas for assisting them as they implement their plan.

Table 3. Pre- and posttest data.

Instrument	Mean Score	Minimum Score	Maximum Score
Pretest	60%	38%	95%
Posttest	84%	55%	100%

The client partner combined data from these forms into a spreadsheet that could be easily used as an inspection and review tool both for individual RMs and the region as a whole. Managers used this report to have proactive discussions with individual RMs about their planned performance, with the result being a healthy discussion to identify any gap between what they planned to do and what their goals were for selling CMG products and services. Figure 1 shows the form participants used at the end of the program, and table 4 shows the spreadsheet showing individual forecasts.

Participants most frequently noted the following planned actions:
- update relationship plans to include strategy for selling CMG products
- ask more probing questions involving CMG issues
- match products by customer needs or wants for customers and prospects
- determine if customer is capable of "buying" products
- identify each CMG product specialist for my market and begin making joint calls with those specialists regularly
- focus less exclusively on credit and deposit products, and place more attention on "personal" opportunities
- regularly review training reference materials to keep my knowledge up-to-date.

Many RMs noted their goal to make specific numbers of calls each month, so they could meet their overall revenue goal.

An equally important part of this study involves exploring specific barriers to successful implementation. These issues give insight into the things that need to be changed, modified, or adjusted so that the new skills or knowledge can be successfully implemented. The following barriers, in participants' words, were the ones they most frequently cited in their feedback to the action plans:
- not getting the necessary commitment from the various product specialists to take action on my referrals
- other job priorities that keep me from focusing on this area
- participation with all services that yield higher revenue $$
- change in corporate strategy or emphasis
- procrastination
- not reviewing info from CMG 101 on periodic basis to reinforce skills
- no self-diagnostic after each sale and lost sale
- not consistently asking the probing questions.

Along with input concerning barriers to successful implementation, participants gave feedback on things that would assist them as they implement the new skills and knowledge from this course. Senior

Figure 1. End-of-program action plan.

Action Plan for CMG Product Training 201: A Sales Approach

Name: _____   Date: _____

Objective: _____

(SMART) Specific, Measurable, Attainable, Realistic, and Time Based

Action Steps		Analysis
Specific Steps: *I will do this*	**End Result: *So that***	*What would the outcome be if you are successful?*
1.	1.	A. What is the unit of measure?
2.	2.	B. What is the value (cost) of one unit? $
3.	3.	C. How did you arrive at this value?

4.

_____

_____

_____

_____

5.

_____

_____

_____

_____

What may prevent you from successfully implementing skills or knowledge learned in this program?

What will assist you as you implement new skills or knowledge learned in this program?

D. How much do you believe this measure will change over the next 90 days? (monthly value)
$ _____

E. What level of confidence do you place on the above information? _____ %
(100% = certainty and 0% = no confidence)

Table 4. End-of-program action plan (usable) data.

Name	Unit of Measure	Value (Cost) of One Unit	Explanation	90-day change (monthly value)	Confidence Level
RM1	One item sold	$5M to $10M minimum	Estimate based on experience with CMG sales	$15,000	70%
RM2	Closed referral	$25M	Estimate of average size of deal in my market, based on experience	$10,000	75%
RM3	Closed business	$15M	Assigned goal—very attainable	$15,000	100%
RM4	One sale	$30M	Estimated values on average of CMG (personal and corporate) of one product	$10,000	75%
RM5	Items sold	$5M	Most products sold can be counted in $5,000 increments of revenue	$7,500	50%
RM6	Improved sales	$10M	Each prospect or customer if sold correctly will address the above	$5,000	70%
RM7	# sales	$25M	SWAG—total two sales in the next 90 days ($50M); six per year (zero last year)	$17,000	85%
RM8	Improved CMG sales	$10M	Referrals currently in pipeline	$3,500	95%
RM9	Sales	$10M	Estimated revenue from product sales to affluent individual	$5,000	75%

RM10	One item sold	$10M	Typical fee for 401K planning stock transfer business	$17,000	66%
RM11	Sales	$10M	By selling more than one or two CMG products per prospect or customer. Personal estate planning (PES) / Investment—money manager	$10,000	85%
RM12	Dollars	$15M	Gross sales of one PES, business valuation and money manager	$5,000	75%
RM13	Sales	$25M	Average CMG sales	$17,000	50%

leaders and the client partner used the suggestions to remove some of the barriers or to provide job aids that would assist in the sales process, or both. These included

- joint calls with product specialists for feedback and coaching
- newsletter with refresher information, success stories, and status or updates on activity
- matrix of products offered
- additional learning opportunities on this topic
- upper management's commitment to this area.

The client partner presented this data along with the quantitative data in table 4 to the leadership team. It was clear to this team that they needed to ensure proper support by product specialists as RMs attempted to use their new skills and knowledge to improve their job performance. It was also clear that they as leaders needed to ensure they remained consistent in their strategic emphasis and commitment to these goals. This was the first initiative that captured this type of forecast data and reported it to senior leaders. The candor of the feedback from participants surprised them, and they felt empowered as leaders to support and inspect progress of the sales force based on this data.

Forecast Business Impact

The most critical and challenging part of this study was to link this training program with specific improvements in business measures. The client partner asked participants to forecast the business impact of successfully implementing their action plans. There were 47 participants enrolled in this program, and 34 of them completed and returned the action plan. Thirteen participants provided usable estimates, all of which focused on increased CMG product sales. This number represents 38 percent of all participants who responded, and 28 percent of all participants attending the program.

The total benefits forecast from the program were calculated by making the following four conservative adjustments to the data:

1. It was assumed that participants who did not provide usable data for these series of impact questions would have no improvement. This is conservative since other participants certainly could have improvements, but for some reason did not want to forecast results.

2. Calculations consider benefits only through the end of the calendar year. The program took place in February, and benefits were calculated on the basis of data forecast from March through December

of that year. Normally, the first year of benefits is captured in analysis. It is assumed that First University programs must have an appropriate return on the investment in the first year of implementation, but skills taught should have lasting benefits beyond the first year. In this case, the benefit calculation is even more conservative than normal.

3. In order to complete an accurate analysis, revenue factors presented were converted to income factors using a 33.2 percent margin.

4. Confidence level percentages are used to acknowledge the subjective nature of these estimates. Downward adjustments on the forecast contribution have been made to reflect the most conservative benefit.

Table 5 provides detail on forecast benefits for the program. After implementation of these adjustments, the total forecast benefits for this program are $336,133 in increased income from CMG product sales.

Costs

The cost to design and deliver this training is an important value because it becomes the numerator of the return-on-investment (ROI) analysis formula and also reflects the overall investment in this program. The philosophy adopted for this study, which is followed by most major organizations using the ROI analysis process, was to be very conservative in cost calculations. This means that costs are fully loaded; when a particular cost item is in doubt, it is included in the analysis. The cost to design and develop both the self-directed phase and the classroom phase of this program was fully loaded into the ROI calculation for this analysis even though the cost could be distributed over future deliveries of this program. This approach helps to ensure that the ROI generated has the credibility of being a realistic and conservative measure.

Figure 2 details costs incurred to design and deliver this program in this region.

Forecast ROI

The client partner calculated the forecast ROI using the forecast benefits value of $336,133 and the total program costs of $51,341. When costs and benefits are combined in the standard ROI formula, the forecast ROI becomes:

$$\text{ROI} = \frac{\$336{,}133 - \$51{,}341}{\$51{,}341} = \frac{\$284{,}792}{\$51{,}341} = 555\%$$

Table 5. Forecast benefits.

Name	Unit of Measure	Value (Cost) of One Unit	Explanation	90-day change (monthly value)	Adjusted Value Reflecting Margins	Confidence Level	Adjusted Monthly Forecast	Adjusted 90-Day Forecast	Adjusted March-December 1998 Forecast
RM1	One item sold	$5M to $10M minimum	Estimated based on past experience with CMG sales	$15,000	$4,980	70%	$3,486	$10,458	$34,860
RM2	Closed referral	$25M	Estimate of average size of deal in my market, based upon experience	$10,000	$3,320	75%	$2,490	$7,470	$24,900
RM3	Closed business	$15M	Assigned goal; very attainable	$15,000	$4,980	100%	$4,980	$14,940	$49,800
RM4	One sale	$30M	Estimated values on average of CMG (personal and corporate) of one product	$10,000	$3,320	75%	$2,490	$7,470	$24,900
RM5	Items sold	$5M	Most products sold can be counted in $5,000 increments of revenue	$7,500	$2,490	50%	$1,245	$3,735	$12,450
RM6	Improved sales	$10M	Each prospect or customer if sold correctly will address the above	$5,000	$1,660	70%	$1,162	$3,486	$11,620
RM7	# sales	$25M	SWAG—total two sales in the next 90 days ($50M); six per year (zero last year)	$17,000	$5,644	85%	$4,797	$14,392	$47,974

RM8	Improved CMG sales	$10M	Referrals currently in pipeline	$3,500	$1,162	95%	$1,104	$3,312	$11,039
RM9	Sales	$10M	Estimated revenue from product sales to affluent individual	$5,000	$1,660	75%	$1,245	$3,735	$12,450
RM10	One item sold	$10M	Typical fee for 401K planning stock transfer business	$17,000	$5,644	66%	$3,725	$11,175	$37,250
RM11	Sales	$10M	By selling more than one or two CMG products per prospect or customer. PES/Investment—money manager	$10,000	$3,320	85%	$2,822	$8,466	$28,220
RM12	Dollars	$15M	Gross sales of one PES, business valuation and money manager	$5,000	$1,660	75%	$1,245	$3,735	$12,450
RM13	Sales	$25M	Average CMG sales	$17,000	$5,644	50%	$2,822	$8,466	$28,220
Total							**$33,613**	**$100,840**	**$336,133**

Figure 2. Program cost data.

Design:

Outside consultant services	$15,400.00
Salaries and benefits—First University staff	3,950.00
Salaries and benefits—subject matter experts (SMEs)	975.00
Subtotal	$20,325.00

Delivery:

Outside consultant services for facilitation	$ 1,800.00
Salaries and benefits—SME (one SME each day)	1,040.00
Salaries and benefits—First University staff (one staff, day 1)	320.00
Salaries and benefits— 47 participants	21,150.00
Travel expense—outside consultant	966.78
Travel expense—First University staff	800.00
Registration support	300.00
FedEx expense	65.00
Hotel expense (meeting room, food, beverage, equipment)	2,683.53
Materials and printing expense (both 101 and 201)	1,890.50
Subtotal	$31,015.81
Total Program Cost	**$51,340.81**

Outcomes From End-of-Program Evaluation Data

The following summarizes observations and recommendations for this program as a result of data analysis:

- First University next actions.
  - modify agenda and workbook based on participant feedback and changes made during pilot
  - modify the pretest scoring mechanism for CMG Products Training 101 (prerequisite to 201) to improve the ease of use for managers as they score the test and provide adequate direction to participants
  - work with corporate CMG contacts to make cases more real life and obtain buy-in
  - create a matrix of CMG products organized by customer needs to be included in course materials and for participants' use as a reference tool after training
  - introduce expectation for participants to complete action plans early in the day and review an example showing how to complete them

— secure the support and advocacy of a senior executive in each state in which the training occurs to set appropriate expectations and kick off the class.
- Leadership team next actions.
  — Each RM should identify qualified CMG prospects and prioritize them to focus on the highest revenue opportunities.
  — Each RM should document a strategy for developing CMG opportunities within his or her market.
  — Each RM should establish calling goals for meeting his or her revenue goals.
  — Managers should ensure calling goals are set and inspect progress frequently and consistently.
  — Managers should go on prospect calls with RMs to provide coaching and feedback.
  — Commercial bankers should continue learning about CMG products by making joint calls with CMG product specialists; inviting CMG product specialists to staff meetings to focus on specific product issues; and reviewing CMG newsletters, success stories, and the like.
  — Managers should cross-functionally discuss and report a status of call activity (actual and planned), deals closed, and success stories monthly at the first Monday meeting.
  — Senior leaders should be consistent in reinforcing the strategic focus around CMG products and resist inappropriate opportunities to divert attention from this goal.
- Evaluation period results. During this 90-day evaluation period, there was intense focus on all activity supporting CMG product sales. The following statistics show marked improvement at various points in time for this period:
  — In the first two weeks following training, average qualified referrals per week increased from 12 to 25.
  — In that same two weeks, almost $100,000 in income was referred and closed, with training being identified as the major contributor for this success.
  — Sixty days following the program, actual income from deals closed approached $225,000 (representing approximately 65 percent of their adjusted forecast annual improvement).
  — Joint calls with RMs and their CMG product specialists increased during this evaluation period by 70 percent over the previous year's results.

Actual Business Impact and ROI

After the 90-day evaluation period was over, performance monitoring showed that RMs had already generated $330,771 in income from CMG products. This improvement far exceeded participants' estimates at the end of the program. It was a result not only of training but also of such other factors as joint calls with CMG product specialists for feedback and coaching, and management support and inspection. Figure 3 shows the increase in income as a result of the training. The results through the end of that year are depicted by the solid line in figure 3.

Isolating the Impact of Training

Several factors often contribute to performance improvement. RMs who participated in this pilot were surveyed by phone and asked to estimate the extent to which a variety of factors had an impact on their success. The percentage of replies to each of the factors is as follows:
- CMG products training, 35 percent
- joint calls with product specialists, 31 percent
- manager's coaching and inspection, 22 percent
- incentives, 9 percent
- other, 3 percent.

The study used the participants' estimation method because rapid deployment and the constantly changing environment made other methods, such as control groups or trend line analysis, impractical.

Increased income attributed to training equates to approximately $115,770 in the 90-day evaluation period, and $529,783 through the end of that year. The broken line in figure 3 represents the amount of actual success participants attribute to training.

The dotted line in figure 3 represents participants' estimates of increased income as forecast at the end of the program, as shown in table 4.

ROI

The client partner calculated the actual ROI for this project using data obtained through performance monitoring. The ROI calculation, which follows, uses data from figure 3 and foregoing cost data:

$$ROI = \frac{\$529,783 - \$51,341}{\$51,341} = \frac{\$478,442}{\$51,341} = 932\%$$

Figure 3. Results of CMG products training.

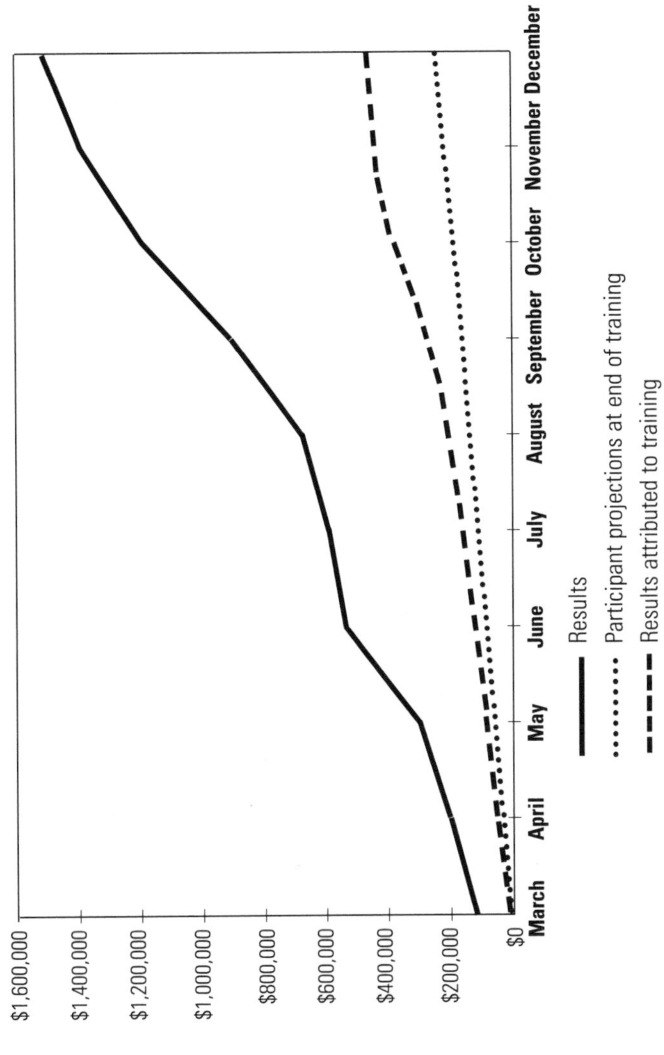

Legend:
— Results
········· Participant projections at end of training
– – – Results attributed to training

Communications Process

Throughout the project, the First University client partner was responsible for communicating with and coordinating the efforts of all parties involved. When the evaluation period ended, the client partner presented a report to the president of this region to describe progress to date as well as the extent to which training had an effect on these results. The report outline follows:

- introduction (including name of program, date delivered, target audience, purpose of study, program objectives, and response profile)
- participants' reactions (including quantitative data from questionnaire used as well as open-ended comments)
- participants' planned actions (including most frequently mentioned planned actions from action plans as well as barriers and enablers)
- projected business impact (including response profile of participants providing usable data, descriptions of adjustments made, costs, and ROI calculation)
- actual business impact (including data from performance monitoring and ROI calculation)
- appendix (including spreadsheets detailing data from action plans and evaluation instruments used during project).

After the client partner presented the findings to the president for this region, they held a meeting with his senior leadership team where the client partner presented the same report. This meeting resulted in continued focus on the business goals as well as acknowledgment of the extent to which training could have an impact on performance improvement. A leader in that meeting said, "This is the way we should do this work. It feels like we really partnered to do the right things, not just what we thought we should do." The leadership team agreed, and this proved to be the first of many similar partnerships for performance improvement.

The presentation of this impact study also produced another important result. This leadership team had always felt there was a link between training and performance improvement, but had never personally experienced a process in which that link was so clearly defined and presented. Feedback from this group included the following comments:

- "I like the fact that you considered RMs' time away from work while attending training. That shows you really understand the impact to our business when those guys aren't making calls. It gives me confidence that you'll only recommend training when training is really the right solution."

- "I like the process you used for determining the business impact and calculating ROI. It makes sense. I think I'll put more emphasis, however, on the information around their planned actions from the action plans. That helped me really focus on what people planned to do, and what I needed to do to direct them or get our of their way so they could succeed."
- "The most helpful part of this process for me was getting data I could use to help me manage my business. This wasn't just about training, but improving processes, improving reporting, improving relationships, and getting distractions out of my folks' way."

Lessons Learned

This was the first project that used action planning as a forecast tool. It proved to be a powerful and useful tool for both First University and the internal clients served. It both provides data that describes the behavioral and quantitative parts of changed behavior and performance improvement, and it forces participants to think about how they will apply what they just learned to their jobs. Action planning has proved to be an important part of the ever-challenging task of transferring training to the job.

In a business world where margins are shrinking, human performance improvement is more important than ever. Providing leaders with data they can actually use to assist them as they lead in performance improvement is often the key to showing the value added. The action planning tool can accomplish this goal and support basic adult learning principles.

Questions for Discussion

1. How is your group positioned to partner with your internal clients to conduct valid and effective performance assessment work?
2. What other types of data collection tools could have been used to gather data in this case?
3. How important is it to identify all things that have an impact on performance and to develop an evaluation strategy to support all interventions, not just training?
4. How does using participants' estimate to isolate the effects of training have an impact on the end result, given the fact that performance monitoring was used to convert the data into monetary value?
5. How credible is the business impact and ROI data? Explain.
6. How could this evaluation strategy have been improved?

The Author

Debra Wallace is the business and performance measurement leader for First Union's First University. She has over 15 years' experience in the banking industry, with the last 10 of those years focused on training and development. Her emphasis for the past six years has been on the development of expertise in the areas of performance consulting as well as on assessment, measurement, and evaluation. She has led her group in developing best practices for reporting the impact of training on the business unit. Wallace holds a B.S. degree in accounting from Clemson University. She can be contacted at the following address: 109 Ashley Oaks Drive, Blythewood, SC 29016; email: d2wall@bellsouth.net.

ROI From Individualized Training for Computer Manufacturing Employees

Focus Corporation

David Barraza

In computer manufacturing the speed of technological change continues to increase while the life cycle of the product continues to decrease. In a build-to-customer-order manufacturing environment, these elements can have a tremendous impact on business. This case study presents the training challenges of a build-to-customer-order computer manufacturing environment and the training intervention the Focus Personal Computer Division implemented to meet the challenge. It details the division's special training needs, its training goals, the training system introduced, the metrics used to measure the effectiveness of implementing the new training system, and the return on investment.

Background

Focus Personal Computer Division built desktop computers, laptops, and small servers for business customers. Top management made the decision to shift the division's operations from build to stock of its product line to build to customer order (BTCO). Instead of building several hundred units with the same configuration, each system built could be different. In BTCO, customers design their own system, specifying a base, nonfunctioning system, and then the options required to meet their unique applications. Customers could select from more than 1,100 options, such as CPUs, memory, drives, input and output cards, and software. Customers could also choose to have their systems customized with hardware and software options that were not released by Focus. Focus configured and tested the specified system. The production process began after the order was received. Under BTCO, customer orders ranged from a quantity of one to a quantity of 1,000, and processes had to be able to handle this wide variation. The manufacturing processes were redesigned to efficiently handle an order quantity of one. This included changing the factory layout and flow. Most orders were small. Even large corporate customers that bought several thousand systems a year from Focus ordered in small quantities to fully utilize the BTCO advantage. More than 70 percent of the orders were for 10 or fewer systems.

As a result of process and factory layout improvements, production did see some improvements in reduced operator assembly and test times under the existing training system. These changes were not good enough.

The Challenge

Manufacturing employees were struggling under BTCO. Instead of one product, a worker now needed to know more than 30 different product families. For one product family, the number of possible configurations easily surpassed a billion. The flexibility of the manufacturing process had to increase significantly. At the same time, the quality of the systems had to go even higher. Again, the need for an effective training program became a necessity.

Another factor was the speed of technological change in the industry. A computer manufacturer must release new products quickly when a new technology becomes available. Frequent major changes in technology made the life cycle of a product relatively short: Nine to 12 months was not uncommon. Products in the personal computer industry changed almost daily. For example, when Intel increased the speed of its processor chip or an integrated circuit chipmaker designed a new chip-set that added a new function to the computer, products using these often required a new motherboard design or in some cases a complete product change. To keep up with this market, Focus had to respond quickly and release new products as soon as a new technology became available. A three-month delay could mean one-third of the life of the product was lost. The need for fast cycle product releases was another reason the production workers had to be efficiently and quickly trained. Improperly trained workers meant low productivity and poor quality. This was an unacceptable situation.

The trigger for the decision to improve training was when the author's boss, the vice president for operations, started getting two or three phones calls a day from the field saying quality was a problem. It was clear that inadequate productivity and factory and field quality were major costs, and cutting them would require an investment in training employees.

The Division's Goals

To remain competitive in this industry, Focus Personal Computer Division needed to release products faster. Although higher productivity was a management goal, it was not one we told our employees. As director of manufacturing engineering and director of manufacturing operations at Focus, the author's idea was that the product quality would go up and productivity would increase naturally if employees received proper training. Our first training priority was quality.

Creating the Training Plan

To meet the needs of a build-to-customer-order environment and other requirements of a fast-paced and ever-changing product line, an extensive training plan was required. The plan called for each production worker to receive 110 hours of training over an 18-month period. Training would require a major commitment from the manufacturing department, from production supervisors, and also from the workers. It would mean that on the average, an equivalent of five workers would be in training on a continual basis. Before embarking on such an ambitious project, the manufacturing operations department had to get commitment from top management.

Management Backing

To secure management's backing, the manufacturing operations department had to justify the training program. The managers in manufacturing operations felt the benefits of the training would be the following:
- higher product quality
- higher productivity
- reaching new-product productivity targets faster
- a more flexible workforce
- a more effective utilization of the workforce.

The author estimated the cost of training versus the savings, and together with the production manager and the training manager designed metrics to measure the effectiveness of the training during the training process and after it was completed. (See the section "Training Metrics" later in the chapter.)

State Funding

The state of California, through its Employment Training Panel (ETP), pays companies in California to train their workers in skills that other companies can use. The state does this because a skilled unemployed worker is more readily hired than an unskilled one. The state also wants to ensure that California companies have a skilled workforce so that they can stay competitive with companies elsewhere. California has determined that it is less expensive to assist in the payment of training costs than it is to pay extended unemployment benefits or lose taxes from companies that leave the state.

This reimbursement to a company does not cover the cost of training, but it does significantly reduce the total training cost. The state accepts only certain types of training and has very strict record-keeping requirements. The state was a helpful and supportive partner in Focus's training project. Our broker for state funding under this program was Katherine Amoukhteh, of Workforce America, a private company, in San Jose and Laguna Hills, California, that provides a wide range of corporate training and obtains training funds for California companies.

BTCO Process

The flow of the build-to-customer-order computer configuration process needs to be understood before the training objectives can be understood.

Focus had two parallel production lines with almost identical processes: one to build desktop and laptop personal computers and the other for small servers. Building in quantities of one started in the kitting area, which is the place for pulling parts in the stockroom for a specific BTCO system. All the parts required to configure one system were placed in a tote box, except low-cost common parts like screws and cable ties. These common, inexpensive parts were stocked at the assembly stations. If the order was for 10, then 10 totes were used. The tote boxes traveled by conveyor to the assembly area. The system was assembled completely by one person in a single-person work cell. Each assembler had to be able to assemble any of the product families on his or her line with any combination of the more than 1,100 options. The assembled products then passed through a labeling area where an employee applied safety agency and system labels.

Next the system entered a computer-integrated test area, called test, where the unit was dynamically tested for several hours and the customer software was automatically loaded onto the hard disk drive.

After successful completion of the test operation the unit went to the cosmetic area where the case works were cleaned. Then the accessory items, such as the keyboard, mouse, and manuals, were placed inside the shipping carton with the system. About 15 to 20 percent of the systems were routed through the final audit area where a technician performed a complete electrical and mechanical inspection. The systems were then boxed and sent to the distribution area. Stand-alone items such as monitors and printers were brought together with the computers and the complete order was shipped to the customer.

It is important to note that there were no separate quality control points; no stations were dedicated to doing independent inspections. Every worker was responsible for his or her own quality.

Training Plan Objectives

The objectives the training program had to meet were as follows:

- *Quality:* Focus customers demanded high quality and did not accept anything less. The build-to-customer-order environment with a large number of variables in each order made achieving a high level of quality much more challenging. Training had the potential to improve quality by helping production workers learn and understand the correct way to build the product and by getting everyone involved to use identical production processes, which would eliminate variation. Uniformity of processes improves overall quality quickly.
- *Flexibility:* The product mix of the systems to be built changed daily. The mix of servers and workstations could change drastically each day. Also in the electronics industry, there is a strong tendency to increase shipments significantly at the end of each quarter. Therefore the workforce had to be flexible and able to handle the daily and monthly production variations. The skill sets for performing the tasks in the assembly, test, and cosmetic areas differed significantly. To have a flexible workforce, employees had to be cross-trained in multiple areas. At that time Focus was not systematically cross-training people. The goal was to have each person cross-trained and certified in at least three areas.
- *Productivity and fast ramp-up:* Focus was releasing new products monthly. It was important that the company increase the volume of shipments of a product immediately after its release. To achieve this, the company had to have a steep learning curve for quality and productivity. For existing products, manufacturing and training managers predicted that the average time required to assemble should

improve significantly by the time all the production workers had been completely trained.

- *Self-paced:* People learn by different methods and at different rates. A few can learn simply by reading or listening. Most require hands-on practice to become proficient. To make BTCO successful with the diversity of people involved, Focus Personal Computer Division needed a self-paced training program that was effective with people who had a wide range of learning styles and speeds.

The Workforce

The educational levels of the production people ranged from not completing high school to two years of college (usually in electronics). Focus was very fortunate to maintain a stable direct labor workforce in a period of high turnover and rapid growth in the computer manufacturing industries of Silicon Valley. The average length of employment for its production workers was over 12 years. The average annual turnover rate for the production workers was about 5 percent compared with 30 percent for the geographic area. Some of the turnover was due to internal transfers and promotions.

A significant percent of Focus's direct labor workforce spoke English as a second language, approximately 65 percent to 70 percent. Most were Asian, although a fair number were Hispanic. It would have been expensive and time-consuming for Focus to develop the training program in multiple languages. Most of the people could read English but often at a slow pace. It was important to develop a training plan that did not penalize employees with an English language deficiency.

Those who wrote procedures, coached, or supervised the training or trainees also needed to get trained. These included manufacturing engineers with educational levels from bachelor of science to graduate degrees in mechanical and electrical engineering.

Existing Training

Manufacturing operations taught two types of classes in the existing training programs: core and production. The core subject classes were the basics taught to all new employees and all other employees annually to reinforce critical process procedures. These were skills required in all production operations, such as proper handling of sensitive electronic assemblies, electrostatic discharge protection, and safety. Training sessions also covered such topics as product marketing strategies and customer applications of the products built at this facility. It was important that the production people understood where and how the products that they created would be used and the importance of their efforts. These core classes usually lasted one or two hours and took place in a classroom environment. The format was lecture, with small video clips and demonstrations to reinforce some of the lecture portion.

Most of the production training used the assembly demonstration method to introduce workers to new products. The manufacturing engineer responsible brought several of the top assemblers into a conference room. Then the manufacturing engineer would use a kit of parts to demonstrate how to assemble a new product. The total time for the instruction was usually less than an hour. Following the demonstration, the engineer would ask if there were any questions. Most of the audience was overwhelmed by the large amount of information they received in a short period of time. Their usual answer was silence because they were embarrassed to show a lack of understanding in front of their peers. This method of training resulted in a familiarity with the product but retention of only about 10 percent. The workers would initially have to refer to the written procedure during the assembly process because they could not retain all the information presented during the manufacturing engineer's presentation. A rapid ramp-up in volume was required when a new product was released to manufacturing. The present assembly demonstration method had a long learning curve, and the initial quality of the product was poor. It did not meet Focus's standard.

Proficiency Training—The New System
Target Area: Production

The company's primary need for training was in production. To improve product quality, the emphasis was on cross-training and job certification. The training approach Focus selected to meet the training objectives was a new system called 100% Proficiency, developed by Effective Training Solutions (ETS) in Fremont, California. ETS bases its training products on research that was conducted by L. Ron Hubbard in the 1960s. It was published as a lecture series and showed that training could be improved by shifting responsibility for learning and the control of learning to the trainee. This training system sets a standard of 100 percent, which depends heavily on training each student or trainee in relevant learning skills. With this system, the trainer's focus shifts from the directive role of teacher or trainer to the more facilitative role of coach and to verification of proficiency.

All Focus permanent production employees became involved in this new ongoing training. It consisted of two parts. In the first part, the production people attended a three-day class that taught practical techniques on how to learn. The how-to-learn process included learning how to identify and overcome learning inhibitors, learning at one's own pace, clarifying words one doesn't understand, and understanding one section completely before moving on to the next. The second part was implementing the job certification and cross-training program. This consisted of using a 100% Proficiency check sheet. The check sheet ensured that trainees practiced, or drilled, with hands-on exercises to become fully proficient during training, not after. The check sheet served as the training instruction or road map. It used the assembly or process procedure as its prime reference document. (The sheet used annotated digital photographs and line drawings instead of word descriptions whenever possible. These images minimized ambiguity and the difficulty some people had with English. The manufacturing engineering group wrote and maintained the assembly procedures.) The check sheet identified the new key words in the procedure, divided the procedure into learnable sections, specified special learning exercises and drills, and provided for the trainer and trainee's sign-off of learned sections. The trainee attests in writing to having achieved 100 percent proficiency upon completion of the check sheet. A filled-out and signed copy of the check sheet was a record of successful completion of training by the individual.

Trainees started by becoming 100 percent proficient in assembling one of the product families of computers or learning a process, such as computer integrated testing. To be certified, trainees had to build a predefined number of BTCO systems without error. The number varied from 20 to 50 depending on the product family.

Before 100% Proficiency training, workers got cross-training by moving to a different area to get the training they needed; there was no certification system. After implementation of this certification system, workers were able to systematically move through their check sheets with minimal lost productivity in their primary production area.

Production training had changed in both subject matter content and learning style, helping manufacturing operations achieve our training objectives and quality goals.

One Training Example in Production

This example of product training in assembly illustrates 100% Proficiency training. An empty assembly work cell receives a kit of parts required to completely build a product as well as the assembly procedure and check sheet. The equipment (such as calibrated power screwdrivers, hand tools, bar code reader, and test computer) and hardware (screws, cable ties, and other free stock items) required for the training are already available in each work cell. The trainees work alone at their own pace during most of the session. They start by familiarizing themselves with the documentation and start the process by logging onto the quality information system. They use the check sheet to guide them through the training. The check sheet is divided into sections. Each section contains a new area to learn and understand. Trainees should be able to complete a section in 20 or 25 minutes. A section may contain new words that a trainee does not understand, in which case the trainee must study and clarify these first. Next, the check sheet identifies a few sections for a trainee to read from the assembly procedure. After the trainee has read and thoroughly understands the section, he or she will practice assembling that part. For instance, the section might be about installing the integrated-circuit processor chip, heatsink, and fan assembly. The trainee assembles and disassembles these parts until he or she completely understands that section. The section may also contain a short written exercise to reinforce a complex assembly technique such as how to configure option boards into a series of printed circuit slots using a priority list in the assembly procedure. After completing a training section, the trainee signs the check sheet and asks the trainer to verify his or her ability to perform the operations in that section. Upon completion of a successful demonstration, the trainer also signs off on the check sheet, attesting to demonstrated trainee competence just for that section. The trainee then moves on to the next section. If a trainee has difficulty with a section, directions advise the trainee to restudy or redrill the applicable part of the section and then be reexamined. When a trainee has successfully completed all the sections in the check sheet, the trainer has the trainee completely assemble the product from the beginning. The duration of one training session is from three to eight hours, depending on the complexity of the product or process and the pace of the trainee.

At the beginning of this training program the line supervisors were trained by Effective Training Solutions as 100% Proficiency trainers. As the implementation of this training system progressed, the top-rated direct labor people received the same training, and also became certified as 100% Proficiency trainers. Becoming 100% Proficiency trainers gave direct labor people new challenges. It also minimized the need to use supervisors or engineers as trainers. The trainers received an eight-hour class on how to perform as trainers. Direct labor trainers did not get an increased grade following completion of their initial training. However, being a 100% Proficiency qualified trainer reflected positively in their performance review. A trainer must have taken all the training and be certified in every area in which he or she is a trainer. The trainer attests that the person in training understands each key word, can perform the drills in each section, and has successfully completed written exercises. The trainer is not a teacher and should not instruct the trainee on how to perform the check sheet drill. The trainer should direct the trainee to the procedure or other learning material so that the trainee can overcome his or her own barrier to learning. The trainer also participates in the certification process by inspecting the students' completed products.

Scheduling Training

Most of the training took place during nonpeak work periods. The exception was when a new product was ready to be released. Training for new products had to occur before engineering released the system to manufacturing. An advantage of single-person assembly cells is that training could occur any time there was a slow period in production. All that was needed for learning was a predetermined kit of parts for the product. The training took place in an unused work cell. A person was certified for that product when the training had been successfully completed and the operator demonstrated competence on production units. By looking ahead at potential large orders for a particular product and at current backlog, production workers could be cross-trained to handle future production peaks of that product.

Core Training Affected

The original plan did not include 100% Proficiency in the core subjects training. As a byproduct of successes implementing this system in production training, however, some of the learning principles and techniques were incorporated into core training. The content did not change, but the format did somewhat. The restructuring was in line with principles like not overloading trainees with information and talk, breaking the class into bite-sized pieces, ensuring that everyone had to understand before the instructor moved on, and clarifying words that some people didn't understand.

A Training Manager Is Key

With an ambitious training program of 110 hours per operator over an 18-month period, it proved critical that someone manage the program. The 100% Proficiency training implementation manager at

Focus was Kristine Lee-Cox. The author and training manager set targets for what percentage of the training plan had to be completed each month, and one person was needed to collect results and publish them to supervisors, production managers, the director of manufacturing operations (myself), and the vice president of operations.

Organizationally, Cox worked directly for me. Still, she was in the challenging position of having all the responsibility to get this training successfully executed in 18 months without the advantage of line authority over those on whose compliance her success depended.

The target in figure 1 is linear. The actual plot (dotted line) reflects results of the training manager's challenge to keep the percentage of training completed on target.

There was a requirement for consistency in product and process procedures and check sheet documentation. For instance, when 10 different manufacturing engineers developed assembly procedures, there might be 10 different formats. Without consistency, the operators receiving the training would be confused, and the effectiveness of the training diminished. Also, to receive reimbursement from the state of California, it was important to have quality documentation. An additional challenge was the natural conflicts between production goals and time allocated to training. Production supervisors' deadlines were short

Figure 1. Training completed versus target (by quarter).

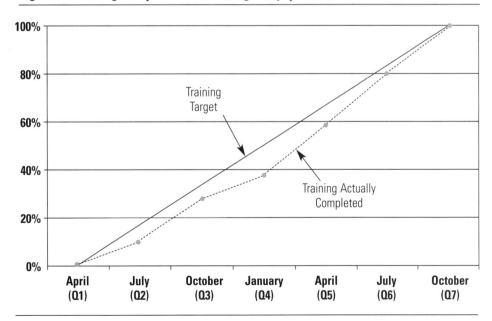

term, so they were more inclined to reason that they could always catch up with the longer term training goals when the immediate problems got resolved. The production supervisors were strong supporters of the training plan, but the training manager had to help them balance conflicting priorities.

Within a quarterly period, training was scheduled to decrease as production targets went up, and to increase again at the start of a new quarter when the production target was lowest. Figure 2 shows the nonlinearity of the training due to peak work periods for a portion of the year. It is a detailed look that shows the variations of the training targets within a quarter. For example, the first month of a quarter, like April, had about 55 percent of the training for that quarter; the second month, like May, had about 35 percent of the training; and the third month, like June, had about 10 percent scheduled. Production volume was typically 20 percent, 35 percent, and 45 percent for the three months of the quarter. Figure 2 was an internal management tool that helped plan a balance between training and production needs.

Training Evaluation

The training program used all levels of training evaluation from 0 to 5.

Through careful analysis at Level 0, manufacturing engineering and manufacturing operations management determined that the factory processes were already effective and efficient for the production of computers. Manufacturing had a data collection system that produced accurate and timely metrics. From an analysis of these metrics, manufacturing determined that an improvement of quality and productivity would have to come from the training of operators.

Level 1 evaluation, which measures the reactions of training program participants, occurred at the end of each 100% Proficiency workshop. The Effective Training Solutions instructor asked each person trained to fill out a written evaluation asking about the workshop content and the trainer's performance. These early written evaluations were helpful because they told us that the employees felt the training program would be useful not only in their work but also in their private lives. Their responses improved our confidence level that they would willingly stay involved in the long training program.

The training method itself contains Level 2, because of the "checkout" in the check sheet method. At the end of each section in the check sheet, trainees must demonstrate that they have reached the expected

Figure 2. Training targets due to peak work periods.

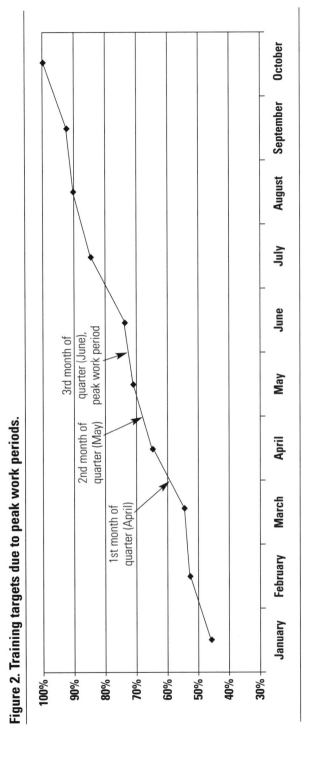

level of knowledge or skill defined as the training objective at the beginning of the check sheet. For a trainee who has not, the trainer refers the person to the exact point of the check sheet that was incomplete for restudy or more drill. When the trainee has mastered the material, the trainer checks the person again. The manufacturing operations department was not focused on measuring how much each trainee improved, but on getting every operator, regardless of where he or she started, up to the same 100 percent standard of proficiency. A byproduct of trainees' accomplishment in achieving such a high performance standard was that their confidence, morale, and willingness to communicate more also improved. These changes in turn increased input from the trainees to their supervisors and process engineers, which made continuous process improvement easier and more effective.

The certification process incorporated Level 3, the evaluation of what changed because of the training. To get certified, an operator had to assemble 20 to 50 units without error. The check sheet training raised the operator to this level of proficiency.

At Level 4, metric results carefully tracked final results in terms of increased production, improved quality, decreased costs, and so forth.

The return-on-investment (ROI) calculation, Level 5, had its basis in the dollarization of the metric results tracked in Level 4.

Training Metrics

Simple and easy-to-understand metrics were needed to measure the effectiveness of the training program. Management had to be kept informed of progress through these numbers gathered on a periodic basis. The data for the numbers needed to be easy to gather and not require explanation or interpretation. The metrics were based on the objectives of the training program: quality, productivity, and flexibility.

Measuring and Isolating the Training Factor

It can be difficult to precisely measure the effects of training in a dynamic business environment in which products are being phased in and out of production monthly. A control group was not practical, in part because each operator had to complete 110 hours of training within 18 months so Focus would meet California's requirements for reimbursement. In spite of these challenges, the author feels that Focus was able to accurately measure the effectiveness of the training.

Before training started, the production processes were in place. These processes remained in place throughout the training with only minor changes, so we considered them a constant. Training being the only major change, the process changes that operators recommended after getting trained were credited to the training.

For instance, immediately after training on a particular PC, a group of operators recommended that the CD drive be installed prior to the hard drive to make it easier for them to see the connectors while installing the cables. This improved the quality of the process and was due to the operators' training.

Focus's measure of quality and productivity in assembly, which saw most of the dollar savings from training, was very accurate. Manufacturing had a state-of-the-art data collection system in place before training started, and it allowed us to do the following:

- measure the number of each type of unit built per hour (desktop, laptop, and servers)
- differentiate between an improvement from automation of the testing process, such as how much was due to the operator's improved knowledge or skill
- know which operators had worked on a specific computer and for each process step
- get individual feedback on any production problem
- accurately measure and isolate the causes of improvements.

Manufacturing used well-defined metrics, established and approved by senior management before the training started, to measure quality, productivity, and flexibility goals. We also decided to graphically track training progress as a management tool, to balance our investment in training against production goals. Quality was the critical objective because of its effect on customer satisfaction, reducing field failures, reducing calls from angry customers and salespeople, and the like. Following is a description of the four main goals that manufacturing operations tracked:

- *Quality:* This metric was the percentage of worker errors found throughout the production process. Quality problems can occur in any step of the process. Our quality tracking system, which tracked each system from the start of assembly until the unit was packed in its shipping container, provided accurate workers' quality data by product and time. The quality yields in final audit improved from just above 94 percent to 99.5 percent, on a measure in which 98 percent is considered world class.

As figure 3 shows, factory quality started at 94 percent at the beginning of training in April (quarter #1, or Q1), then reached a high of 99.5 percent, and remained at that level. The training implementation lasted 18 months. However, the division continued with training and saw further improvements. Maximum payback was in 24 months.

Field quality improved from 93 percent to 98 percent, as figure 4 shows. Field "turn-on" quality measures the percentage of systems that had no reported problems within the first 30 days after shipment to the customer.

Field quality started at 93 percent and reached 98 percent in 24 months. It was less smooth than factory quality because of sporadic reporting and the significant factor of customer-added hardware and software, which was common in large volume orders.

- *Productivity:* Improved productivity reduced direct labor time. It directly saved the company money by lowering the cost of goods sold. The calculation for the average time to build a system was the number of systems built in a shift divided by the number of direct production hours. In assembly, time will vary depending on the type of product and the number of options to be installed. The time can vary from 10 to 25 minutes per unit. Over an eight-hour period, however, the variations tend to even out the average time, as figure 5 shows. At the start of the training program the average assembly rate was about 3.6 systems per hour. Within 18 months it was 4.6 per hour, which was a 28 percent increase in productivity. The increase occurred without the addition of people or equipment.

  Figure 5 illustrates the increase in assembly productivity to 4.6 units per hour in 24 months. The curve is not smooth, particularly at the beginning of the training project, because employees were just learning the methods and getting cross-trained. The productivity increases resulting from 100 percent proficiency training more than made up for the time invested in it. Direct labor in the test process was reduced by 10 percent due to training. Productivity in the minor production areas such as labeling, cosmetics, accessory kitting, and packout increased on the average 15 percent.

- *Flexibility:* Cross-training increased flexibility in production by allowing us to move properly trained people to a production bottleneck area. Bottlenecks would change daily and sometimes hourly. Increased flexibility was important because it allowed us to improve our on-time delivery percentage. This metric is the number of production areas each person has been certified in. The goal was to cross-train every direct labor person in at least three different areas by the end of the program. After 18 months into the program, 100 percent of the people had been trained in three or more areas.

  The graph in figure 6 shows the percent of people who met that goal or the percent of people who were successfully trained and certified in at least three areas. The graph starts slowly in the beginning

Figure 3. Workers' quality in the factory (by quarter).

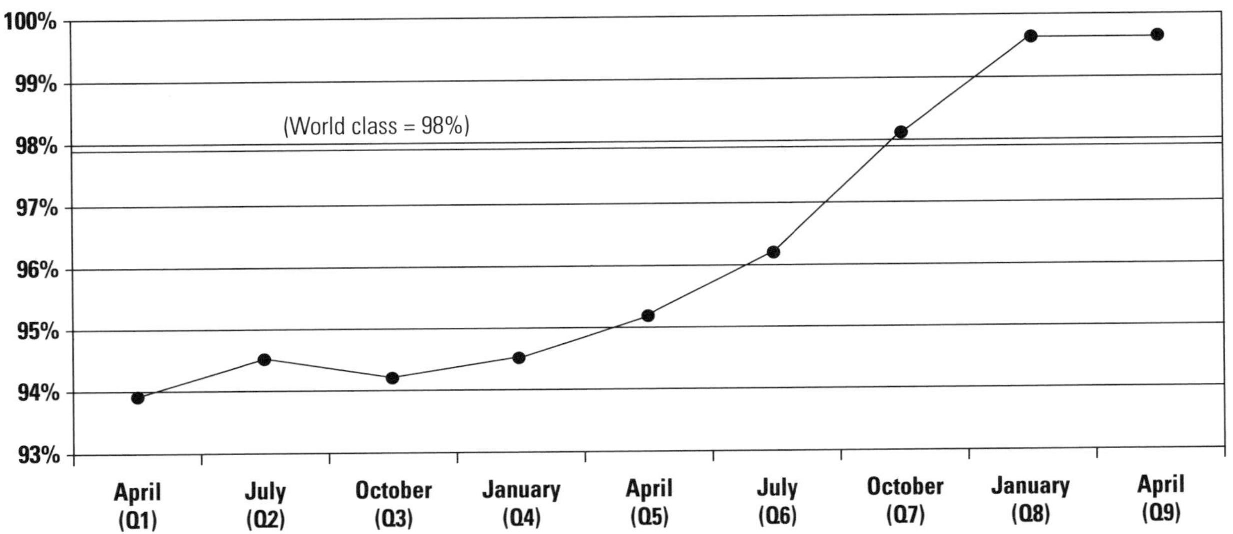

(World class = 98%)

100%
99%
98%
97%
96%
95%
94%
93%

April (Q1)
July (Q2)
October (Q3)
January (Q4)
April (Q5)
July (Q6)
October (Q7)
January (Q8)
April (Q9)

Figure 4. Field "turn-on" quality (by quarter).

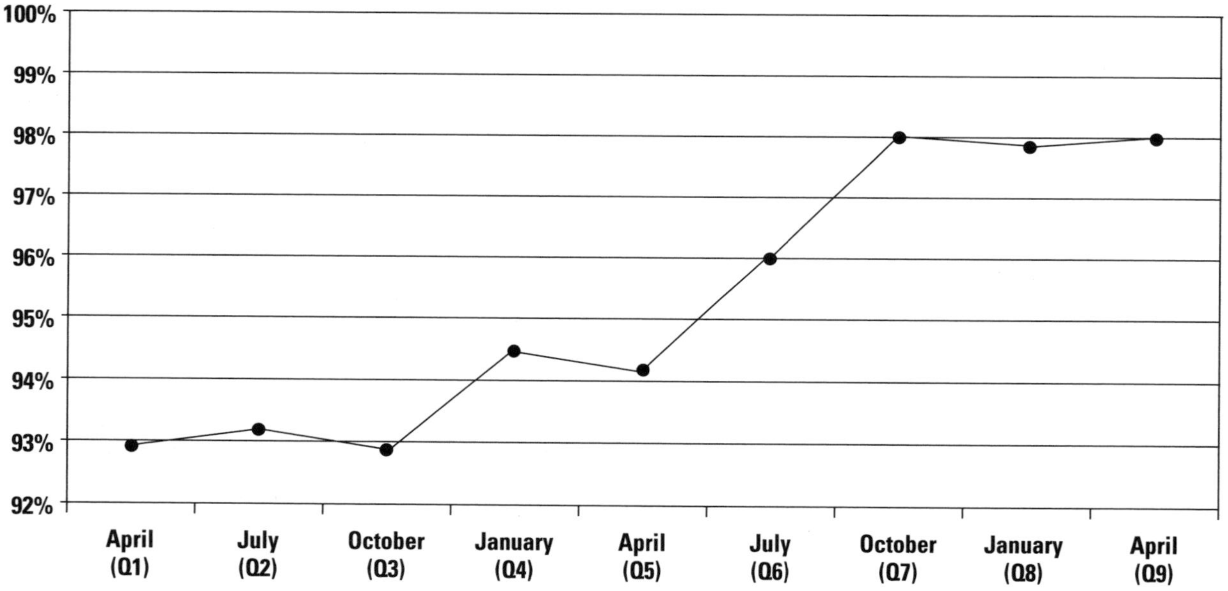

Figure 5. Assembly productivity in units per hour.

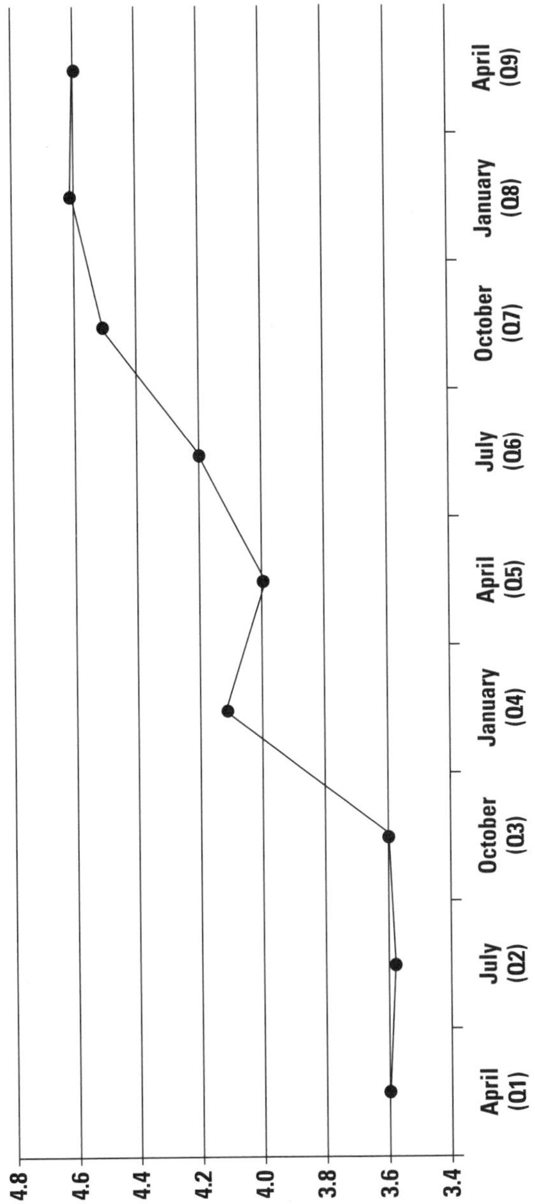

because of the initial time invested in cross-training. It then rises rapidly as more trainees complete cross-training, reaching 100 percent within 18 months.

Some workers received certification in as many as five areas. Because of this increased flexibility, the line supervisors were able to move people from one area to another in the same day to meet on-time delivery targets. Moving people where they were needed also decreased idle time. There was a 2 percent productivity gain, strictly due to the decreased idle time.

- *Hours of training:* We tracked the record of the hours of training completed versus the monthly target and percent of total training plan hours completed. Manufacturing operations had to complete training within 18 months to receive the maximum funds from the state ETP. Each quarter we plotted the target date against the actual, using the percentage on the Y-axis because that was more descriptive than the number of hours of completed training, as figure 1 shows. For the first nine months, we were slow to get started and lagged behind our target. In the last nine months we were able to catch up. Although not a metric factored into ROI, this was a critical management tool that our training manager and I used to track actual training progress in relation to the target. Also, the monthly target for training hours may not be linear because of predictable peak work periods. In the electronics industry the last month of the quarter is always the busiest, so less training is scheduled during that month. (See figure 2.)

Return on Investment
Selling the Training Program to Top Management

Prior to beginning the training program, the author, as director of manufacturing operations, presented to top management the projected ROI in order to secure its approval and authorization for the funds required. Top management would require an ROI of 100 percent for justification. The best approach for that was to use only the tangible easy-to-measure cost benefits in the calculation and to describe in detail at the presentation the expected nontangible benefits. Top management accepted the proposal because it met the 100 percent ROI minimum and addressed their priorities.

There were two primary factory improvement goals for this training program: workers' quality and productivity. These were of major interest to top management, especially quality, which was a top priority for the vice president of operations. The metrics had baseline and improvement targets for each. The quality goal was to improve from a

Figure 6. Workforce cross-trained in three or more areas.

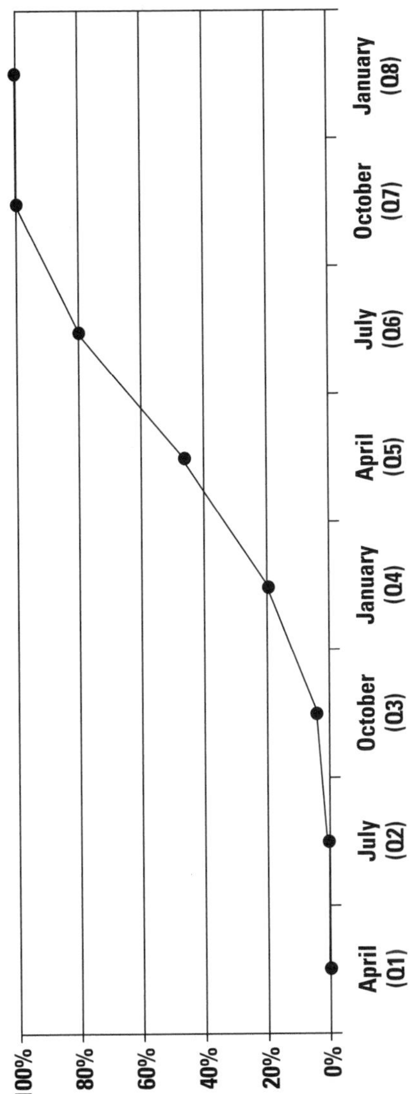

baseline metric of 94 percent to a world class 98 percent, an increase of four percentage points. The assembly productivity improvement goal was to increase by 20 percent, starting from a baseline of 3.6 units per hour. Improvement goals also included other minor production areas, which had a combined improvement target of 10 percent. The factors that had to be considered when doing the calculation were the primary targets (quality and productivity), projected build rates (quantity), and standard times (the average time to build each unit or complete an operation within a product family). The dollar figure used to calculate labor costs for both return and investment sides of the calculation was the average direct hire pay rate for a standard eight-hour day. The investment side of the ROI equation was the sum of the external and internal costs less the projected reimbursement from the state of California. The external costs included Effective Training Solutions and Workforce America, which helped us apply for the ETP grant, helped us set up the proper training records required by the state, and reviewed our record keeping prior to the quarterly ETP audit. The internal costs included lost direct labor time during training (an average of five full-time workers); trainers' time; one full-time training manager; time dedicated to writing check sheets, and the like; and a small materials cost. The projected factory ROI was 230 percent.

Results

Results exceeded expectations in every category. In the factory, quality rose from 94 percent to 99.5 percent, higher than the 98 percent targeted. Productivity rose by 28 percent in assembly, which had a 20 percent improvement target. The other areas had a combined productivity increase of 15 percent, which had a 10 percent improvement target. As a result, actual factory ROI was 310 percent. If the state reimbursement had not been considered, the factory ROI would have been 190 percent.

Field savings (from reduced costs to perform product repairs and service after delivery to customer) were not part of the original projections. They are also more difficult to accurately determine because deliveries are worldwide. We do know that there was a drop from 8 percent to 3 percent in the reported field failures following implementation of quality and production improvements in the factory. Some of the field failures are customer induced because of the custom software and hardware they install. The customers' contribution to the failures makes it hard to determine an accurate percentage of total field failures caused by the manufacturer. Cost savings could be calculated, however, based on fewer service calls, fewer customer visits by field engineers, and fewer systems returned to the repair centers. If these numbers are taken into account, the combined factory and field ROI was 570 percent.

The improvement most difficult to measure in terms of dollar return, but by far the most important, was increased customer satisfaction due to improved on-time delivery and quality. The improved workers' quality meant higher quality in the field. This translated into increased sales. Unfortunately, this number was impossible to calculate. The value of eliminating daily calls to the vice president of operations from angry customers and salespeople, however, was priceless.

ROI Calculations

Focus measured the ROI both for the factory and the field. Following are the calculations, beginning with the returns for the factory:

Productivity improvement reduced cost of goods sold: In assembly, there was a 28 percent increase for desktop, laptop, and small server computers.

(37 assemblers @ average salary of $15.00/hour and 2,080 hours/year) $\times$ 28% = $323,000

In other areas of production (labeling, cosmetic, accessory kitting, and packout, but not test, repair, and final audit), there was a 15 percent increase:

(35 operators @ average salary of $15.00/hour and 2,080 hours/year) $\times$ 15% = $164,000

Quality improvement reduced rework and retest time: Quality yield went from 94 percent to 99.5 percent, or a 5.5 percent improvement.

(Reassigned five operators who analyzed failed systems to find fault, repair, retest system, and handling of defective materials) = $156,000

Flexibility decreased idle time by 2 percent.

(130 operators @ average salary of $15.00/hour and 2,080 hours/year) $\times$ 2% = $81,000

Total factory returns = $724,000

Following are ROI calculations for the field:
Warranty cost reduction: Repairing a failure in the field is up to 10 times more costly than finding it in the factory.

Using average costs for field calls and on-site repair × 5% less calls = $201,000

Major system repairs: Failed systems are returned to repair facilities for rework and many have to be resold at a substantially lower price.

2% fewer systems returned to repair facilities = $406,000

Customer satisfaction: Increased sales due to improved quality and increased on-time delivery was not estimated due to the subjectivity of those kinds of calculations.

Total field returns = $607,000

Total returns = $1,331,000

Following are the investments, first internal:

110 hours of training for each direct labor person plus costs for trainers, training manager, materials, and check sheet writing (not including writing process procedures, which occurred before training) = − $262,000

Following are external investments:

Effective Training Solutions and Workforce America = − $120,500

Total investment = − $382,500

Reimbursement from the State of California Employment Training Panel = $149,000

Net investment = − $233,500

The ROI for factory and for factory and field are as follows:

Factory = $724,000 / $233,500 = 310%
Factory + Field = $1,331,000 / $233,500 = 570%

Conclusion

The Focus Personal Computer Division completed its 18-month plan on schedule and attained its training and business goals. Work cell assemblers in the complex and challenging BTCO manufacturing system achieved a higher level of quality and productivity building new products than when the simpler build-to-stock system was in place. Once the new 100% Proficiency training system was implemented, the employees felt more comfortable and less frustrated thanks to self-paced learning using check sheets and the how-to-learn techniques. Less trainer time was then required to reach the same level of proficiency. The cross-training allowed production to become more flexible in handling the daily product mix variations. It permitted an increase in production levels, quickly and efficiently, particularly at the end of the quarter.

Other benefits occurred with the implementation of this training system, including the involvement of the production workers in improving the training program and production processes. Certification using 100% Proficiency training made them confident in their skills and knowledge of the processes. They became more willing to assist in process improvement. We had tried work groups and quality groups in the past with very little success, and they were soon abandoned. The new training program made the production workers less reluctant and even made some eager to participate in production process improvement.

The author's theory was supported by the results of this case. By training people correctly, the quality of their work went up and, without making increased productivity a goal, their productivity also went up.

Questions for Discussion

1. Why was a training manager important to the success of the project?
2. Flexibility was an indirect goal established to improve on-time delivery. If the performance of multiple departments affected on-time delivery, do indirect goals such as this one make sense?
3. Should such an important goal as productivity improvement be kept from the workers for fear of a negative effect on another goal—quality? Do workers have difficulty with multiple and possibly conflicting goals?
4. This plant had a high number of English-as-a-second-language workers. Would self-paced learning be as important for people fluent in English?
5. The complete ROI was not calculated due to cost and data availability. Should these less tangible parts be estimated and added to the calculation or should they be ignored? Will management believe difficult-to-verify estimates?

The Author

David Barraza is an industrial engineer with 40 years of experience, specializing in high-tech manufacturing operations and manufacturing process improvement. While serving as director of manufacturing engineering and director of manufacturing operations at a major computer company in San Jose, California, he led the conversion of manufacturing operations from mass assembly to the BTCO computer manufacturing method, and he designed the production processes that enabled the company to become an industry leader in this challenging and complex manufacturing sector. In 1996, as a direct result of his leadership and engineering innovations, the San Jose division received the Corporate Achievement Award for over $1 million annual savings in direct labor, reduced test time, and improved product quality. Presently he is a part-time consultant specializing in manufacturing processes. Barraza has a B.S. and M.S. from San Jose State University in industrial engineering. He can be contacted through Effective Training Solutions, Attn: Diana Doiel, 39355 California Street, Suite 207, Fremont, CA 94538-1447; phone: 800.949.5035; Diana@trainingsuccess.com.

Measuring ROI for Telephonic Customer Service Skills

Verizon Communications

David J. Keuler

The Enterprise Business Group of Verizon Communications purchased and implemented an intervention designed to provide representatives with advanced training in customer service skills. The group expected this training curriculum (R3 service) to reduce the number of calls that escalated to the supervisory level. Verizon's Measurement and Evaluation team evaluated three sites using a mixed design prior to and after the training intervention. Self-report, direct observation, and return-on-expectation data were gathered in support of the impact evaluation. Representatives as a group did not perceive that their skills had improved as a result of training, though their team coaches perceived modest improvements. Direct observations showed no skill increase. Return-on-investment analyses revealed a negative 85 percent return for year one and a negative 54 percent return for year two. As a result of this impact study, the Enterprise Business Group discontinued the program. This study clearly demonstrates that more elaborate research designs may strain measurement resources; however, they can prove to be quite valuable in light of costly expenditures on certain training interventions.

Organizational Profile

Verizon Communications, formed by the merger of Bell Atlantic and GTE, is one of the world's leading providers of communications services. Verizon companies are the largest providers of wireline and wireless communications in the United States, with more than 101 million access line equivalents and more than 26 million wireless customers.

This case was prepared to serve as a basis for discussion rather than to illustrate either effective or ineffective administrative and management practices.

A *Fortune* 10 company with more than 260,000 employees and approximately $60 billion in 1999 revenues, Verizon's global presence extends to 40 countries in the Americas, Europe, Asia, and the Pacific.

Program Description

The Enterprise Business Group purchased the R3 service training curriculum from a vendor, and Verizon instructors implemented it. Training objectives included improving Verizon customer feedback and reducing the overall number of calls that escalated to the supervisory level. A formal needs assessment, if conducted, was unavailable to the Measurement and Evaluation (M&E) team, which included the author, at the time of the request to measure the impact of training.

Anecdotal accounts prior to and during the training intervention indicated that the expected benefits of the training would be minimal. The training manuals were generic and not tailored to the specific needs of the company, and course participants were skeptical of another "customer contact skills" training program.

The R3 service training curriculum was a two-day, leader-led course. M&E was asked to determine the degree of skill transfer to the field, and whether or not the goals for this new curriculum were being met.

Evaluation Methodology

Given the program expense, M&E was determined to use an experimental design that would capture any improvement representatives made in their skills after training. Control groups were used to isolate the impact of training. Moreover, a within-subjects design allowed for comparisons before and after training of both the experimental and the control groups. M&E used direct observation in addition to self-reports to determine any skill gains. Figure 1 outlines the design of this study and the timeline for assessments.

M&E selected three sites to participate in the impact study. We selected approximately 20 representatives at each of these sites to serve as the experimental and control groups for the impact study. At each site, M&E assigned approximately 10 representatives to the experimental group and 10 representatives to the control group. We made these assignments to the groups on the basis of matching criteria such as years of experience, performance level, age, and gender so as to equalize the groups. We chose not to rely on random assignment to the experimental and control groups since the number of study participants was too small to engender confidence in this procedure.

Figure 1. Timeline and experimental design.

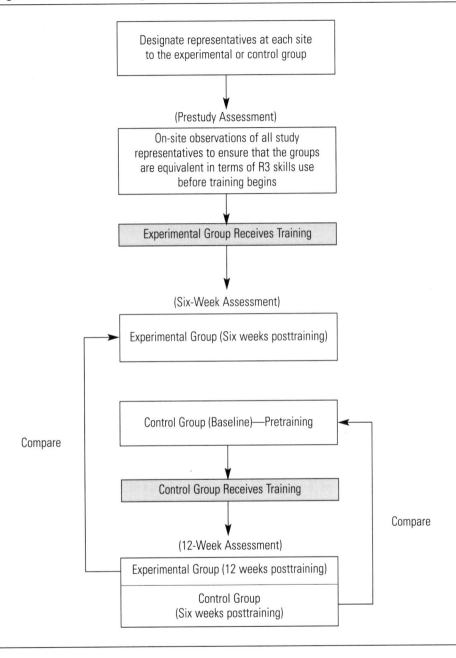

The group designated as experimental received the training at the beginning of the study, and the control group received it six weeks later. M&E assessed both groups prior to any training (the prestudy assessment) and again six weeks after training. At this six-week assessment point, the experimental group had completed training, but the control group had not yet begun training. It was then possible to compare the skill usage and effectiveness of the experimental group with their pretraining baseline as well as with the control group, as figure 1 shows.

Immediately after the six-week assessment, the control group received training. Six weeks later, M&E assessed the control group and compared those results with the pretraining baseline. At the same time, the experimental group (which had had training 12 weeks earlier) was assessed again; these results were compared with the experimental group's results at the six-week assessment point to measure any skill loss or gain between six and 12 weeks posttraining.

M&E collected the following data:

- *Reaction data (Level 1) (Phillips, 1997):* M&E administered the Verizon postcourse questionnaire (PCQ) to course participants immediately following training. We reviewed the PCQ data and summarized the verbatim comments to assess participants' reactions to training.

- *Learning data (Level 2):* M&E developed a knowledge-based test of R3 service skills to determine whether course participants were emerging from training with the required knowledge and skills. The department had purchased this course from a vendor, but it did not include a Level 2 assessment in the course design. Time constraints prevented M&E from formally validating the test; as such, the data was used only in conjunction with other data.

- *Job application data (Level 3):* Trained observers used an observer checklist that M&E developed for evaluating all representatives six weeks following their R3 training. Observers spent eight hours prior to the formal evaluation observing phone calls and comparing scoring to ensure some measure of interrater reliability.

The observer checklist focused on the following six skill areas:
— opening the call
— diagnosing problems and identifying needs
— assessing progress and updating the plan
— recommending approaches for results
— closing the call
— overall listening skills.

Each section of the checklist consisted of a list of R3 skills that the observer rated with a yes if he or she observed it during the call or with a no if he or she did not. Each representative was observed once at each assessment, and the number of R3 skills used during the call was divided by the total number of skills that the representatives had an opportunity to use. In this manner, each representative was assigned one score for each of the six sections. Observers had access only to the representative's side of the conversation and were not able to hear the customer. The observer checklist was designed with this limitation in mind. In addition, observers were blind to the experimental or control group assignments of the study participants in order to avoid bias.

M&E administered a follow-up survey on site to the experimental group and the control group six weeks after they completed the training. The team designed the survey questions to assess the extent to which the participants perceived that they had applied on the job the knowledge and skills they had acquired during training. The survey was unusually long and thus was administered in person with supervisory support to ensure a high return rate.

- *Business impact (Levels 4 and 5):* M&E developed a customer escalation log to monitor the number of call escalations for the experimental group and the control group. Team coaches collected data on this form over a three-month period. This was the only expected tangible benefit of training that team coaches identified. Thus, the success or failure of the training program was contingent on the log's ability to show improvements in customer contact skills that would lead to a decrease in the absolute number of customer call escalations to the supervisory level.

- *Return-on-expectation (ROE) interviews:* M&E conducted these interviews (Hodges, 1998) with each site's team leader at the completion of training to determine if his or her expectations had been met.

- *Return-on-investment (ROI) calculation:* M&E calculated an ROI analysis by dividing net program benefits by program costs. Costs included purchase price, delivery, and facility costs. Tangible benefits included cost savings associated with reduced call escalations. Intangible benefits were isolated from follow-up surveys and ROEs.

An excerpt of the results of this study follows. It retains the details to provide readers with a flavor of the statistical approach and with the means of isolating the impact of training. The results appear by site since there were some expectations that the individual sites may vary in their response to the training. The site-by-site analysis also demonstrates how pooling samples to increase sample size may obscure important differences relevant to the isolation of training impact.

Reaction Data (Level 1)

Verizon PCQs were obtained from all R3 service classes available for analysis. From these R3 service classes, 231 PCQs were returned. M&E rated 21 positively worded questions on a scale ranging from one, for strongly disagree, to five, for strongly agree. Questions 17 through 20 were as follows:

17. My knowledge and/or skills increased as a result of this course.
18. The knowledge and/or skills gained through this course are directly applicable to my job.
19. I feel confident of my ability to apply what I learned in this course.
20. This course was valuable as a development experience for future work.

These questions were to capture perceptions of course impact. These questions received the lowest ratings. In particular, the mean rating of 3.47 on question 17 was markedly low relative to the other PCQ questions and to Bell Atlantic reaction data in general. Historically, mean scores on the PCQ items at Bell Atlantic rarely dip below 3.90. Overall satisfaction with the course (3.65) also indicated notable dissatisfaction. The highest ratings were reported for the instructor's skills in teaching the course.

Verbatim comments from the PCQs focused predominantly on perceptions that the course was inappropriate to the representatives' level of experience with customer service skills.

Learning Data (Level 2)

Mean test scores from all available regions were collected and scored. Test scores were low, with several regions reporting mean scores below 70 percent. Across regions, test scores ranged from 40 percent to 100 percent, with 75 percent being the most frequently achieved test score.

Job Application Data (Level 3)

Assessments occurred prior to training (prestudy assessment), at six weeks (the six-week assessment), and at 12 weeks (the 12-week assessment). Results are presented in this order.

PRE-STUDY ASSESSMENT. Core questions and their answers, which follow, represent the focus of the statistical analysis within each section.

Core Question: Were the experimental and control groups equivalent in terms of R3 skill usage before either group received training?
Answer: Yes

Prior to the formal beginning of the impact study, observers, using the observer checklist, watched study participants at each of the three study sites. These prestudy observations provided an opportunity for observers to improve their consistency when assessing individuals, and it also provided data that would be used to determine whether the experimental and control groups were equivalent in terms of R3 skill usage prior to training. Observers assessed each individual (hereafter referred to as a "representative") on one phone call. Within each of the six R3 service skills areas, each representative was assigned a score that reflected the number of R3 skills used on the call divided by the number of skills the representative had the opportunity to demonstrate. For example, the "opening of the call" had 10 skills. If a representative correctly demonstrated five of the R3 skills, and two of the R3 skills were not applicable to the call, the representative would have received a "percent correct" of $5/8 = .63$ (63 percent).

Table 1 shows the mean percentages of R3 skills in the experimental and control groups. There were no significant differences between the experimental and control groups prior to training in any of the R3 skills area, all p's $< .05$. These findings support the notion that the matching procedure for designating the experimental and control groups was successful. Representatives as a group demonstrated the highest proficiency in overall listening skills prior to R3 training and demonstrated the lowest proficiency in closing the call, according to R3 principles.

SIX-WEEK ASSESSMENT. Six weeks after the experimental group received training, M&E observed both the experimental group and the control group, and each group completed the follow-up survey.
• *On-site observations at the six-week assessment:*

Core Question: Was there any difference in R3 skill usage between the group that had received training (the experimental group) and the group that had not yet received training (the control group) as assessed by on-site observation?
Answer: No

Table 1. Mean percentage of R3 skills used prior to R3 training.

R3 Service Skills	Experimental	Control
Opening the call	60%	56%
Diagnosing problems and identifying needs	63%	63%
Assessing progress and updating the plan	52%	55%
Recommending approaches for results	55%	52%
Closing the call	35%	40%
Overall listening skills	67%	70%

Again, M&E observed both groups on-site six weeks following the experimental group's training. M&E expected that the experimental group would demonstrate significantly more R3 skill usage than the control group, which had not yet received training. As table 2 shows, there were no significant differences between the groups at six weeks post-training, indicating no observable improvement in the use of R3 skills in the experimental group, all p's $< .05$. Comparisons with the prestudy assessment also indicated that the expected shift in the experimental group's use of R3 skills was not observed, all p's $< .05$.

- *Follow-up survey results at the six-week assessment:*

  Core Question: Was there any difference reported between the group that had received training (the experimental group) and the group that had not received training yet (the control group) in their perceptions of effectiveness in performing R3 skills?
  Answer: No

M&E assessed each of the six R3 service skills areas. We provide section one, "opening the call," from the follow-up survey as an example of the evaluation strategy.

- *Opening the call:* Table 3 lists the R3 service skills that make up the opening of the call. No significant differences were found between the two groups within a region, across regions (all regions combined), or across skills (all skills combined). The exception was skill

Table 2. Mean percentage of R3 skills used, six-week assessment.

R3 Service Skills	Prior to Training (Prestudy Assessment)		Six Weeks Posttraining in the Experimental Group	
	Experimental	*Control*	*Experimental*	*Control*
Opening the call	60%	56%	59%	56%
Diagnosing problems and identifying needs	63%	63%	62%	56%
Assessing progress and updating the plan	52%	55%	57%	52%
Recommending approaches for results	55%	52%	49%	66%
Closing the call	35%	40%	35%	31%
Overall listening skills	67%	70%	75%	80%

three, which was significantly higher in the control group. In general, both groups reported being "very effective" in performing the skills listed in table 3. Further analysis of frequency ratings indicated that subjects in both the experimental and control groups reported using these skills on most calls. No systematic differences were found between the experimental and control groups on the frequency of skills use, all p's < .05.

TWELVE-WEEK ASSESSMENT. At the 12-week assessment, M&E gave both groups the follow-up survey with the same list of R3 skills that asked them to rate their effectiveness in performing those skills. A comparison of the control groups' baseline assessment at six weeks (just before receiving training) with their reassessment six weeks after training provided a measure of skill increase that could be directly attributed to the R3 training. M&E found no significant difference between baseline and six weeks' posttraining, all p's < .05.

> Core Question: Did the experimental group report any loss or gain in effectiveness in performing R3 skills from the six-week to 12-week assessments?
> Answer: Yes, the experimental group from Site B reported significant decreases in R3 skill usage.

At the six-week and 12-week assessments, members of the experimental group gave their perceptions of their effectiveness in performing R3 skills. These two assessments allowed for a comparison to determine any skills loss or gain over the six-week period. (Note that there was no 12-week assessment for site C participants since the control group did not complete the impact study. Data was available only for sites A and B.) As table 4 shows, there were no significant differences between the six- and 12-week assessment of R3 skill effectiveness. However, several skills showed significant reductions in site B from the six- to the 12-week assessment. Effectiveness in multiple areas decreased from the "very effective" to "moderately" effective range of the scale, as the shaded areas with bold numbers in the table show.

- *General survey questions.* M&E asked several general questions as part of the follow-up survey.

> Core Question: What did the study participants as a whole think of the R3 training 6 weeks after training?
> Answer: Participants as a group, but particularly those representatives in Site C, reported low levels of consistency between R3 training and what happens on the job, low levels of helpfulness of the

Table 3. Six-week comparison of perceptions on R3 tasks, opening the call.

How effective are you in performing each skill listed?

Not at all 0% — 20% — 40% — Moderately 60% — 80% — Very Effective 100%

Skill	Site A		Site B		Site C		Combined	
	Experimental (n = 6)	Control (n = 8)	Experimental (n = 6)	Control (n = 9)	Experimental (n = 6)	Control (n = 9)	Experimental (n = 18)	Control (n = 26)
1. Greeting the caller	98	94	94	98	96	97	96	97
2. Introducing yourself	98	95	96	99	96	97	97	97
3. Using enthusiastic tone of voice	83	92	81	95	94	95	86	94
4. Listening to customer without interrupting	85	88	92	93	94	96	90	92
5. Conveying empathy by acknowledging difficulty customer is having	83	90	93	93	98	95	91	93
6. Establishing yourself as a resource by actually telling the customer that you can help with the problem or issue	85	87	85	94	93	93	88	92

(continued on page 142)

Table 3. Six-week comparison of perceptions on R3 tasks, opening the call (continued).

Skill	Experimental (n = 6)	Control (n = 8)	Experimental (n = 6)	Control (n = 9)	Experimental (n = 6)	Control (n = 9)	Experimental (n = 18)	Control (n = 26)
7. Avoiding trying to diagnose or resolve problem/issue before agreeing on a purpose for the call	83	87	87	81	90	97	87	87
8. Defining the purpose of the call within the first few minutes (e.g., "I'll make an adjustment to your account")	87	85	89	88	95	88	90	87
9. Communicating what the initial plan for the call will be to the customer	86	88	89	92	95	94	90	91
10. Checking to make sure customer agrees with your initial plan for the call	80	85	92	88	90	94	87	89

Table 4. Mean percent ratings of R3 training at six and 12 weeks, experimental group.

How effective are you in performing each skill listed:

Not at all 0% — 20% — Moderately 40% — 60% — 80% — Very Effective 100%

Skill:	Site A Six weeks Posttraining (n = 6)	Site A 12 Weeks Posttraining (n = 4)	Site B Six weeks Posttraining (n = 5)	Site B 12 Weeks Posttraining (n = 4)	Combined Six Weeks Posttraining (n = 11)	Combined 12 Weeks Posttraining (n = 8)
1. Greeting the caller	98	91	94	96	96	94
2. Introducing yourself	98	91	96	99	97	95
3. Using enthusiastic tone of voice	83	88	81	71	82	78
4. Listening to customer without interrupting	85	87	92	83	88	85
5. Conveying empathy by acknowledging difficulty customer is having	83	91	93	83	88	87
6. Establishing yourself as a resource by actually telling the customer that you can help with the problem/issue	85	80	85	88	85	84
7. Avoiding trying to diagnose or resolve problem/issue before agreeing on a purpose for the call	83	88	87	66	85	77
8. Defining the purpose of the call within the first few minutes (e.g., "I'll make an adjustment to your account")	86	81	89	85	88	83
9. Communicating what the initial plan for the call will be to the customer (e.g., "Let's begin by getting your account on the screen")	86	79	89	88	87	84

(continued on page 144)

Table 4. Mean percent ratings of R3 training at six and 12 weeks, experimental group (continued).

	Site A		Site B		Combined	
10. Checking to make sure customer agrees with your initial plan for the call	80	79	92	67	85	73
11. Asking what has been tried before when diagnosing a problem and issue	78	79	93	75	85	77
12. Asking about timing issues during diagnosis of problem/issue (e.g., "When was it that you...")	85	86	90	76	87	81
13. Gathering information from customer using questions that require more than a "Yes" or "No" answer (e.g., "Can you tell me what you did?")	87	94	85	83	86	89
14. Avoiding using the word "but" when discussing issues with customer	84	78	78	57	81	69
15. Asking questions that clarify the issue/problem	92	95	89	85	91	90
16. Checking back with the customer to make sure you understand the issue/problem	85	82	93	85	89	83
17. Explaining to customer at each step along the way, any progress you have made as you work toward resolving the issue/problem	75	82	91	74	83	78
18. Reconfirming purpose/priorities of the call with the customer	85	86	81	79	83	83
19. Verbally updating the plan for the call as you progress through the call	86	89	83	65	84	77
20. Checking that customer agrees with the updated plan for the call	87	89	90	69	88	79
21. Explaining to customer the reasons behind any observation you make, before making the observation	84	83	92	78	88	80

	Site A		Site B		Combined	
22. Asking for the customer's perspective before making any recommendations	74	75	91	65	81	70
23. Making recommendations after achieving a shared perspective with customer	78	84	91	83	84	84
24. Checking to make sure customer agrees with your recommendations	91	87	93	87	91	87
25. Summarizing the call by reviewing what has been accomplished during the call	86	90	87	70	86	81
26. Using "we" language when summarizing the call (e.g., "We've agreed that you want me to add 5 lines")	84	95	87	75	85	85
27. Checking that customer agrees with your summary of the call	88	94	87	73	87	85
28. Communicating any follow-up steps that need to be taken by you or the customer	84	87	86	80	85	83
29. Checking to make sure customer agrees with any follow-up steps	78	89	89	84	83	87
30. Displaying patience throughout the call	91	90	91	83	91	86
31. Concentrating intensely on the conversation (e.g., taking notes, not having to ask customer to repeat information)	84	91	95	90	89	91
32. Listening empathetically by communicating at least one empathic statement during the call (e.g., "I understand why you need that done today")	85	90	89	82	87	86

(continued on page 146)

Table 4. Mean percent ratings of R3 training at six and 12 weeks, experimental group (continued).

	Site A		Site B		Combined	
33. Avoiding internal or external finger pointing (i.e., not blaming Bell Atlantic or other persons for any problems that may have occurred)	91	85	91	73	91	79
Opening the Call (1-10)	87	85	90	82	88	84
Diagnosing Problems (11-16)	85	86	88	77	87	81
Updating Progress (17-20)	83	86	86	72	85	79
Recommending Results (21-25)	81	82	92	77	86	80
Closing the Call (26-30)	84	91	87	77	85	84
Overall Listening Skills (31-33)	88	89	91	82	89	85

training materials in performing on-the-job duties, and low to very low levels of coaching or feedback, or both, with applying R3 skills on the job.

As table 5 shows, study participants as a whole reported that they had moderate opportunities to use the R3 skills on the job and, to a moderate extent, they reported actually applying them. Training provided participants with moderate to frequent opportunities to practice handling customer contacts effectively. Participants as a group, but particularly those representatives in site C, reported significantly low levels of consistency between R3 training and what happens on the job (question four), low levels of helpfulness of the training materials in performing on-the-job duties (question five), and low to very low levels of coaching or feedback, or both, with applying R3 knowledge and skills on the job (question six). While representatives reported that they had high expectations of applying the knowledge or skills, or both, on the job (question seven), they reported low levels of belief that R3 skills were positively influencing customer satisfaction (question eight) or were useful in avoiding potential conflicts or negative escalations (question nine).

- *Written comments.* In general, comments focused on the perception that R3 skills were already in the representatives' repertoire of customer service skills and therefore training was not particularly useful.
- *Specific R3 skills.* Study participants were asked to rate how effective training was in preparing them to perform the specific R3 service skills.

Core Question: What did the study participants think of the effectiveness of R3 training in preparing them to perform each of the R3 skills listed below?
Answer: Site C reported significantly less R3 effectiveness than Site A, which reported slightly higher ratings than Site B.

M&E asked the experimental and control groups six weeks after their respective training to rate how effective the R3 training was in preparing them to perform each of the 33 skills listed in table 6. Since both groups had received training, no differences were expected, and their ratings were again combined within each site. (Note that the control group in site C did not complete the impact study. The seven participants from site C were all part of the experimental group.)

Table 5. Mean percent ratings on general follow-up survey questions, six weeks postraining.

Never/Rarely		To a Moderate Extent		Often/Always	
0%	20%	40%	60%	80%	100%

To what extent...	Site A (n = 11)	Site B (n = 13)	Site C (n = 8)	Overall (n = 32)
1. have you had *the opportunity* to use the knowledge and/or skills presented in the R3 training?	62	60	57	60
2. have you actually applied the knowledge and skills presented in the R3 training on the job?	63	65	60	63
3. did the training provide you with enough practice in handling customer contacts efficiently?	79	70	42	67
4. did the content of R3 training accurately reflect what happens on the job?	45	46	21	40
5. were the training materials helpful in performing your on-the-job duties (e.g., the 10-week follow-up reminders)?	42	38	10	33
6. have you received help, through coaching and/or feedback, with applying the knowledge and/or skills on the job?	41	33	4	29
7. are you expected to apply the knowledge and/or skills covered in R3 training on the job?	76	77	72	75
8. do you believe R3 training positively influenced Customer Satisfaction in your department?	37	33	12	30
9. do you believe R3 training assisted you in avoiding potential conflicts or negative escalations with your customers?	50	36	10	36

Table 6. Combined mean percent ratings of R3 training effectiveness, six weeks after training.

Not at All   Moderately   Very Effective

0%   20%   40%   60%   80%   100%

How effective was R3 training in preparing you to perform each skill listed:

	Site A (n = 11)	Site B (n = 12)	Site C (n = 7)	Overall (n = 30)
1. Greeting the caller	55	34	5	35
2. Introducing yourself	53	34	5	34
3. Using enthusiastic tone of voice	52	39	5	36
4. Listening to customer without interrupting	60	37	9	39
5. Conveying empathy by acknowledging difficulty customer is having	58	39	5	38
6. Establishing yourself as a resource by actually telling the customer that you can help with the problem or issue	59	38	16	40
7. Avoiding trying to diagnose or resolve problem or issue before agreeing on a purpose for the call	68	39	10	44
8. Defining the purpose of the call within the first few minutes (e.g., "I'll make an adjustment to your account")	57	40	7	40
9. Communicating what the initial plan for the call will be to the customer (e.g., "Let's begin by getting your account on the screen")	59	38	7	40
10. Checking to make sure customer agrees with your initial plan for the call	62	44	13	44
11. Asking what has been tried before when diagnosing a problem or issue	61	39	19	42
12. Asking about timing issues during diagnosis of problem or issue (e.g., "When was it that you....")	63	42	17	44

(continued on page 150)

Table 6. Combined mean percent ratings of R3 training effectiveness, six weeks after training (continued).

How effective was R3 training in preparing you to perform each skill listed:	Site A (n = 11)	Site B (n = 12)	Site C (n = 7)	Overall (n = 30)
13. Gathering information from customer using questions that require more than a "Yes" or "No" answer (e.g., "Can you tell me what you did?")	61	41	7	41
14. Avoiding using the word "but" when discussing issues with customer	51	42	29	42
15. Asking questions that clarify the problem or issue	63	43	10	43
16. Checking back with the customer to make sure you understand the problem or issue	63	41	8	42
17. Explaining to customer at each step along the way any progress you have made as you work toward resolving the problem or issue	65	43	18	45
18. Reconfirming purpose and priorities of the call with the customer	61	40	14	41
19. Verbally updating the plan for the call as you progress through the call	59	40	19	43
20. Checking that customer agrees with the updated plan for the call	61	40	9	42
21. Explaining to customer the reasons behind any observation you make, before making the observation	62	38	12	42
22. Asking for the customer's perspective before making any recommendations	67	39	21	46
23. Making recommendations after achieving a shared perspective with customer	62	39	11	42
24. Checking to make sure customer agrees with your recommendations	61	40	8	42
25. Summarizing the call by reviewing what has been accomplished during the call	60	42	11	42
26. Using "we" language when summarizing the call (e.g., "We've agreed that you want me to add five lines")	60	44	16	44
27. Checking that customer agrees with your summary of the call	66	42	8	44
28. Communicating any follow-up steps that need to be taken by you or the customer	70	36	15	45

29. Checking to make sure customer agrees with any follow-up steps	69	39	**10**	7
30. Displaying patience throughout the call	49	39	**7**	36
31. Concentrating intensely on the conversation (e.g., taking notes, not having to ask customer to repeat information)	55	40	**13**	40
32. Listening empathetically by communicating at least one empathic statement during the call (e.g., "I understand why you need that done today")	50	42	20	40
33. Avoiding internal or external fingerpointing	63	41	**15**	44

As the table indicates in the bolded regions, significant differences emerged between ratings of training effectiveness in site C, with site C reporting significantly less R3 effectiveness. Ratings in site A on average fell in the moderate range of the scale, whereas ratings for site B tended to fall in the low-moderate range. Site C ratings fell in the not-at-all-effective range of the scale. A few skills ratings did not differ significantly with site A, in particular skill 14, which dealt with avoiding using the word *but* when speaking to customers. Overall, ratings across regions ("overall") fell in the low-to-moderate range of the scale, but were clearly influenced by the extremely low site C ratings and consistently higher site A ratings. Both the site B and site C ratings indicated very low perceived R3 effectiveness in skill preparation.

- *Written comments from the follow-up survey.* An overwhelming majority of written comments conveyed representatives' opinion that they already possessed the R3 skills prior to training.
- *Factors contributing to the ability to perform R3 service skills.* M&E asked study participants to estimate the percent that a particular factor enabled them to perform the R3 service skills. Table 7 shows the mean percentages that participants noted for each factor. Within and across regions, representatives reported that past experience was the greatest enabling factor.
- *Positioning of R3 training.* M&E asked study participants to describe what they were told about the R3 training before they attended. Of the 24 participants who provided written comments, 50 percent said "nothing," 25 percent said they were told that it was a class on "customer service skills," and the remaining 25 percent said they were told very little if anything about the course, other than assignment to a control or experimental group. Only one of the 24 responses concerning positioning was positive in nature: "The training would help in dealing with all types of customer contacts and help to delight our customers."
- *Opportunities to diagnose problems.* The final question on the follow-up questionnaire was, "On what percent of calls do you have the opportunity to diagnose customer problems/issues?" The mean percent response to this question was 52 percent with a range from 3 percent to 100 percent, indicating moderate opportunities to diagnose problems. However, on-site observations indicated that across regions, there were few calls that allowed for opportunities to diagnose problems.

Table 7. Factors contributing to performance of R3 service skills, by percent.

Factor	Site A	Site B	Site C	Overall
Knowledge, skills, or experience you had *before* training	62	77	69	**70**
Knowledge, skills, or experience you gained *from* the training	10	5	5	**7**
Knowledge, skills, or experience you acquired on your own *after* the training	4	2	2	3
Procedural documents or job aids	7	7	6	7
Coaching or feedback from peers	5	3	9	5
Coaching or feedback from your team leader	6	3	5	4
Observing others	6	3	6	4

Business Impact (Levels 4 and 5)

Team leaders completed the customer escalation log inconsistently, and, therefore, it could not be used for this study. In addition, the customer contact interviews, which would have provided a measure of the quality of representatives' calls, were not able to be tracked to the individual representatives and thus were unusable for business impact analyses. As a result, management estimates had to be relied on to calculate the tangible benefits of training. This perception data was derived from the ROE interviews.

ROE Interviews

ROE interviews were conducted with each of the four team leaders (two from site A) from the sites participating in the impact study. When asked their expectations for the R3 training, the leaders responded that they expected improved customer relationships or reduced escalations and that their expectations had not changed from the beginning of the program. When asked if they had observed any behavior changes that they could attribute to the training, their responses and the percent to which they believed the behavior had changed were as follows:

- more probing and willingness to go the extra mile to help the client, 30 percent
- ability to identify customers' needs, 30 percent
- knowing when and being able to say no, 5 percent
- getting back to the customer in a more accountable way, 25 percent.

In response to a question about their perception of any financial benefit that could be attributed to the R3 training, the four team leaders reported that they perceived escalations were reduced by 20 percent, 25 percent, 0 percent, and 10 percent. These estimates were used as the tangible benefits to calculate the ROI since the escalation logs were not completed by team leaders. The degree to which they believed their expectations were met was 80 percent, 30 percent, 90 percent, and 60 percent. The 30 percent rating was due to the opinion that the training vendor would have delivered and followed up the training more effectively than the company personnel and that those attending the training were not willing to improve their skills since they believed they already possessed them. The 60 percent rating was due to the opinion that there were escalations that should not have occurred.

ROI Calculation

For the first year of the R3 training, when the original purchase of the product and the evaluation costs were used in the calculation, M&E expected to see an ROI of negative 85 percent (that is, 15 percent of the investment of $488,027 would be returned in year one, with a loss of $416,459). In year two, we expected an ROI of negative 54 percent (that is, 46 percent of the investment of $314,551 would be returned in year two with a loss of $171,415). The year two calculation does not include any program maintenance that may be required and, therefore, the negative ROI is likely to be larger. Table 8 provides the figures used for the ROI calculations for year one, and table 9, for year two. Note the following assumptions made in the calculations of the ROI analyses:

- An average of 15 representatives are at each site.
- The total population of representatives is approximately 600; therefore there are approximately 40 total sites.
- Each site has an average of 15 escalations per month, or 180 escalations per year.
- Perceived reductions in escalations at the study sites were 20 percent, 25 percent, 0 percent, and 10 percent. The estimated overall reduction in escalations is therefore equal to the mean of the estimates (20 + 25 + 10 + 0/4) = 14 percent.
- The value of each escalation is one hour of team leader time, two hours of representative time, and one hour of clerical support.
- The number of representatives receiving training in year two is the remainder of the representatives who have not received training in year one.
- The value of the training does not include potential sales value, but only the hourly wage of the time participants are in training, and therefore not on the job.

In addition to the tangible benefits of reduced escalation used for the ROI calculation, intangible benefits include increased customer satisfaction and possible customer retention.

Recommendations and Outcome

Based on the results of this impact study, M&E strongly recommended that the program be discontinued. The program was in fact discontinued shortly after the results of this impact study were disseminated.

Conclusions

This impact study demonstrates the potential value that more elaborate designs can contribute to the evaluation process. The M&E team at Verizon comprises only a handful of individuals. Nevertheless, four individuals were able to conduct this impact study. The strain on evaluation resources was clearly evident; however, the cost of this

Table 8. Year one ROI calculations.

Cost of the R3 Training Program	Tangible Benefits of the R3 Training Program
Year One	**Year One**
• Purchase price = $157,900	• Reduced escalations:
• Instructor costs = $24,780	
(Loaded labor hourly rate × number of hours per session × sessions per year)	Mean reduction (14%) × number of escalations per year (3,600) × cost of each escalation ($142)* = $71,568
• Student costs:	
Participation time = 185,071	* Mean hours of senior management × loaded labor hourly ($45.27) + mean hours of representatives × loaded labor hourly rate ($36.26) + mean hours of clerical × loaded labor hourly rate ($23.68)
(Loaded labor hourly rate per student × hours attending training × number of students per year)	
• Materials = 104,700	
• Evaluation costs = 15,576	**Total Benefits for Year One =** $71,568
Total Costs for Year One = $488,027	

$$ROI = \frac{Benefits - Costs}{Costs} \text{ or } \frac{\$71,568 - \$488,027}{\$488,027} = -.85 \text{ or } -85\%$$

Table 9. Year two ROI calculations.

Program Cost		Program Benefits	
Year Two		**Year Two**	
• Student costs:		• Reduced escalations:	
Participation time =	$185,071	Mean reduction (14%) × number of escalations	
Materials =	104,700	per year (7,200) × cost of each escalation ($142) =	$143,136
Instructor time =	24,780		
Total Costs for Year Two =	**$314,551**	**Total Benefits for Year Two =**	**$143,136**

ROI = **Benefits − Costs** or **$143,136 − $314,551** = −.54 or −54%

Costs   **$314,551**

particular program was high, and the impact this study eventually realized clearly justified the efforts. Rarely does M&E engage in such elaborate efforts; yet occasions do arise in which more thorough evaluations are plausible and even doable. Despite certain academic compromises in the evaluation process outlined here, the results were consistent across reaction, learning, job application, and business results data. Covering several bases in one study can sometimes mean the difference between a good argument for program retention or discontinuation and a great argument. A great argument here resulted in the discontinuation of an expensive program, a feat not so easily achieved in our corporate environment.

Questions for Discussion

1. How would you critique the evaluation design and method of data collection?
2. What did you think about the strategies used to isolate the impact of training?
3. What other strategies for isolating the impact of training could have been employed here?
4. How credible does the ROI calculation seem to you?
5. How would you have approached this evaluation differently?

The Author

David J. Keuler is a practicing behavioral psychologist in Silver Spring, Maryland, and is an expert in behavioral analysis and research methodology. He is a former research fellow from the National Institute of Mental Health and has served as the primary evaluation consultant to Verizon Communications over the past several years. His expertise in clinical research has played a central role in defining Verizon's award-winning measurement and evaluation philosophy and process implementation strategies. He earned his Ph.D. in clinical psychology from the Catholic University of America and received his clinical training at Bellevue Hospital in New York City. He can be reached at Verizon, 13100 Columbia Pike, Suite B-32, Silver Spring, MD 20904; email: david.j.keuler@verizon.com.

References

Hodges, T.M. (1998). "Measuring Training Throughout the Bell Atlantic Organization." In *In Action: Implementing Evaluation Systems and Processes,* Jack J. Phillips, series editor. Alexandria, VA: ASTD, pp. 45-54.

Phillips. J.J. (1997). *Handbook of Training Evaluation and Measurement Methods* (3d edition). Houston: Gulf.

How Much Is Performance Improvement Really Worth?

A Major Global Automotive Corporation

Gwendolyn G. Berthiez and Dietrich Klusemann

This return-on-investment (ROI) impact study was conducted on a sales training program, one element in the pan-European launch of a new automobile. The primary project objective focused on the following question: Exactly what financial effect did this specific launch training have on the overall, bottom-line sales of the new car? What percentage of new sales, if any, could training claim?

The results are substantial and unquestionably beneficial to executives in determining how to wisely allocate shrinking budgets to gain maximum return on human performance for dollars invested. Results are also of value to performance improvement and training professionals interested in building a business case for executive expenditure on performance improvement initiatives.

Background

Raytheon Professional Services works with many prominent global corporations as a long-term strategic partner in matters relating to human performance improvement. One such client is a large automotive corporation with a far-reaching, extensive global presence in virtually every country in the world.

To respect client confidentiality, the subject company will remain unnamed in this impact study. Additionally, this case study does not display actual impact figures, although all the ratios and percentages represent accurate relationships among the numbers. The percentages have been rounded either up or down to make graphical representations easily legible.

Raytheon plays a significant role in the design, development, delivery, and evaluation of new-vehicle-launch sales training. There are a number of factors that influence car sales, such as advertising, promotional activities, sales incentives, competitive car models, retail distributor launch activities, as well as the styling, engineering, and price of the car itself. Additionally, the training for sales consultants is a determining factor in the sales of new cars.

Sales launch training precedes the actual launch and release of the new vehicle into the marketplace. Sales launch training is designed to educate sales consultants on the unique features and benefits of a specific car, so that they can clearly illustrate why that car better meets prospective buyers' needs than a competitive model. The bottom line is that the sales consultant represents the ultimate contact point with the customer. If the consultant cannot sell the car, then revenue will not be generated either for the retail distributorship or for the manufacturer. Therefore the sales launch training becomes strategically important in generating actual car sales.

Both the number of people involved and the size of budgets required to launch a new automobile are under ever greater scrutiny by executive management. Launch initiatives have become so large that conducting an ROI on initiative outcomes is necessary to justify continued outlay of funds and employees' downtime from work to attend training.

Purpose of Evaluation

The impact study was conducted to illustrate the difference between the effectiveness and the efficiency of a performance improvement initiative. Most training is effective to some degree in that at least some students will learn something and take it away from the training. However, was the training efficient? The following question needed to be addressed: "Did the cost of the training dollars invested warrant the financial expenditure required?" In other words, "Did the investor or investors realize the anticipated bang for their buck?" This case study illustrates that the investors did indeed realize a payback for capital invested and that it can be measured in monetary terms. Secondary objectives for undertaking the study were as follows: to present clients with objective, factual, and decisive data to implement corporate strategy utilizing training to affect performance improvement initiatives, and to determine and prove the value of training and performance improvement measurement as a legitimate and effective product-line offering to clients.

As a solutions and performance improvement provider, Raytheon Professional Services (RPS) was expected to deliver tangible and rational data to validate its value-added capabilities to the customer. RPS provided data indicating that our launch training clearly increased car sales by enhancing sales consultant product knowledge. RPS also responded to the customer need to link training and performance improvement solutions directly to its strategic business measures to validate current and projected investment in large-scale, global performance improvement initiatives. The objective was to guide customers to invest training and performance improvement dollars more efficiently with measurable results to take to the executive bargaining table. By contributing to the customer's achieving a key objective for this product launch—"To become the number one best-seller in Europe"—RPS established greater credibility and opened doors for additional business opportunities.

When Raytheon and the client reviewed the New Model Launch Program to determine appropriateness for a Level 5 ROI impact study, they considered Phillips's seven key determining criteria. As figure 1 shows, six of the seven criteria applied. The case to conduct an ROI impact study appeared to be substantial.

The initial scope of the project included the following criteria:

- *Volume:* Delivery was projected for approximately 233 training days throughout Europe. Although issues such as volume are often relative, 233 training days represented a considerable effort, even for a global player. The volume was also large enough to provide a reasonable base from which to draw statistically significant conclusions.
- *Size:* The program involved over 20,000 participants throughout Europe. The issue wasn't merely total head count, but rather the fact that this population represented the entire European retail sales force.

Figure 1. Key criteria for project selection.

Volume	☑ **233 Training Days, European-wide**
Size	☑ **> 20,000 Participants, European-wide**
Visibility	☑ **Training on a Very Important Product**
Cost	☑ **A Multimillion Dollar Program**
Strategic Link	☑ **Mission "To Be #1 Best Seller in Europe"**
Duration	☑ **Product Launch Recurs**
Senior Management	▬

- *Visibility:* This vehicle launch represented a high-exposure initiative of vital importance to our customer. This was a high-volume, bread-and-butter, must-win automobile, which had to be successful if the automotive company was to not only maintain but also exceed sales and margins. The key to the success of the vehicle launch initiative was the training of sales personnel on the unique features of the new car in comparison with the features of the competitive model.

Cost

The cost of vehicle launch training was budgeted at several million dollars to the manufacturer alone, which absorbed all design, development, and delivery costs. If training were to be provided for subsequent launches on a recurring annual basis, the investment of considerable time and millions of dollars merited a thorough ROI study.

- *Strategic link:* The company's mission, for this automobile to be the number one best-seller in Europe, clearly reflected strategic relevance. By definition, the sale of this car was inseparably linked to the company's strategic goals. All too often the connection between company strategy and training initiatives is inadequately considered. And, of course, when cause-and-effect relationships between initiative and corporate strategy are unknown, any attempted measurement becomes guesswork. In this case the success or failure of auto sales would clearly have a direct impact on the company's position in the marketplace.

- *Duration:* It is possible to consider this criterion from several angles. Launch initiatives, including training on the unique benefits and features of the new car, typically span approximately eight months from conception to implementation to evaluation to conclusion. While individual vehicle launches may be viewed as discrete, short-term events, numerous vehicle launches occur every year as an integral and key strategy of the client's business cycle. In this context it was particularly interesting to see whether we could validate that automotive launches serve as key indicators in terms of their contribution to a given car's success in the marketplace.

The scope of the pan-European program was the original focus and was to include a host of Western European countries, such as the Netherlands, Belgium, Germany, France, Italy, Spain, and the United Kingdom (UK). For purposes of this particular study, we chose to focus specifically on the UK. The figures in the remainder of the study are based on the UK marketplace (for example, the target population was distilled down from 20,000 to 1,800 participants). If cultural differences were negated, we found the subject population sufficiently statistically valid, 95 percent, to be able to extrapolate results for the rest of the Western European community.

Evaluation Methodology
Model
This impact study uses Phillips's (1997) model. In addition to his overall ROI model, we found it useful to add an additional component at the beginning of the process model, the training needs analysis (TNA). Prior to investing in an extensive ROI study, too many companies fail to strategically link training initiatives to the overall business thrust. The focus on a TNA helps to clearly identify exactly what needs to be accomplished with a given training initiative. A TNA also identifies critical success factors that link to corporate strategy. The ROI study must be based on these identified critical success factors, such as key business indicators.

The methodology steps are as follows: data collection, training effects isolation, data conversion to monetary value, intangible benefits identification, and program costs tabulation and ROI calculation. As the reader will note throughout this study, data for each of the steps is investigated and applied with consequent success.

Data Collection Methodology
Table 1 shows the eight-month data collection plan, March through October, for the UK launch team.

The authors and their team collected data at four levels to thoroughly validate the impact study and to provide information to several interested parties. Due to the geographical distribution of trainees, we used questionnaires to collect data in conjunction with published sources such as annual reports, price lists, and actual sales records. For cost reasons we could not conduct observations of on-the-job application, interviews, or focus groups. Instead, we ascertained the key metrics that would drive business impact (number of units sold and margin per unit realized) from the questionnaire and then validated the metrics with actual figures confirmed by the client.

Therefore, for purposes of this study, focus was directed to the posttraining and six-month follow-up questionnaires, which yielded the percentages and numbers needed to directly calculate the ROI. Both questionnaires contained exactly the same questions except for a change in tense for the six-month follow-up version. The questionnaires

Table 1. Data collection plan for the UK new product launch.

Level	Broad Program Objectives	Data Collection Method	Timing of Data Collection	Responsibilities for Data Collection
1. Reaction, satisfaction, and planned actions	Determine participant satisfaction (meeting logistics, training content, and facilitator delivery) Distribute and collect posttraining questionnaire	Standard participant satisfaction questionnaire	End of training day	Moderator and facilitator
		Posttraining questionnaire on job application and business results and impact	End of training day	Moderator and facilitator
2. Learning	Lesson objectives per leader's guide	Posttest on knowledge (electronic handset) (No pretest)	End of training day	Moderator and facilitator PC operator and programmer
3. Job application	Distribute and collect six-month follow-up questionnaire Sell product based on consultative selling techniques Conversion of competitive brand Test drives conducted Prospect-to-sales ratio	Six-month follow-up questionnaire to sales consultants, based on sales consultants' estimates and confidence factor (Level 3 and 4 data)	Six months after training session and product release to specific country	Launch team Objective third party—agency
4. Business results	Distribute and collect six-month follow-up questionnaire Increase conversion rate Increase margin Increase sales	Six-month follow-up questionnaire to sales consultants, based on sales consultants' estimates and confidence factor (Level 3 and 4 data)	Six months after training session and product release to specific country	Launch team Objective third party—agency

asked the respondents for their perceptions, though it is clear that these "perceptions" were much more precise after the experience of six months in the field. In addition these figures were subsequently compared with actual, hard figures collected by the manufacturer.

Questions four and five on the questionnaire provided actual percentage and numerical data for an ROI calculation. The data collection plan focused on conversion rate, margin, and sales to get the data for Level 4, business results.

Participants received the questionnaire twice and returned it twice. They received the first questionnaire by hand at the end of the initial vehicle launch training day along with, but separate from, the standard participant satisfaction questionnaire. Then, six months after the original training, they received by mail the second distribution. Due to an extensive, conscientious, and carefully instructed distribution and collection network, 366 questionnaires were returned, 50 more than the 316 required to maintain statistical validity representing a participant population of 1,800.

Training Effects Isolation Methodology

Of the 10 traditional approaches currently in use (Phillips, 1997) to isolate the cause-and-effect relationship between training and performance improvement, the following three approaches were utilized here:

- *training impact:* sales consultants' perception of the influence of sales launch training on actual car sales
- *confidence factor:* sales consultants' certainty of their estimates about the influence of training and other factors, such as advertising, sales incentives, promotional activities, and competitors' initiatives, on actual car sales
- *customer validation:* final sales data collected by the customer and used to substantiate sales consultant estimates.

These approaches were selected for ease of use and realistic credibility of sources. We considered the sales consultants resident experts on when, how, and how many additional cars each sold due to increased vehicle knowledge and awareness. The consultants' estimate provided an adequate indicator of additional sales, since we correlated these estimates with actual sales figures. We could have used alternative approaches, such as control groups, monitoring on-the-job application of principles learned in training, and trend-line analyses. Though we chose not to in this instance, in future ROI initiatives it will be beneficial to compare and contrast other methods of isolating data wherever practical and cost efficient to do so.

Data Conversion Methodology

The conversion of data was relatively easy since units of cars sold can be multiplied by a given unit price and unit margin to establish the monetary benefits. One way to determine a retail organization's benefits is to express the benefit as the delta between unit margins. In this case, it is possible to express the benefit as the delta between unit margins realized on the old model versus the margins to be realized with the new model. With the figures for the UK example, the calculation would look like this: $540 per unit multiplied by the number of incremental units to be sold as a result of the launch training (2,052 units) plus all the other units sold anyway, to which the better margin would also be applied (51,848). Please see figure 7, ROI for the retail distributor, and figure 8, Calculations for retail distributor, which are described in more detail in the section "Program Costs Tabulation and ROI Calculation."

Intangible Benefits Identification Methodology

Intangibles are those benefits and measures that cannot be expressed easily in monetary terms. In our case, we asked a number of questions to provide more general feedback on the value of the training intervention. The questionnaire posed the following three important questions about intangible benefits:

1. "Did the sales launch training help you to sell the new model car?" As figure 2 shows, 96 percent of sales consultants who had received training on the new car indicated that training helped them to sell the new model, not just the day immediately after sales training occurred, but six to eight months after as well. Their response indicates that the training was effective and well received, but in itself this result cannot be expressed in dollars and cents.

2. "To what extent has the training influenced the following measures in your work: sales volume, customer satisfaction, conversion ratio?" Figure 3 graphically illustrates the answers to question two. While an answer to this question does not provide conclusive proof, it does furnish a good indicator of the influence and positive results from the sales consultants' training. Future studies can use alternative methods and questions. Responses about the impact on volume, customer satisfaction, and conversion ratio (ratio of prospects to actual sales) in themselves do not translate into monetary values. We did not expect very high ratios, so were pleased to note that all three dimensions were nearing the midrange of moderate, or three. This

Figure 2. Replies to intangible results question: "Did the sales launch training help sell the new model car?"

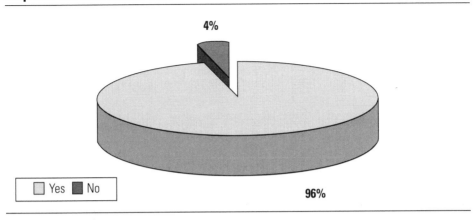

4%

Yes ☐ No ■

96%

response indicated sales consultant awareness that the launch training had a noticeable influence on sales volume, customer satisfaction, and conversion ratio. A substantial and positive indicator was now available for consideration and correlation with other data points.

3. "Please indicate the percentage of effect that each of the factors listed has had on sales of the new car." The factors were training, sales incentives, dealer promotions, advertising, price, the product itself, and other. The total percentage for the seven factors had to add up to 100 percent. The fact that the sales volume in question two was affected to a "moderate" extent supports the responses to figure 4, which indicates the relative importance of training to issues such as price and the car itself. Obviously the most brilliant training would have no effect if the car were poor; therefore the car itself and its price are incontestably key success factors in the sale of any vehicle. Together, the "car itself" and the "price" claimed 47 percent of the influence on car sales. The second largest influence on sales was the "other" category at 20 percent. The "other" category covered various factors that were insignificant by themselves. The remaining significant factors such as advertising (9 percent), retailer promotions (7 percent), and sales incentives (9 percent) claimed a collective 25 percent influence on sales. While the factors training, advertising, and sales incentives are very close, it is significant that training was rated equally as important as advertising and sales incentives. The bottom line is that sales consultants indicated that training affected a solid 9 percent increase in specific car sales.

Figure 3. Replies to intangible results question: "To what extent has the training influenced sales volume, customer satisfaction, and conversion ratio?"

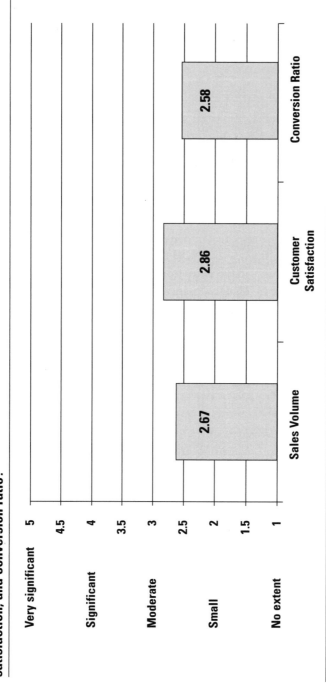

Figure 4. Replies to intangible results question: "Please indicate the percentage of effect that each of the factors listed has had on sales of the new product."

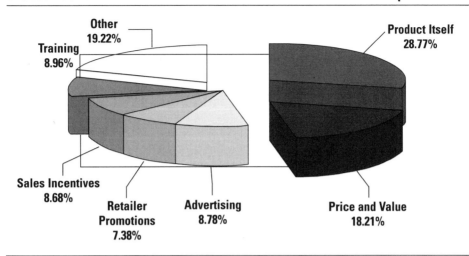

Other
19.22%

Training
8.96%

Product Itself
28.77%

Sales Incentives
8.68%

Retailer
Promotions
7.38%

Advertising
8.78%

Price and Value
18.21%

Program Costs Tabulation and ROI Calculation

The basis for our calculations on program costs and ROI were the most accurate and precise information we could obtain from annual reports, industry statistics, confidential information from our client, and competitive numbers available from marketing and brand management departments and subject matter experts. The evaluation strategy, depicted in table 2, focused on three data points: conversion ratio, margin, and actual sales expressed in units. For each data item, the table shows the methods by which we isolated the effects of the program, the methods by which we converted the data to monetary values, as well as the cost categories and intangible benefits, other influences, and the communication target.

Subsequent calculations are based on the estimates of the sales consultants on the showroom floor. The initial posttraining questionnaire established a baseline of additional incremental projected sales due to sales launch training. The six-month follow-up questionnaire helped validate these expectations, which we finally compared with actual data from the manufacturer.

In our study two major parties incurred costs and also benefited from the training and performance improvement initiative in different ways. The primary party was the manufacturer of the car to be launched, and the other was the retail distribution network that would sell the car. The manufacturer paid for the vehicle launch training to be designed, developed, delivered, and translated. The retail distribution

Table 2. Evaluation strategy and ROI analysis plan for the UK new product launch.

Data Items	Methods of Isolating the Effects of the Program	Methods of Converting Data	Cost Categories	Intangible Benefits	Other Influences and Issues	Communication Targets
Conversion Ratio (ratio of prospect to sale)	Training participant and sales agent estimation with confidence factor	Expert estimates	• Fixed: —design —development —delivery —cars • Variable: —evaluation —food and beverage	Perception of retail organization by wholesale organization; Sales consultant confidence and satisfaction	Competitor activity; Product availability; Product quality; Press reports; Weather	Brand management team; Participants; Retail organizations; Various management groups; Launch team; Internal and external customer briefings; Conferences
Margin	Training participant and sales agent estimation with confidence factor	Actual improvement in monetary values	(Capture all the costs)	Customer satisfaction		
Sales	Training participant and sales agent estimation with confidence factor	Standard value per industry and brand management team		Will not tie a value to the following: • communication • team work • efficiency		

Figure 5. ROI for the manufacturer.

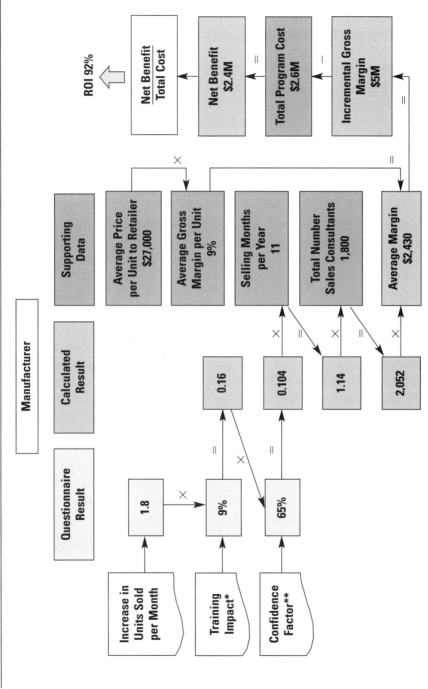

*Training impact—Sales consultants' perception of influence of sales launch training on actual car sales.
**Confidence factor: Sales consultants' certainty of their estimates about the influence of training and other factors on actual car sales.

network paid for travel and lost labor costs for sales consultants to attend training. In the end, as is the case with many vehicles new to the marketplace, the success of the manufacturer's effort was integrally tied to the efforts expended by the sales force, the diverse pan-European retail distribution network. Since the costs incurred by both parties differed somewhat, two separate but related ROI calculations are presented, one for the manufacturer at 92 percent ROI, and one for the retail distributor, at 325 percent ROI. Figure 5 shows the calculations for the manufacturer's ROI at 92%. The calculation is separated into the questionnaire result, the calculated result, and the supporting data (supporting data is industry specific).

Three key results from the questionnaire are as follows:
- Sales consultants anticipated they would sell 1.8 additional cars per month.
- Sales consultants said that they sold an average of 9 percent more cars due to the sales launch training.
- Sales consultants were 65 percent confident in all estimates that they provided.

The average price per car to the retailer was $27,000. The true gross margin is a closely guarded industry secret. Based on industry expertise, for this case we chose to run the calculations using an average gross margin of 9 percent. Let's step through the actual calculations to validate the methodology used, as figure 6 shows.

Since results are of little value if no one believes them, the final ROI figures were discounted and modified based on a number of credibility factors. For example, we discounted results by the training impact and the confidence factor, disregarded extreme data values, used the lowest value in a range, assumed no impact if the respondent registered no answer, verified key data, and differentiated between tangible and intangible data (Phillips, 1997, pp. 198-201).

The findings were handled in the following manner:
- The data was calibrated and cross-checked against actual car model sales results reported in the company's annual report, objective industry statistics, and internal company sales reports.
- The findings were discounted by a training impact of 9 percent taken from questionnaire responses. Training impact represents sales consultants' perceptions of the influence of the sales launch training on actual car sales.
- The findings were discounted by an average confidence factor of 65 percent. The confidence factor represents sales consultants' certainty of their estimates regarding the influence of training and

other factors such as advertising, sales incentives, promotional activities, and competitor initiatives on actual car sales.
- As in all good statistical data, we excluded any values that were outside of realistic possibility. If the average number of cars sold per sales consultant per month was between two and four units and a

Figure 6. Calculations for the ROI for the manufacturer.

Increase in cars sold per month			1.8
Training impact*		×	9%
Number of additional cars sold above estimated target per sales consultant		total	0.16
Discounted by confidence factor**		×	65%
Number of additional cars sold above estimated target per sales consultant		total	0.104
Selling months per year		×	11
Number of additional cars sold above estimated target per sales consultant		total	1.14
Total number of UK sales consultants		×	1,800
Total number of additional cars sold per all UK sales consultants		total	2,052
Average price per car to retailer	$27,000		
Average gross margin per car	× 9%		
Average margin per car sold	= $2,430		
Average margin calculated using 9% average gross margin per unit		×	$2,430
Gross margin for all additional UK cars sold		total	$5,000,000
Less total design, development, delivery costs		−	$2,600,000
= Net benefit of sales launch training		**TOTAL**	**$2,400,000**

$$\frac{\underline{Program\ Benefits}}{Program\ Costs} \quad \frac{5,000,000}{2,600,000} \quad = \ 1.923\ benefits\text{-}to\text{-}cost\ ratio$$

$$\frac{\underline{Net\ Program\ Benefits}}{Program\ Costs} \quad \frac{2,400,000}{2,600,000} \quad = \ .923 = 92\%\ ROI$$

*Training impact—Sales consultants' perception of influence of sales launch training on actual car sales.
**Confidence factor—Sales consultants' certainty of their estimates about the influence of training and other factors on actual car sales.

respondent indicated 50 cars sold, that response was deleted from the calculations.

- When a question was left unanswered, we assumed that the dimension queried on that question had no impact on sales and therefore inserted a value of zero to further adjust results downward.
- We differentiated between tangible and intangible data. While we noticed and were gratified by intangible data, intangible results were used only as an additional sanity check against tangible figures.

As indicated above, a second impact study was calculated for the retail distributor with a resulting ROI of 325 percent. The retail distributor calculation required several additional factors to be included, such as discount on old versus new model, total new units sold, and salary, travel costs, and training fees, as figures 7 and 8 show.

Sales consultants normally have a few percentage points with which to work in closing a car sale. We determined that in order for consultants to sell the old model, they had to give an average discount of 4 percent. Because the new model was more attractive than the old model, consultants expected sales to be more brisk, and they expected the buying public to be willing to accept only a 2 percent discount in order to acquire the new model car. Subtracting the new model discount of 2 percent from the old model discount of 4 percent left a 2 percent delta, which, multiplied by the recommended retail price (RRP) of $27,000, left an incremental margin of $537. If we had used $537 as the average adjusted retailer margin and multiplied it by 53,900, all the new cars sold in 1998, our calculations would have yielded an astronomical and improbable 1,100 percent ROI. Therefore, we applied the same conservative approach to the $537 figure as we did in the manufacturer calculations. We further discounted the $537 figure by the training impact (9 percent) and confidence factor (65 percent), which yielded a more credible average adjusted retailer margin of $32. Multiplying $32 by 54,000, new units sold in 1998, resulted in an incremental gross margin of $1,600,000, which we could claim as having been generated due to consultants attending our sales launch training. Or could we?

Considering cost to the retail distributor, we took the average annual salary of a sales consultant and broke it down to a day rate of $180; added to $180 the travel expenses of $42 per consultant and training fees of $0 and came up with a total cost of $222 per consultant to attend the sales launch training. All that remained was to multiply $222 by 1,800, the number of sales consultants who attended the launch training, to net a total cost to the retailer network of attending launch training of $400,000. By subtracting $400,000 from

Figure 7. ROI for the retail distributor.

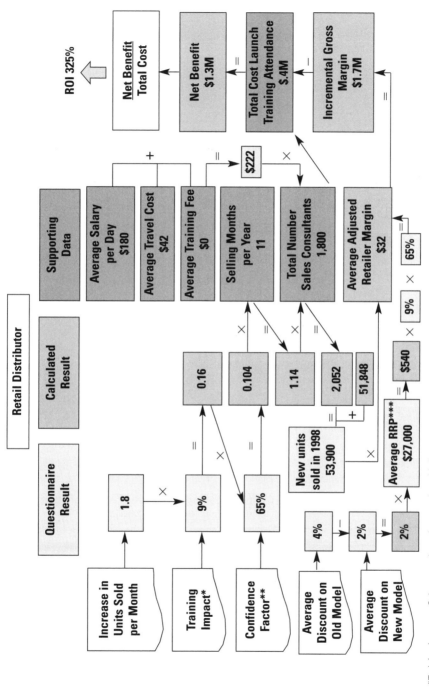

*Training impact—Sales consultants' perception of influence of sales launch training on actual car sales.
**Confidence factor: Sales consultants' certainty of their estimates about the influence of training and other factors on actual car sales.
***RRP—Recommended retail price.

Figure 8. Calculations for retail distributor.

Increase in cars sold per month		1.8
Training impact*	×	9%
Number of additional cars sold above estimated target per sales consultant	total	0.16
Confidence factor**	×	65%
Number of additional cars sold above estimated target per sales consultant	total	0.104
Selling months per year	×	11
Number of additional cars sold above estimated target per sales consultant	total	1.14
Total number of UK sales consultants	×	1,800
Total number of additional cars sold above estimated by all UK sales consultant	total	2,052
Projected number new units sold in 1998	+	51,848
All new units sold in 1998	total	53,900

Average discount on old model		4%
Average discount on new model	−	2%
	=	2%
Recommended retail price (RRP)	× $27,000	
	=	$540
Training impact	×	9%
	=	$49
Confidence factor	×	65%
Average adjusted retailer margin	=	$32

Average adjusted retailer margin calculated	×	$ 32
Gross margin for all additional UK units sold	total	$ 1,700,000
Less total design, development, delivery costs	−	400,000
= Net benefit of sales launch training	**TOTAL**	**$ 1,300,000**

Program Benefits	**1,700,000**	=	**4.25 benefit-to-cost ratio**
Program Costs	**400,000**		
Net Program Benefits	**1,300,000**	=	**3.25 = 325% ROI**
Program Costs	**400,000**		

*Training impact—Sales consultants' perception of influence of sales launch training on actual car sales.
**Confidence factor—Sales consultants' certainty of their estimates about the influence of training and other factors on actual car sales.

the incremental gross margin of $1,600,000, we arrived at the total net benefit of $1,200,000, a number that we felt we could reasonably claim as a number the sales launch training had indeed generated. In other words, without the sales launch training attended by 1,800 consultants, $1,200,000 of incremental margins would not have otherwise been generated.

Conclusion

After running the numbers, our retail distributor ROI was 325 percent, conclusive evidence that the investors, the manufacturer, and the retail distributor did realize a significant payback for capital invested and that the impact of training on performance improvement can indeed be measured in credible monetary terms.

Our sales launch training was not only effective but also efficient. Sales consultants learned and increased their knowledge about the new car model being brought to market; therefore, our sales launch training was effective. Additionally, the training dollars invested justified the financial expenditure required and investors realized the anticipated bang for their buck; so our sales launch training was also efficient.

Subjecting one's investment in human performance improvement to the scrutiny of an ROI evaluation is becoming more and more an inescapable requirement for most training professionals today. With the increased importance of the stock market's valuation of companies' performances, stakeholders are more often asking the hard questions as to why certain investments are necessary if the stock market cannot "see" the results and thus cannot honor the investments.

While managers today may acknowledge that some form of measurement is probably necessary, many still maintain that the effectiveness of training cannot actually be measured. At Raytheon Professional Services we believe differently. We maintain that when debating the merits of measuring training efficiency, one ought to consider a continuum. On one side of the continuum is the statement that measuring the efficiency of training is impossible. On the other end of the continuum is the statement that measurement of training is an exact science producing accurate results 100 percent of the time. The truth, as always, lies somewhere in between.

While one cannot generally take calipers and measure the effectiveness of a training intervention to six digits of accuracy, especially in the soft skills areas, it is nonetheless possible and desirable to move along this continuum toward the measurement side. Any measurement is worth much more than no measurement at all.

The key criteria to keep in mind are as follows:

- Don't make it a theoretical exercise; be pragmatic about what you want to achieve.
- Accept reasonable results.
- Make sure you conduct the study in a cost-efficient manner.
- Be quick. Results must be available in a timely fashion, or they represent mere academic interest.

If you still have doubts, consider how much money is being spent in areas such as marketing and advertising without any exact ways of measuring the results. Yet decisions are made about significant investments every day of the week, often based on relatively imprecise and unscientific information. Our basic contention is that training can no longer afford to operate totally in the dark and that some measurement, imperfect though it might be, is a step in the right direction. With time, experience, and historical data, future training and performance improvement investment decisions will become more sound and more targeted than in the past. Training and performance improvement as disciplines will take their rightful positions at the corporate executive table.

Communication Process

A key aspect to keep in mind when conducting a study that attempts to measure the results of a training initiative is that it puts those responsible under a microscope. Many training managers are uneasy about the idea of suddenly having to face a tool or methodology that objectively measures their activities. Depending on the culture of the company this uneasiness and concern need to be taken into account.

First, one must sell the benefits of such a measurement system to all the stakeholders—managers, developers, trainers, and participants. If staff perceive measurement as a threat, they are not likely to be cooperative. This study had support from the very top of the organization right through to departmental managers and the field force. This pervasive support proved instrumental in the collection and return of data from the sales consultants. The authors worked with customer management up front to establish project expectations to ensure that what was measured was precisely what was credible to the customer; changes in customer expectations were carefully monitored and adjusted throughout the project life cycle.

Second, questionnaire respondents need to understand the purpose of the exercise. They must clearly see their contribution as nonthreatening to themselves or to their immediate colleagues. When feedback is requested, the participants ought to be involved in the dissemination of the results.

Third, communication must be an ongoing activity. It is not sufficient to announce the initiative and then leave it at that. Rather, it is important to establish a consistent communication plan from the start. That plan should inform stakeholders of the progress at every step along the way.

Finally, all communication must address the question, "So what?" If any of the recipients of this information cannot see the relevance to their job and responsibilities, the communication will have been in vain.

Lessons Learned

It is possible to summarize the lessons from this case study with seven succinct points, as follows:

1. Begin with the end in mind.

During the planning process, be very certain of what the training project's end objectives are. Ask yourself—and, more important, ask the project sponsor—the following questions:

- "Exactly what do you want to accomplish?"
- "What would success look like at the conclusion of this project?"
- "What are the expected deliverables?"
- "What are the cause-and-effect relationships of the key business drivers?"
- "What would have been accomplished for you to say, 'The project has been a success. Now let's talk about the next one.'?"

2. Decide whether or not you can actually deliver.

Can you handle the request? Do you have the expertise, or do you know where to find it? Are the parameters reasonable yet challenging? Numbers can very quickly get out of hand, but it is important to carefully consider whether or not the scope is realistic to achieve. In determining the feasibility of meeting a request, take your time and think through each step carefully. Do not give managers unrealistic expectations about how quickly you can provide useful ROI data to them. Be careful and thorough. You will need to get it right the first time in order to secure funding for subsequent projects.

3. Start out small.

As you begin selecting your first viable ROI project, try to think small. If you don't, unanticipated challenges will almost immediately present themselves. Limit your scope to an arena that is 100 percent within your control or that of the project sponsor. Select a manageable project that is almost guaranteed to be successful and provide good, solid results on which you can build subsequent projects. Consider keeping the project as low key as possible. Early unwanted publicity may force you to share inconclusive and immature data, resulting in project derailment or even cancellation. Though critics are an important part of the road to success, make certain that you choose the time and place to engage with them.

4. Be certain that all pertinent data and numbers are accessible.

An ROI project is rarely a unilateral activity. As the project scope is fully determined, it will become evident that a number of people and functions will have to be involved to a lesser or greater degree. What data will you be allowed to access? Is any of it confidential and to which functions? Is the head of the function that houses the data a supporter of yours and of the ROI project? How can you sell the idea to the holder of the data, and how can that individual use it to further functional or company objectives?

You will also need to find out whether or not you have ready access to the data with which you will need to compare your ROI results, such as departmental numbers and highly proprietary company statistics. Not all pertinent data is available in the company's annual report. Check this aspect out thoroughly before launching into the ROI project. You might be surprised to find how difficult it is to obtain some of the meaningful numbers, ratios, and percentages you need.

5. Develop a budget and get it approved.

This is all part of successfully managing the ROI project. You need to be regarded as a numbers guru in order to build credibility with the customer (whether internal or external; management, sponsor, or critic). A solid budget must be established upfront, since ROI projects can be expensive and take time. A key part of many people's jobs is that they be smart about money and numbers. Make these skills part of your tool kit, too, if you want to be successful. In many cases you have just one opportunity to establish credibility, so mistakes are not an option where finance is concerned.

In determining resource costs, think through resource needs carefully at each step. As you plan, be brutally realistic about the scope and actual time required. Is this a full-time job for you? Do you have other resources at your disposal to deploy on the actual "doing" of the work and the gathering of the data, or are you a one-person show? Is this an additional job on top of the other three full-time responsibilities you have?

Do you have the resources required for data entry and number crunching? Is someone available who has an excellent command of Excel, Access, or Lotus 123 to manipulate the data accurately? Who will analyze and make sense of the findings? Who has the requisite MS Project or FastTrack expertise to create a time line? What about other employees' time and costs to oversee data distribution and collection? Make no mistake: Conducting an ROI study requires time and concentration. Progress will not occur with a stolen few minutes, especially if you are still in the learning mode.

6. Respect politics and the buy-in process.

Everyone who touches the process needs to understand and buy into the reasons for the ROI study and its importance. Explain what it will mean to them and their jobs. How will they benefit from the results of the study? Never forget that you do not live and work in a vacuum. Your company is a highly integrated and sensitive system of interconnected people and processes on which you rely for your data—sponsors, local champions, administrative people, critics, and the like. Be careful to obtain approval from all power brokers concerned, especially if you are asking for sensitive numerical data from them or from their employees.

7. Select the appropriate vehicle to enable ease and accuracy of data collection.

Review all possible options and then select the approach that best meets the needs of the project. Will you use questionnaires, surveys, tests, interviews, focus groups, observation, performance records, or something else? Keep credibility foremost in mind when choosing a data collection vehicle. Consider the approach as well as the participant audience that is most likely to supply the information needed to build a credible ROI case. Careful and thoughtful preparation saves backtracking, confusion, and wasted time and effort.

Questions for Discussion

1. What is the value of looking at the ROI in training and human performance improvement?
2. What can an ROI study realistically provide and what can it not provide?
3. What are some of the critical success factors to consider before embarking on an ROI study?
4. Why is the cause-effect relationship between variables important?
5. What are some of the methods used to link training outcomes to monetary values?
6. What has politics got to do with measuring the effectiveness of training?
7. What is the difference between "effectiveness" and "efficiency" of training?

8. When does it pay to conduct an ROI study?
9. How should one deal with intangible factors?
10. When is a factor "intangible"?

The Authors

Gwendolyn G. Berthiez is a senior consultant with Raytheon Professional Services, Consulting Group, based in Troy, Michigan. For six years, she worked in the international arena implementing large-scale leadership and strategic change initiatives for global corporations. She has been active in the areas of organization change management, strategic learning, performance improvement, human capital development, and corporate university consulting for approximately 15 years. She has spoken on the topic of ROI at various international conferences and human performance gatherings in Italy, Germany, Australia, the UK, and the United States.

Approaching change initiatives, as well as training, with a practical business management focus, she emphasizes the link between bottom-line ROI and development of an enterprise's human capital to drive identifiable quality within companies. Berthiez can be reached at Raytheon Professional Services, Consulting Group, 1650 Research Drive, Suite 100, Troy, MI 48083; email: gberthiez@rps.com.

Dietrich Klusemann is Raytheon's director, Consulting Services, and is based in Ruesselsheim, Germany, where measurement and testing of training initiatives is an integral part of the consulting offering. He has worked most of his professional life in the training field both in Australia, where he spent 15 years, and Germany, primarily in the automotive industry. Since joining Raytheon in 1995, he has been in charge of several multi-million-dollar training projects and has specialized in the strategic evaluation of such investments in human performance improvement. Klusemann has spoken on the topic of ROI at various international conferences both in Germany and in the UK. He is an economist by training and holds an M.B.A.

Note

The authors would like to thank the following for their editing suggestions and helpful comments: Paul C. Swinscoe, director, Consulting Services, Raytheon Professional Services, London, UK, and Maurice J. Ryan, director, Marketing & Business Development, Delta College Corporate Services, Saginaw, Michigan.

References

Phillips, Jack J. (1997). *Handbook of Training and Evaluation Measurement Methods* (3d edition). Houston: Gulf.

Suggested Readings

Berthiez, Gwendolyn G. (March 2000). "Take It Step by Step: How to Improve Your ROI Projects." *Training*, p. 18.

Brinkerhoff, Robert O. (1987). *Achieving Results From Training*. San Francisco: Jossey Bass.

Dixon, Nancy M. (1990). *A Tool for Improving HRD Quality*. San Diego: University Associates.

Fitz-enz, Jac. (1984). *How to Measure Human Resources Management*. New York: McGraw-Hill.

Flamholtz, Eric G. (1985). *Human Resource Accounting* (2d edition). San Francisco: Jossey-Bass.

Head, Glenn. (1994). *Training Cost Analysis*. Alexandria, VA: ASTD.

Kirkpatrick, Donald L. (1994). *Evaluating Training Programs*. San Francisco: Berrett-Koehler.

Newby, A.C. (1992). *Training Evaluation Handbook*. San Diego: Pfeiffer.

Phillips, Jack J. (1996). *Accountability in Human Resource Management*. Houston: Gulf.

Phillips, Jack J. (1997). *Return on Investment in Training and Performance Improvement Programs*. Houston: Gulf.

Phillips, Jack J. (Ed.). (1994). *In Action: Measuring Return on Investment* (volume 1). Alexandria, VA: ASTD.

Phillips, Jack J. (Ed.). (1995). *In Action: Conducting Needs Assessments*. Alexandria, VA: ASTD.

Phillips, Jack J. (Ed.). (1997). *In Action: Measuring Return on Investment* (volume 2). Alexandria, VA: ASTD.

Phillips, Jack J. (Ed.). (1997). *In Action: Transferring Learning to the Workplace*. Alexandria, VA: ASTD.

Phillips, Jack J. (Ed.). (1998). *In Action: Implementing Evaluation Systems and Processes*. Alexandria, VA: ASTD.

Phillips, Jack J. (Ed.). (1999). *In Action: Measuring Learning and Performance*. Alexandria, VA: ASTD.

Phillips, Jack J. (Ed.). (2000). *In Action: Building Learning Capability Through Outsourcing*. Alexandria, VA: ASTD.

Phillips, Jack J. (Ed.). (2000). *In Action: Leading Knowledge Management and Learning*. Alexandria, VA: ASTD.

Phillips, Jack J. (Ed.). (2000). *In Action: Performance Analysis and Consulting*. Alexandria, VA: ASTD.

Robinson, Dana Gaines, and James C. Robinson. (1989). *Training for Impact.* San Francisco: Jossey-Bass.

Rust, Roland. (1994). *Return on Quality.* Chicago: Probus.

Spenser, Lyle M., Jr. (1986). *Calculating Human Resource Costs and Benefits.* New York: John Wiley.

Measuring ROI of Computer Training in a Small to Medium-Sized Enterprise

Slick Manufacturing

Mike Devaney

This case study examines the role that return-on-investment (ROI) evaluation could play in Irish small to medium-sized enterprises (SME). (An SME is an enterprise with fewer than 250 employees.) The study was to examine the feasibility and compatibility of ROI evaluation in a company with limited resources and no formal HRD structure. The study shows that ROI can be implemented and illustrates the important link between HRD activities and business results to company management.

Background

The idea for this study originated in my experience as an HRD advisor for client companies as part of my work for a government development agency (Enterprise Ireland). It was evident that little or no Level 4 evaluation was being undertaken in small to medium-sized companies. If such an undertaking were possible and successful, it would contribute to the process of convincing the management of these companies that HRD activities are an investment and not a cost and can make an important contribution to business success. In addition the increased demand for accountability from the government- and European-funding agencies requires some mechanism to measure and reflect the benefits accruing to the different shareholders.

The criteria for selection were that the company be an Irish SME, with no full-time training manager or formal training department. The selected company should have some history of training.

This case was prepared to serve as a basis for discussion rather than to illustrate either effective or ineffective administrative and management practices. Names, dates, places, and organizations have been disguised at the request of the author or organization.

The company should undertake training to meet perceived immediate needs, and the company's management should believe ultimately that training is relevant but not an ongoing priority. Survival of the company should dominate management thinking. Training in the company would historically focus on individuals, and its training budget would be haphazard and limited.

In the west of Ireland, the majority of industrial companies employ fewer than 50 persons. I decided to select for this case study one of those companies as being typical of the norm. This company was Slick Manufacturing (not its real name for reasons of confidentiality).

Slick Manufacturing employs 42 people full-time who work on the design, manufacture, or sales of industrial products. The company was founded in 1979 and is owned by the managing director. Currently Slick manufactures a large range of different products and exports to global markets. The company experienced huge sales growth in the past 26 months, and its sales turnover is currently less than IR£10 million (Irish pounds).

Historically, Slick restricted its training to craft apprenticeship training, and the drive for it came from individuals, to meet immediate needs, and from the company, to meet statutory requirements. The company recruited a new financial controller in January 2000 and gave him the responsibility for training in addition to his financial duties.

Triggering Events for Training Program

The upsurge in company turnover was creating increased strain on the company's internal systems of operation. The existing computer system was first generation with a hard-drive capacity that was too limited to meet the company's requirements. Relevant employees did not have access to the system, so it was incapable of generating accurate management reports. Employees and management were straining under the stress, as staff turnover, absenteeism, and low morale were becoming growing problems.

Needs Assessment

The financial controller-training manager urged management to undertake a survey among the employees to assess the magnitude of the problem and the potential causes and solutions. Management agreed to this proposal. The survey consisted of informal oral interviews with all employees to ascertain barriers to the achievement of work tasks and suggested solutions. The employees indicated that there was too much work and not enough employees. This was evident from increased errors, increased customer complaints, inaccessibility of management information when required, and widespread inefficiencies.

The company also undertook an analysis of the past 12 months' worth of customer complaints and found that they were linked to inefficiencies. For example, from the time a customer ordered a product until it arrived at production was taking on average 10 days. Eight employees were involved in that process, and errors, such as lost orders and incorrect calculations, were high. Customer complaints were running at four per month with 50 percent of those orders being lost to the company.

The company also undertook exit interviews with departing staff. They found that five of the six said their primary reason for leaving the company was that the work had become too difficult and they were unable to handle it. They also cited work-related stress as a major factor.

Management's Plan of Action

The company realized it was facing a grave problem. Its reputation as a world-class manufacturer was being tainted, its image as a good employer was being affected in its traditional sourcing area for labor, and its sales and profitability could be under threat. Members of management identified the administration system and the administrative staff as the key areas in which to focus. They decided to purchase a new computer system and train all management and relevant employees on that system.

Program Costs

An integrated computer system was purchased to replace the older computers and the training costs appear in table 1.

Table 1. Training costs for computer system.

Category	Cost
External trainer (tuition, documentation, and so forth)	£37,500
Employee and management salaries	£4,941
Miscellaneous (travel and subsistence, room hire, and so forth)	£6,000
Needs assessment	£949
	£49,390

The program costs were straightforward and came from actual cost statements, receipts, and payroll rates. They include external trainer costs, salary costs, miscellaneous costs for travel-related expenses, and the cost of the needs assessment. These costs did not include those for the evaluation because the only cost incurred was for management time, and management said the company would recoup that cost with the knowledge and learning it gained from the evaluation and the application of the new knowledge and learning to future training. The needs assessment cost was an estimate based on direct times and expenses involved in the process. The development costs were low and were included in the external trainer's costs because they were provided by the trainer. Participants' salaries costs were included as a training expense because the training per participant worked out at an average of six days.

On-the-Job Application

It was evident that management's response to a difficult problem had yielded results, as table 2 shows. The training enabled workers to complete many procedures in much less time than they had spent before the training. Before training, workers spent as many as six days per month processing goods inwards (that is, receivables) statements, invoices, debtors and creditors statements, inventory, and profit calculations. That paperwork now took only two days per month. One measure of success is how others see you, and, by that standard, Slick was doing well. In the past, it received four complaints per month, but those complaints were now eliminated.

Conversion of Benefits to Monetary Values

Table 3 shows the calculations for the monetary benefits from the training intervention. Values could be based on improved productivity, labor savings, improved quality, improved morale, and the like. This analysis focuses on labor cost savings, which are linked to all the others. The focus is important because management has identified survival as the key priority, and to management, it is strongly linked to cost savings. If a further link can be created between cost savings and training, the importance of training can be consolidated. Thus the total benefit of training, including the results of maximizing the intellectual capital within a company, can create a momentum that might give small companies a competitive advantage in the marketplace.

Table 2. Changes since training.

Pretraining	Posttraining
Time Saving Six days per month to be up-to-date on information (goods inwards, invoices, debtors and creditors statements, stock reductions and profit calculations)	Two days per month
Sales Invoices One person full time on processing invoices	One hour per day for assistant storeman
Product Costing Five days	Two days
Overtime Large overtime bill	Overtime eliminated
Sales Reports One day to do one report	10 minutes to do one report
Product Planning Three days	1 1/2 days
Sales Orders Processing Time Eight people (10 days per month)	One person 10 minutes per day
Customer Complaints Four per month	Eliminated
Number of Sales Lost Two per month	Eliminated
End-of-Month Calculations Six days by 2 1/2 administrative people	1/2 day by one person

In this case study the total value of the benefits of each measure was calculated, leaving management with the decision of which measure to use. Because of the interest within the company in the area of sales, management decided to use those measures. Thus the total monetary value of the benefits of these measures (sales invoices, £11,775; sales reports, £6,501; sales order processing, £46,770; and customer complaints and losses, £72,000) amounted to £137,046.

Isolating Training Effects

The company's training appeared to increase its bottom line significantly. While the change in performance may be linked to the training, other nontraining factors may have also contributed. In this case

Table 3. Monetary benefits from training.

	Savings
Time Saving Saving on time: two employees worked six days per month on processing documentation pretraining. Posttraining reduced to two days, saving four days per month (48 days per annum) Employee hourly cost = £7 Cost per working day = £49 Saving per annum (two employees) £98 × 48 days =	£4,704
Sales Invoices One person full-time on invoices Cost per annum = £12,000 Assistant storeperson, 10 minutes per day £6/hr = £225/per annum. £12,000 − £225 =	£11,775
Overtime Four employees (£6 per hr.) for one hour per day Four hours per day at £6/hr. = £24 per day £24 × 225 days = £5,400 per annum overtime eliminated	£5,400
Sales Reports 60 reports per annum at one day to do report Cost £111 × 60 = £6,660 per annum 10 minutes to do report 1/42 × £111 × 60 = £159 £6,600 − £159 =	£6,501
Production Planning Three days for a manager to complete a production planning project = £333 Three reports per annum × £333 = £999 now takes one day = £333	£666
Product Costing Product costing time reduced from five to two days 30 managers' days save 30 × £111	£3,330
Sales Order Processing Eight persons over 10 days per month • £56/hr. × 7 × 10 = £3,930 per month £3,920 × 12 = £47,040 per annum • One person 10 minutes per day = £1.16 £5.60 per week × 48 = £270 per annum £47,040 − £270 =	£46,770
Customer Complaints and Losses Cost of four customer complaints = £800 per month, £9,600 per annum Lost sales and customer complaints eliminated Loss of profit on 26 lost sales per annum = £62,400	£72,000
Total	**£151,146**

study management has identified the introduction of the new computer system itself and the training as the two reasons for the performance improvements. How much did each factor contribute to the improvement? Various techniques and calculations may answer this question: trend line analysis, use of control groups, forecasting methods, and participants' and management's estimate of training impact. Management at Slick decided that it knew its business well and was in the best position to ascertain the impact of training. Management believed that the effects of training could not have occurred without the purchase of a computer system, but they pointed out that they had purchased a state-of-the-art system in 1989 but did not formally train the staff on it. This resulted in a number of problems and no evident improvement in performance, individual or organizational, in the short to medium term. They felt strongly that the recent measured improvements were 90 percent the result of the training. I asked the managers to revisit this 90 percent estimate.

The efficiencies accruing from the installation of the computer must have fed into the benefits. The consensus arrived at was that the competent use of the computer by the user is hugely important and there are in-built efficiencies and system improvements resulting from the computer system itself, but management still held the view that training was a significant cause of the positive benefits that accrued to the company. However, they agreed to analyze their confidence level.

Management considered the two factors contributing to the improvements and then applied experience and subjective thought to the process. While not scientific, the managers have an intuition about their business and markets that must not be underestimated. In addition, they are the target group who must be convinced about the value of training.

Table 4 shows an analysis of management's confidence level in relation to the 90 percent figure (training cause of improvements). Note that all the managers were program participants.

Estimates of Training Impact From Managers

By factoring in a confidence level, I was able to maintain the conservative approach. Managers estimated that 90 percent of the sales order processing time improvement was due to training, but they were only 80 percent confident about that estimate. I multiplied the confidence percentage by the improvement percentage and then divided by 100 for a confidence level of 72 percent. Then I multiplied that

Table 4. Improvement from training.

Improvement Measures	£ Improvement	% Estimate of Training's Impact	% Confidence	£ Improvement Due to Training
Sales invoices	11,775	100	95	11,186
Sales reports	6,501	95	75	4,632
Sales orders processing time	46,770	90	80	33,674
Customer loss and complaints	72,000	90	95	61,560
Total	137,046			111,052

figure by the monetary amount of the improvement in order to isolate the portion attributable to training.

The total monetary value of the improvements due to training is estimated at £111,052.

ROI Calculation

I used that figure to calculate the ROI. The formula for the ROI is as follows:

$$\text{ROI} = (\text{value of benefits} - \text{cost of training}) / (\text{cost of training})$$
$$= (111{,}052 - 49{,}390) / (49{,}390)$$
$$= 61{,}662 / 49{,}390 = 1.248 = 124.8\%$$

For every £1 Slick Manufacturing invested in this training program, the company received £1.25 over the cost of the program. The ROI model places training on the same level as other investments that company management undertakes. The managers found the model easy to understand, and they were involved throughout the process.

The question of what is a good ROI now arises. There are many different answers, and only the company management knows what is right for its situation. The achievement of a 125 percent return is very satisfactory. Indeed some companies, including Slick Manufacturing, believe that as long as it breaks even, the training is worthwhile.

To maintain the credibility of the ROI findings, it is important to ensure the following:

• The exercise is based on some form of needs assessment.
• The effects of training are isolated so that training does not get credit for improvements that other variables caused.
• You are conservative in the assumptions.
• Management is involved in the total process.
• Results are communicated to all employees.

The benefits of training in this study are quite large and include reduced stock, increased morale, and efficient use of management time. The measures selected for the ROI exercise suited management and made the exercise less complex. A more complex analysis would have yielded an even better ROI.

Case Study Findings

In this study the Phillips ROI model was adapted to an SME's size and needs. The case study focused on calculating the monetary benefits of a training program and isolating the effects of training from other benefits.

Without regard to any financial benefit, training should satisfy the following: It should be relevant to the company's needs; it should achieve its objectives; sufficient budgets should be available; and trainees should make use of their learning. If these criteria are met, then training would probably be worth the investment, even without measuring the ROI.

The purpose of undertaking the case study in Slick Manufacturing was to apply a variation of Phillips's ROI framework to a typical Irish SME. It was to ascertain if
- an ROI exercise was possible in that type of organization
- benefits could be positive and measured
- a link could be created between training and organizational objectives
- the management of an SME would see the value of an ROI framework.

SMEs and ROI

The application of the ROI framework in Slick Manufacturing was successful. Management was keenly aware of the existing problem that the organization faced and was desperate to know if its solution was successful. Many SMEs would have similar problems and needs.

To undertake an ROI exercise similar to the case study, the organizational environment must be receptive. If ROI is imposed as a condition of grant aid, an organization may be overly optimistic in the data it supplies. It may be that the data supplied will ensure a greater ROI, but if organizations are selected and monitored carefully for ROI, projects could be accurate and meaningful. From this case study a number of factors have been identified that are required if ROI is to work and be accurate. These factors include
- the commitment of executive management
- clear management commitment
- identification of an evaluation champion, preferably a manager
- explanation of the purpose and reasons for evaluation to all employees
- process plan
- a training event that has a strong link to the organization's business plan
- conservative assumptions applied to calculation
- communication of results.

In this case study I simplified the ROI framework to match the organization. I recognized factors such as the needs of the organization, the resources available, and the level of training capability within the organization. The level of accuracy need not be compromised by not applying the full model. In benchmarking before-and-after scenarios without formal "before" measurements, the results were no less accurate because management was capable of making such calculations for the case study. In an organization with the resources to dedicate to such an undertaking, more scientific calculations could be used.

For SMEs without a full-time training manager or HRD staff, this case study shows that a ROI framework could be used to measure the impact of training on business results. Management in Slick Manufacturing confirmed the findings and was more than satisfied with the return. Management was impressed with the overall savings in particular. A return of 125 percent was more than the group had hoped for. The elimination of overtime, customer complaints, and customer loss was a huge gain for Slick. The more efficient use of management and employee time was a very positive outcome. The management believed that training was much more important than it had originally perceived it to be. The final ROI percentage was a powerful persuader once it was credible. In this case it confirmed what management already thought.

The evaluation data from Levels 1, 2, and 3 in the case study was easy to access. No new data was created for the case study. I do not believe that this affected the accuracy of the ROI. The full Phillips framework uses data from these levels, but if the data were to be created in an SME, it would put a strain on the organization's scarce resources. The identification of key problems and use of training to solve these problems resolved management's major concern. Training worked in an effective and efficient manner. The case study illustrated that it worked and was cost efficient.

Since completion of this evaluation, the staff turnover in the organization has reduced. An analysis of the reasons for people leaving postevaluation shows that it is not because of work-related stress but rather for other employment opportunities. This indicates that there were other problems resolved in addition to those measured in the evaluation. Other benefits that were not measured because of the need for soft data include improved morale and less absenteeism.

This case study could have been applied to any SME undertaking training linked to a business plan. It proved that the application of an ROI framework is possible and that SME management will embrace the concept if the managers perceive it to be relevant to their business. It shows that benefits can follow training and that those benefits can be measured in monetary terms. The application of an ROI exercise like this proves that if properly planned and executed the ethos of training within Irish SMEs will be enhanced.

Questions for Discussion

1. How can evaluation be used to illustrate the relevance of HRD activities to the achievement of organizational objectives in a company that employs fewer than 250 people?

2. Discuss the importance and benefits of incorporating evaluation into the assessment of the training needs process. How can business impact measures be included?

3. Identify two key reasons for undertaking ROI in a small company that does not undertake systematic training.

4. "Executive management will only support those training programs which have a positive ROI." Please discuss the advantages and disadvantages of this approach.

5. Develop the case for using managers' estimates in isolating the effects of training in a small organization.

The Author

Mike Devaney has a B.A. in education and training from the National University of Ireland, Galway. He is an HRD advisor with Enterprise Ireland, Glasnevin, Dublin, the national organization charged with assisting the development of Irish enterprise.

Its core mission is to work in partnership with client companies to develop a sustainable competitive advantage, leading to a significant increase in profitable sales, exports, and employment. For over 18 years, Devaney has assisted client companies to develop HRD best practice by implementing a capability-building strategy in order to improve business competitiveness. He can be contacted at Enterprise Ireland, Mervue Business Park, Galway, Ireland; email: michael.devaney@enterprise-ireland.com.

Suggested Readings

Garavan, T., P. Costine, and R. Hegarty. (1995). *Training and Development in Ireland*. Dublin: Oak Trees Press.

Phillips, J.J. (1997). *Handbook of Training Evaluation and Measurement Methods* (3d edition). Houston: Gulf Publishing.

Resisting Measurement: Evaluating Soft Skills Training for Senior Police Officers

Nassau County Police Department

Robert J. McCarty

It is difficult to bring about culture change in a police department, especially when the goal is for the officers to have more open communication and proactive participation. Police organizations are traditionally driven from the top down in a military-like hierarchical structure. However, police work often requires the exercise of independent judgment within limited time frames; because this exercise of independent judgment must also follow proscribed procedures and protocols, it can often lead to frustration. When officers perceive that a change is not in their best interest and is a contradiction to well-established processes, they are likely to resist it. This case illustrates the problems of implementing and evaluating a program focused on interpersonal skills training in a highly structured, often resistant, police department.

General Information
The Nassau County Police Department

The Nassau County Police Department (NCPD) serves western Long Island, N.Y. The area is contiguous to New York City and bordered on two sides by water. The county has a population of approximately 1.3 million people, primarily working-class and middle-class families. Income per capita is higher than the national average. Most people must drive to work or drive to a Long Island railroad station to commute to New York City. A vast network of highways and blacktop roads connects the many towns that cover the area. The police department of approximately 2,500 is among the highest paid in the country.

This case was prepared to serve as a basis for discussion rather than to illustrate either effective or ineffective administrative and management practices.

In 1997, under newly appointed leadership, the NCPD wanted to improve the way its officers worked together. The leadership was endeavoring to open up the work environment and make it more participative. Its goal was to tap the collective experience and knowledge of the NCPD's officer managers in order to improve operations and effectiveness.

Background and Rationale for Review

After unsuccessful attempts to create change through traditional adult learning courses, the NCPD engaged Dale Carnegie & Associates, now known as Dale Carnegie Training (DCT), to train 70 men and women, ranging in rank from lieutenant to police commissioner, in the Dale Carnegie course. This course focuses on improving interpersonal relationships and performance through the development of soft skills.

Both parties agreed to conduct a Level 5 impact study to evaluate the effectiveness of the course. DCT would conduct this study in association with Performance Resources Organization (PRO), now the Jack Phillips Center for Research.

The study had three specific objectives:
1. to assess the specific impact of the Dale Carnegie course in measurable business contributions to the extent possible, up to and including calculating the return on investment (ROI) for the NCPD
2. to determine the extent to which participants applied what they learned in training on the job
3. to identify specific barriers to successful application of training-related skills within the NCPD job environment.

The Dale Carnegie Course
Needs Assessment

Before the training, the instruction team conducted a needs assessment to accomplish the following:
- confirm top NCPD officials' appraisal of the need for a cultural change in a traditional top-down closed system
- determine the appropriateness of the Dale Carnegie course in this context
- ensure that the instruction team had firsthand knowledge to guide them in adopting the course to satisfy the participants' needs. The instruction team was headed up by two successful long-term male instructors (the female participants numbered less than 8 percent), both of whom had significant professional experience as members of the New York Police Department. One was also a highly regarded

Dale Carnegie executive, and both had outstanding reputations in the classroom.

The team conducted the needs assessment in interviews with a cross-section of officers, including senior officials. The assessments took place in both group and individual settings. The team found a culture in which officers were reluctant to volunteer or contribute suggestions for change and improvement. Officers questioned the wisdom of offering ideas when they might be interpreted as criticism of a superior and result in problems affecting future assignments and promotion. There was a decided lack of suggestions for improvement in meetings with superiors. The interviews demonstrated that the majority felt that their priority was "not to rock the boat" in order to succeed in performance appraisals and promotions.

The Course

The Dale Carnegie course training is interactive and highly participatory. It focuses on building soft skills effectiveness in the areas of communication, self-confidence, leadership, and teamwork. Revised at appropriate intervals in order to be contemporary, the course has produced over 4.5 million graduates in more than 70 countries since its introduction more than 60 years ago. It has been highly effective in a variety of settings including business and government, and it has been a self-improvement vehicle for individuals. The course is often customized to focus on areas determined to be of critical importance in needs assessments.

At NCPD, the course was delivered once a week, in three-and-a-half-hour sessions, over a 12-week period. Each session focused on two aspects of the Dale Carnegie human relation principles. Participants had to give a brief talk to the class during each session. The 70 officers were divided into two classes. Each class had a wide cross section of departmental responsibilities represented; their ranks included lieutenants, captains, inspectors, and chiefs as well as the head of the department, the commissioner. Group one began two weeks prior to group two, allowing flexibility for participants desiring to make up a session they were unable to attend at the regularly scheduled time. The course was delivered at a DCT facility in Hauppauge, New York.

Purpose

The purpose of the course was to assist participants in developing the following additional skills:
- improved business and personal relationships
- enhanced communication skills

- strengthened leadership skills
- leadership goal setting and planning
- better cooperation from others
- more skillful and effective public speaking
- increased self-confidence
- better listening
- techniques that help to enhance memory
- better results from meetings
- more positive outlook on life
- enthusiasm
- control of excessive stress
- new ways to solve problems
- more effectiveness at motivating others
- helping others be more results versus task oriented.

Model for Impact Study
Measuring Course Satisfaction at DCT

In 1995, under the direction of then vice president of instruction, Frank Ashby, DCT partnered with Motorola to evaluate customer satisfaction (Level 1) of their courses. They conducted over 170,000 Motorola surveys, most of them for the Dale Carnegie course. The survey has 31 questions relating to relevancy, course design, learning, the quality of instruction, and overall course satisfaction. Motorola determined the customer satisfaction rate of the 170,000 surveys as 96 percent. The next step was to introduce more sophisticated measurement of the effectiveness of DCT training.

Levels of Evaluation

Frank Ashby initiated a relationship with PRO in the year before the NCPD study. It provided DCT with the ability to perform more in-depth measurement of training effectiveness. Internal training and the development of guideline manuals followed.

The PRO involvement gave DCT the ability to offer its clients Level 5 ROI evaluations based on the methodology developed by Jack Phillips, founder of PRO. Phillips's methodology provides a five-tiered framework for the evaluation of training and development, as shown in table 1.

Orientation

Prior to the start of the course, all participants attended an orientation meeting where the instruction team and the author described the purpose of the training and provided an overview of the evalu-

Table 1. Evaluation levels.

Level	Questions
1: Reaction and planned action	Measures participants' satisfaction with the program and captures potential action
2: Learning	Measures changes in knowledge, skills, and attitudes
3: Job applications	Measures changes in on-the-job behavior
4: Business results	Measures changes in business impact variables
5: Return on investment	Compares program benefits to the costs

ation process and of how the training and the evaluation tied in with the goals of the NCPD. Topics of discussion were as follows:
- the purpose of the training and the NCPD's goals
- NCPD's intention to evaluate the benefits and value of the training
- action plans, including their use in tracking the application and measurement of skills
- conversion of skills and behavior to monetary values
- comparison of benefits to costs so PRO/DCT can conduct an ROI study
- benefits of the training and ROI study for individual officers and NCPD.
     By participating in the evaluation, participants would:
- see the results of their efforts in this course and the added value they bring to the workplace
- be able to understand the connection between the Dale Carnegie course and their improvement on the job
- know about the success of the entire class
- help the NCPD obtain information about the ROI in this training program
- help determine the impact of the Dale Carnegie course across a variety of functions.
     Overall, the orientation was upbeat, due in part to the camaraderie and networking that took place.

ROI Process

This study used an ROI process that Jack Phillips developed, PRO provided, and Ron Stone administered. (Formerly with PRO, Stone is now the chief consulting officer for the Jack Phillips Research Center.)

Phillips's ROI model illustrates steps in the process and highlights the issues addressed in the study. The first step is to collect data after completion of the training program. A variety of data collection methods are possible, depending on the situation.

Isolation of the effects of training is of paramount importance. Many outside factors can have an effect on the output measurements when there is an evaluation of the business impact of training programs. Examples of outside factors that can influence outcome data include the many forms of reward and recognition including bonuses, advancement, reassignment to a better position, and citation through organizational recognition programs.

Data must then be converted to monetary values. Conversion enables a comparison of the dollar values produced by the training with the cost of the training in order to develop the ROI.

Tabulations of program costs must be inclusive. These may include administrative costs, a dollar value for the participants' classroom time, and tuition.

Finally, as Jack Phillips (1997) says in his explanation of the ROI methodology, "Costs and benefits come together in an equation for the ROI. Net benefits (the program benefits minus costs) are divided by the total investment in the training program. This provides an ROI formula comparable to ROI calculations for other investments. These typically show the net earnings divided by the average investment.

"A final step lists intangible benefits that are very important but not translated into monetary values for the program benefits." This study identified and reported on intangible benefits.

The framework for this model can be used to measure the ROI in any type of training and development program. It is the model used in this study.

The most difficult aspects of this study were, as follows:
- establishing an understanding by participants of how they could use the action planning process
- establishing and maintaining a willingness among participants to provide data
- calculating the ROI with minimal data from the officer participants.

The circumstances involving these critical difficulties are described in the following section.

Data Collection Methods
Action Plans

Two methods were used to collect data in this impact study: action plans and questionnaires.

Participants first learned about the action plans during the orientation session. I provided further instruction on how to use them at regular intervals during the 12-week course, as described below. Guidelines and illustrations of action plan implementation were also developed in collaboration with Ron Stone of PRO. I also explained these materials to the participants and provided copies to them. Participants used the action plans to track progress and collect actual performance data over a three-month period following the final training session. The action plans included the following information:

- objective
- action steps
- unit of measure per value of unit
- how unit value was determined
- change in unit value
- percent of change caused by training
- level of confidence participant places on the validity of the data contained in his or her action plan.

Questionnaires

The second method of data collection was a follow-up questionnaire designed by PRO for the Dale Carnegie course and customized for the NCPD. Participants received it by mail three months after the final session so that they could return it with the action plan to PRO. It provided data regarding the extent to which participants had used the training on the job and the results that came from these applications. The questionnaire included the following evaluation items:

- Rate the success of the course in meeting 25 objectives, including recognizing achievement, communicating under pressure, and gaining cooperation.
- Rate the relevance of the following program elements to your job (presentation, group discussion, reading materials, program content, and networking opportunities).
- Indicate the degree to which your use of 25 skills (named in the questionnaire) in the following five categories was enhanced: self-confidence, communications, human relations, leadership, and stress control.
- Identify the three most used skills or abilities acquired in the training; how the application of these skills has changed the way that you work (specific behavior change, action items, new projects, and the like); identify specific accomplishments that can be linked to the training (job performance, project completion, response times, and so forth); and identify how these applications relate to the action plan.

- Was the Dale Carnegie training a good investment for the NCPD? Explain.
- Identify barriers, if any, that have prevented application of skills or knowledge acquired in the training. Explain, if possible. A checklist of six items was provided, including "not enough time"; "My work environment does not support these skills"; and "This material does not apply to my situation."
- Indicate the extent to which you think this course has influenced the following measures in your own work or those of your work unit. The questionnaire included a 15-item checklist with such items as supervisory time, union complaints, cycle time of reports, teamwork, and citizen complaints. It requested examples and details.
- Identify and explain how the application of skills from the training has influenced the quality of police service to the public.

The final questions dealt with the participants' feelings about the quality of the course, including whether they would recommend it, suggestions for improvement, and other comments.

Isolating the Effects of Training

There are several strategies available to isolate the effects of training, but most were not feasible in this situation. It was agreed that input directly from participants would be most appropriate in this situation. Participants' estimates of the impact of training are a reliable indicator when appropriate steps are taken to collect data. Their judgment is subjective, but the participants have direct experience to guide their estimates and have firsthand knowledge of other influences that have an impact on performance measures. Participants' estimates have proved to be extremely reliable in studies where they are compared to results from control groups. Participants were asked to give the confidence level that they had in their estimates.

Conversion of Data

In this study, the primary strategy for converting data to monetary values was to ask participants to make estimates and calculations based on improvements in their work units. Of the action plans submitted, many participants used accepted standards and conversion factors to arrive at monetary value. In some cases, however, it was necessary for PRO to make adjustments to ensure the reliability of the data. Some of the action plans were incomplete or otherwise flawed, invalidating the data for purposes of calculating the ROI. However, there were still indications of performance improvement.

Data Collection Strategy
Issues
The data collection strategy of using action plans and a questionnaire was designed to meet the three objectives of this study. Both data collection methods focused on impact, not process. This information was obtained with Level 3 and 4 data collection, although some data was collected on the delivery process and mechanisms. Data was only collected from police officers who actually participated in the training.

Timing of Data Collection
The Dale Carnegie course is designed to have a long-term impact, but valid data about specific improvements from the training is difficult if not impossible to capture years after the program is completed. With time, it also becomes more difficult to isolate the effects of training because additional variables affect output measures, clouding the cause-and-effect relationship between training and improvement. Based on PRO's experience and recommendation, DCT decided to measure the success of the training three months after completion of the last of the 12 training sessions.

A standard practice in ROI evaluation is to capture the first-year benefits after the training is completed and compare them to the cost of the program. This limits the ROI calculation to benefits of the first year. As Ron Stone stated in his final PRO report, "While in some cases this could slightly overstate the results, PRO's experience shows that it usually understates them. In the case of the Dale Carnegie course, it is highly probable that this practice understates the results. . . . This does not imply that these programs are not having a long-term impact at the NCPD. Some individuals responded that these programs actually have shaped their thinking and behavior for the remainder of their career with the NCPD." Limiting the benefit results to one year represents a conservative approach since the benefits that might be acquired in subsequent years are not used in this calculation.

Questionnaire and Action Plan
PRO customized a questionnaire for the NCPD to provide data on the extent to which officer participants actually applied what they learned in the Dale Carnegie course and the success they achieved with their application. The questionnaire provided data addressing the following key areas:
- success of training objectives
- relevance to job

- usefulness of the training
- knowledge and skills increase
- actions taken, accomplishments, and impact
- barriers to implementation
- supervisor support
- business measures linked to training
- recommended changes.

PRO sent the questionnaire to the 70 participants three months after the last session of the training. They were to return the questionnaires with the action plans. The action plans would provide the data for calculating a dollar value of savings achieved through individual applications of skills acquired through the training. The response rate for this documentation was very low, as shown in table 2. Open resistance to cooperating with the evaluation study had been an ongoing issue for some time.

At the orientation session, participants learned the rationale for the action plan and received related printed materials. There was no indication at that time that there would be difficulties with cooperation and implementation of the ROI study.

During session three, I distributed sample action plans and blank action plans. These were discussed and examples were given. I asked participants to complete the left side of the plans covering objective, action steps, and intangible benefits, and turn them in for review at session six.

A turning point occurred before the start of session six. Several participants, many of them high ranking, told the head of the instruction team that the action plan process should be eliminated. They found it self-serving for the Dale Carnegie organization, who they believed would use the results for sales and marketing. They did not feel it would be of benefit to the participants or the NCPD. Moreover, many were resentful of the extra work for everyone. I held conversations with participants during the coffee break and after session six. I found that

Table 2. Response profile: resistance to change.

Data Collection Document	Number Provided or Mailed	Number Participants Responding	Percent Returned
Action Plan Documents	70	17	24%
Questionnaires	70	35	50%

although this criticism was not a universally held sentiment, many others were in strong agreement. In addition, there was no strong individual sentiment to go against the wave of negative opinion. And junior ranking officers were not going to disagree with those of higher rank who had decided that they did not want to participate in the ROI evaluation process.

I discussed the problem openly with the class during the session. Meanwhile, as planned, I reviewed their action plans and introduced more sample action plans. I also passed out and reviewed questionnaires and explained Levels 4 and 5. I reached out for help. A respected chief inspector, who saw the benefits of the training, the action plan process, and the ROI evaluation, organized a meeting of four respected members of the department to explore the possibilities of moving forward as originally planned. They were supportive, would continue to participate, and were willing to be identified as being with the program. They also suggested that the questionnaire be customized and that more action plan examples and more customized guidelines be developed. Working with PRO, I carried out all of these suggestions. Despite these efforts, however, dissension remained among many of the participants.

Another turning point occurred when the department announced promotions and new assignments affecting 40 percent of the participants. The announcement occurred when group one was in week nine of its training and group two was in week seven. Reactions varied from satisfaction to disgruntlement. Many of the disgruntled group said it confirmed their belief that the NCPD was not going to change and that they would not be the beneficiaries of the evaluation study.

As the course continued, I reviewed more action plans and provided written and verbal comments and encouragement to the authors (ultimately these preliminary action plan proposals would total 43). Customized guidelines and more action plan examples were developed in cooperation with an experienced and well-informed NCPD inspector. Most of these were examples of time savings that were converted to dollar values.

In addition, at my request on behalf of DCT, both the police commissioner and the chief of operations, representing the senior official in their respective class groups, endorsed the value of the course and the evaluation study. Ultimately, individual participants themselves chose whether or not to cooperate. The department held no one accountable. Only PRO saw the returns, and the organization maintained strict confidentiality about the identity of those who cooperated in the study.

Although additional letters from both PRO and the chief of operations encouraged participants' cooperation, their appeals seemed to have only a modest effect. The low number of respondents was disappointing, but a positive ROI was obtained. It was also possible to get a substantial amount of Level 4 information.

Program Costs

This study used a fully loaded cost profile. The inclusive cost elements are as follows:

- NCPD administration costs
- tuition (including both instructors' fees, facility, books, awards, and refreshments)
- participants' salaries and benefits (adjusted on the basis of 75 percent attendance)
  - The total cost of the foregoing elements for two classes (70 participants) was $273,060.
  - The cost per participant was $3,901.
  - The cost of the training program for one class was $136,530.

DCT absorbed the costs of conducting the evaluation study as part of its ROI development program. The absorbed costs included all of my liaison and classroom work with the NCPD, as well as the costs of data collection and analysis, and development of the management report.

Results
NCPD-Motorola Level I Study

The Motorola Level I Study was administered by the instruction team during the final session of the training. The survey had 57 respondents. The overall rating of group one was 89 percent satisfaction, and the overall rating of group two was 87 percent satisfaction.

It is instructive to compare the NCPD satisfaction figure with the overall course satisfaction rating of 96 percent by 170,000 DCT graduates. The large majority of the 170,000 surveyed received training in the Dale Carnegie course, but not all of them.

Table 3 shows the five areas of measurement that comprise the overall Level 1 satisfaction ratings.

These figures suggest that the participants felt that the application of the human relations principles that provide the foundation for this course were not a good fit with their perception of the NCPD culture. The feedback from the questionnaires confirmed that impression.

Table 3. NCPD-Motorola Level 1 satisfaction ratings.

	Relevance	Learning	Course Design	Instructor	Overall Course
Group 1	67%	95%	88%	97%	96%
Group 2	63%	90%	88%	98%	85%

Questionnaire

Results on Application of Knowledge and Skills

The response rate to the action plan (24 percent) and questionnaires (50 percent) was low, as shown in table 2. Nevertheless, the questionnaires were a source of valid data because all feedback was anonymous and participants were under no pressure to impress superiors.

The impact of skills and knowledge on behavior was significant to very significant in five areas, as table 4 shows. While these are subjective evaluations, they reflect the respondents' perceptions of the connection between the training and the application of skill in the work setting.

A significant number of respondents reported little or no change in their use of certain skills from the training, as table 5 shows.

Results on Business Impact

Responses to the questionnaire indicate that a very high percentage of the participants felt that the training had limited influence on measures in their work or work unit. Communication, teamwork, problem solving, meetings, and personal productivity ranked the highest of 14 areas. However, they averaged only 2.63 on a five-point rating scale in which one was no influence; two, some influence; three, moderate influence; four, significant influence; and five, very much influence.

Table 4. Application of knowledge and skills.

% Responding	Skills and Behavior With Significant Change
22.9	Being a better listener
25.7	Looking for and expressing positives rather than negatives toward others
25.7	Maintaining a positive attitude, appearance, and demeanor toward others
20.0	Speaking more effectively to groups, in meetings, and one on one
45.7	Being more clear and concise

Table 5. Behavior application with little or no change.

% Responding	Skills and Behavior With Little or No Change
57.1	Making life more interesting or satisfying
57.1	Willingness to take on more challenges or risks
55.9	Being more decisive at making decisions
54.3	Being seen as friendly or cooperative
54.3	Managing excessive stress and tension

Participants were also asked to identify specific accomplishments and improvements that could be linked to training. The following typical comments are among those that suggested areas where positive results were taking place:

- I try to look at things from the subordinate's perspective. I gain more willing cooperation. I get greater satisfaction when I make others feel important.
- I am more concerned with completing my work in a timely manner and am making progress in reducing investigation completion time.
- Better community relations and communications with minority community.
- Success in fostering a cooperative effort among groups with diverse opinions and interests.
- Able to inspire others to accomplish more by being more interested in them and their work.

Relevancy and Benefits and Shortcomings

The questionnaire asked respondents if they would recommend the Dale Carnegie course to others, and 82.4 percent said yes.

In response to the question if this training represented a good investment for their employer, 57.1 percent of respondents said yes.

The following represent typical comments by those who replied yes:

- It improved verbal communication skills of various members. It provided an opportunity for upper management to interact and gain exposure to subordinates that disclosed strengths on both sides.
- Participants got to know and appreciate each other better and learned skills that could improve their personal and professional performance.
- Supervisory personnel rarely get the opportunity to interact on a repeated personal level. The networking and personal interactions were invaluable.

The following represent typical comment by those who replied no:

- Did not address civil service working environment.
- Not relevant to the organizational and political dynamics that exist in this agency. Skills taught were basic—nothing new.
- It had little relevance to the real-world (1990s') police work and society.

ROI Calculation

To calculate the ROI, the benefits from group one were compared with the fully loaded cost of the program for group one, as follows:

- The total benefits from group one are $333,168.
- The cost of the program for group one was $136,530.
- The ROI becomes:

$$\text{ROI} = \frac{\text{Net benefits}}{\text{Costs}} = \frac{\$333,168 - \$136,530}{\$136,530} = 144\% \text{ for group one}$$

- This yields an ROI of 144 percent for group one.

The ROI values are based on participants' estimates in the action plans. They are conservative, having been adjusted downward, also based on participants' estimates from the action plans that isolate the effects of the training. The participants further reduced their estimates to reflect their confidence in the estimates.

The high yield for a small number of contributors is indicative of the type of results manifested when senior officials whose actions have a large sphere of influence participate in action plan improvements.

Because PRO takes a very conservative approach to calculate the ROI, the participants who did not return monetary data are not included in the benefits portion of the above ROI calculation. They are included only in the cost component of the formula.

A discussion of the possible reasons participants did not return action plans or provide monetary data appears in the section "Questionnaire and Action Plan."

Results—Intangible Benefits

Intangible benefits are those that are not assigned a monetary value or where an assigned value is questionable. Nevertheless they are important to the goals of the organization. The questionnaires produced many positive comments. These and information from the action plan reporting provided many intangible substantial benefits in several areas. A sampling of these follows:

- improved understanding and appreciation of each other leading to improved operations
- a more positive atmosphere and work environment
- improved relationships with subordinates
- improved communications and personal relations within the department
- improved job satisfaction resulting in improved morale and a more positive image projected to the public
- improved verbal communications skills resulting in more satisfactory resolution of complaints and problems in less time
- interaction among participants resulting in follow-up groups to further explore issues raised during the program.

Communications

Communications were ongoing at all levels during the training. The completed ROI study was sent by PRO to DCT and, after internal review, was sent by DCT to the NCPD.

Lessons Learned

Based on this and one previous ROI evaluation, the following actions, suggestions, and guidelines were recommended for all future Level 5 evaluations of the Dale Carnegie course:
- Following needs analysis, top client management *must agree upon and support* ways to measure soft skills application and impact (prior to orientation).
- Top client management must establish one or more *operations manager-champions who will support the implementation of the action plan process.*
- Review and coaching of action plans will require a serious commitment of time and energy by ROI-trained instructors.
- Revise session six to include a module for action plan commitment (tying in with human relations commitment and report).
- Customized action plan illustrations may be needed.
- Item 10 of questionnaire regarding application of training may need to be customized.
- Bill some or all of the costs of the ROI study to the client. Clients who feel there is value in the evaluation study should be willing to help pay the costs. High-level management may also invest more effort in supporting the action plan process.

Questions for Discussion

1. Should this type of organization take part in a soft skills ROI evaluation?

2. Would it have been appropriate for the police commissioner or the chief of operations to have made action plan participation mandatory?

3. What other steps could have been taken to remedy the situation when the first group of officers announced that they felt the ROI study was not in their best interests?

4. What other steps could have been taken to reduce the negative impact on many officers created by the announcement of promotions and reassignment?

5. How credible is the business impact and ROI data in this case study?

The Author

Robert J. McCarty is an executive coach, ROI consultant, and an award-winning corporate video producer. He is a former adjunct professor at Teachers College, Columbia University. He is a graduate of Princeton University with an A.B. in history.

McCarty is a member of the American Society for Quality (ASQ), Society for Human Resource Management (SHRM), ASTD, Writers' Guild of America, and the Writers Roundtable. He can be reached at: RJM Associates, Suite 205, 82 Chestnut Street, Rutherford, NJ, 07070-1939; phone: 201.804.9161; email: RJMBIZZ@cs.com.

Reference

Phillips, Jack. (Ed.). (1997). "Evaluating Leadership Training for Newly Appointed People Managers." In *Measuring Return on Investment* (volume 2). Alexandria, VA: ASTD.

Measuring Return on Investment for a Mandatory Training Program

Miami VA Medical Center

Eileen Marcial and Timothy W. Bothell

Seasoned trainers in the federal workforce know to stay calm whenever a new initiative is announced. They know for a new initiative there will be "MANDATORY TRAINING FOR ALL EMPLOYEES," as printed announcements make clear. Determining a plan to train 3,000 diverse co-workers in an era of severe budget constraints requires a trainer with nerves of steel. This case illustrates how the Veterans Health Administration measured the return on investment (ROI) calculated for a mandatory program on self-mastery. The program evaluates the impact of using a specific training delivery methodology and its ability to catalyze employees to participate in and contribute to the organization.

Background of the Industry

Health-care delivery in the United States has changed dramatically over the past decade. Health-care providers are currently faced with somewhat distrustful patients who demand quality care that is affordable. The trend in the health-care sector shows a decrease in employee training expenditures. The training events that are being conducted focus on licensure requirements and are oriented toward developing and enhancing technical skills (McMurrer, Van Buren, and Woodwell, 2000).

Background of the Government Agency

The Veterans Health Administration is held to the same standards and accreditations as any other health-care provider in the United States. It also faces the same challenges: quality care and cost containment.

This case was prepared to serve as a basis for discussion rather than to illustrate either effective or ineffective administrative and management practices.

As the largest component of the Department of Veterans Affairs (VA), it must also meet all of the requirements for federal agencies. It has gone through a major restructuring and downsizing and has a flat line budget despite inflation and new medical technologies. For it to survive, the VA has to become completely patient focused in all of its processes. Its traditional top-down, bureaucratic model is outdated and cannot foster the organizational culture necessary to meet the challenges. It has to reinvent itself.

Toward Becoming a High-Performing Organization

A national VA task force set out to identify the characteristics and best practices of high-performing organizations. Based on their research, the high-performance development model, shown in figure 1, became the human resource initiative to foster and encourage, recruit and retain the workforce necessary for the new VA. The model suggests employees should begin by first enhancing technical skills and self-mastery.

Toward New Learning Methodologies

The VA has introduced several Learning Maps in the past two years. Learning Maps are large visuals that tell a story or depict a process. They are highly interactive and allow employees to be introduced to a specific concept or process by following the visual and discussing the various points along the map. The VA has several different maps on different topics. They are viewed as a tool to help employees understand and accept the realities of change and enhance participation in it. These maps are the products of the VA's nationwide Employee Education System and a vendor partner, Root Learning, in Perrysburg, Ohio. The latest map introduces the high-performance development model (HPDM) and the importance of self-mastery. The map had undergone several beta tests and revisions before it was ready for release.

Assessment of Need

The HPDM was an important initiative of the VA, and it was mandatory that all employees be introduced to it. For the Miami VA Medical Center, that meant nearly 3,000 learners of diverse backgrounds. Certain leadership levels and job functions were the target audience. Their shared characteristics included extreme stress—from having to do more with less, from coping with stressed co-workers, and from having to cope with yet another mandated training program. The soft-skills content of this program was definitely not a selling point for

Figure 1. High-performance development model.

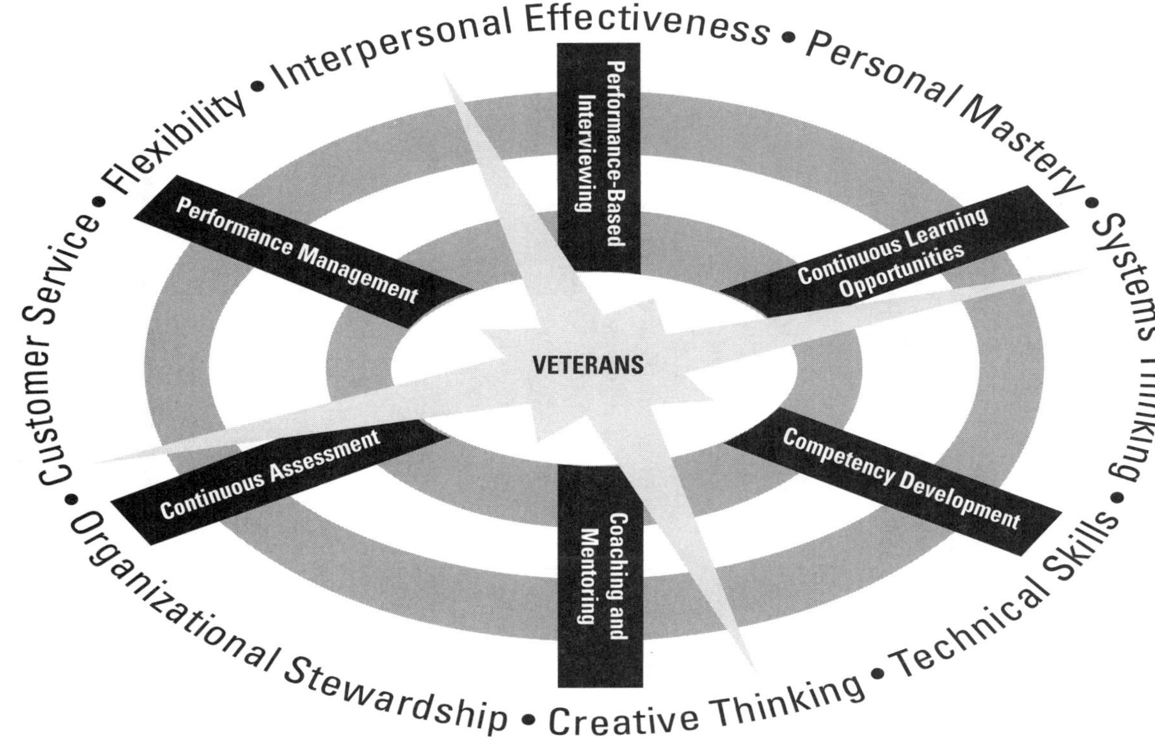

this group. The topic was critical to both the organization and employees, however, so time had to be spent to properly introduce the model. But this audience would probably have to be dragged to the program, kicking and screaming all the way.

The Medical Center director, T.C. Doherty, agreed that a two-hour briefing would be necessary to introduce the model and explain the necessity of the changes required for the workforce. He wanted the program to be encouraging and inspirational in hopes that the employees would be able to buy in to the new philosophy the HPDM represents. Eileen Marcial, one of the authors, served as Learning Map program coordinator and ROI research coordinator on the project, and co-author Tim Bothell was the ROI advisor.

Purpose of the Evaluation

But what if employees did buy in to the philosophy, did understand why it was so critical for the organization and themselves, and did find the program an enjoyable and worthwhile experience? That was Eileen Marcial's hope in using the Learning Map. There is anecdotal information that Learning Maps are a valuable experience and participants find them helpful in understanding complex concepts. A new map had just been developed to explain the HPDM. A problem with using Learning Maps is that the format in which sessions are delivered is highly interactive, necessitating small groups of approximately 10 participants per map and facilitator. The typical map event runs one and a half to two hours. They are not very time-consuming per session, but they are relatively labor intensive and time-consuming over all sessions and over the time it takes to train many people; thus medical center directors have questioned their value. Doherty had assumed employees would be herded into the auditorium in groups of 100 over several months. Fortunately, after he learned about the ROI process, he gave permission for the medical center to conduct a pilot program using the new HPDM Learning Map.

The pilot program used two groups. One group was trained using the Learning Map, and the other was trained using lecture, video, and typical classroom delivery. The purpose of the two groups was to compare Learning Map delivery with lecture, activity-based, classroom delivery.

Evaluation Methodology

In February 2000, Marcial received a prerelease copy of the HPDM Learning Map. It included the 3-by-5.5-foot pictorial map as well as the following:

- *Workplace change sheet:* This sheet has participants list changes they see occurring in the workplace within and outside the VA.
- *How we learn sheet:* This has participants list ways people learn formally and informally.
- *Teammate skills sheet:* This sheet has participants list skills and abilities they think people will need in facing the workplace changes.
- *Development approach sheet:* This has participants brainstorm and list ways they think each of the 8 Core Competencies described in the Learning Map can be developed.
- *Information guide:* This has a resource guide for building each of the core competencies.
- *Personal opportunity plan:* The plan helps participants get started on building each competency.
- *10 Ways to Quick Start the HPDM in Your Life:* This sheet suggests doable actions to get someone going on the HPDM.

Learning Maps are designed to be informational. They have broad objectives and do not have a process for evaluation. All of the materials used during the sessions were incorporated into the data collection plan, and some other measures were necessary. In addition to the program each person was asked to

- complete a questionnaire, shown in figure 2, that asked participants to respond on a scale of one to five, where one represented strongly agree; two, somewhat agree; three, average or undecided; four, fair or somewhat agree; and five, poor or disagree
- return to debrief with the group for an hour follow-up session in five to six weeks
- identify one thing he or she could contribute or do (no matter how large or small) that could make a difference to the facility and say what would have to happen for that person to do it; this exercise was called "How I can help" on the data collection sheet
- tell two co-workers what he or she has learned about the HPDM and ask them to e-mail Marcial or return a postcard telling her "Who Told!"; the VA has a collective learning initiative based on the idea that learning is social and can be informal and that employees can learn from their co-workers.

There were no significant differences in the responses between groups. There were trends favoring the Learning Map group.

The data collection methodology was set up to take advantage of all of the data generated in the sessions. Marcial had several meetings with the chief and assistant chief of human resources management to explain the ROI process and her data collection plan. A significant constraint was that bargaining unit employees would be participating. The

Figure 2. Questions used for the Level 1 evaluation.

Directions: Please respond on a scale of 1-5, where 1 represents strongly agree; 2, somewhat agree; 3, average or undecided; 4, fair or somewhat agree; and 5, poor or disagree.

As a result of this training activity, I:

Am able to identify some of the changes occurring in the workplace
Am able to understand the concept of the HPDM
Am able to list the 8 Core Competencies
Am able to understand the importance of Personal Mastery
Am able to define action steps toward developing a personal plan
Am able to identify ways to contribute to the organization
Know more about the HPDM now because of this class
Know more about the 8 Core Competencies because of this class
Intend to begin a Personal Improvement Plan
Would recommend this class to a co-worker

use of a pre- or posttest for Level 2 evaluation and the use of supervisors as possible data sources for Level 3 evaluations could create uncomfortable labor relations. Civil service does not allow "testing" for all positions. Marcial decided that even the appearance of employees being tested or questioned after the sessions would not advance or promote the high performance development model. She also did not want the chief of human resources to have any concerns about the study or the ROI process.

For a further review of the evaluation methodology, see table 1, which outlines the data collection plan for the study.

Isolating the Effects of the Program

A comparison group arrangement was set up to isolate the effects of the Learning Map. Multiple sessions were advertised. Every other class was a Learning Map session, and the alternate offered the same information, using lecture, video, and discussion rather than the map. Employees were assigned into either group based on which date they chose. Class sizes were limited to up to 15 participants, and employees were instructed to preregister. At that time they were asked to commit to return for the one-hour follow-up. The follow-up sessions were also paired so that comparison group participants could select any time

Table 1. Data collection plan.

Level	Broad Program Objectives	Measures	Data Collection Method and Instruments	Data Sources
1	Overview of the HPDM and promote Self-Mastery	Satisfaction survey	Questionnaire at end of session	Participant
	To complete Personal Opportunity Plan	Personal Opportunity Plan	Personal Opportunity Plan or summary self-assessment	Participant
	To complete "Quick Start"	Quick Start sheets	Quick Start sheets	Participant
2	Identify why changes in the workplace?	In-session workplace changes sheet	Observation and collection of workplace changes sheet	Facilitator and participant
	Identify 8 Core Competencies	In-session teammate skills sheet	Observation and collection of group skills list	Facilitator and participant
		Self-assessment	Questionnaire at end of session	Participant
		Self-assessment	Observation and collection of development approaches sheet	Facilitator and participant
		In-session		
	Identify ways to contribute and help	In-session	Observation	Facilitator
	Identify formal versus informal learning	In-session how we learn sheet	Observation and collection of how we learn sheets	Facilitator and participant

(continued on page 222)

Table 1. Data collection plan (continued).

Level	Broad Program Objectives	Measures	Data Collection Method and Instruments	Data Sources
3	Begin "living" HPDM	Completed plans	Personal opportunity plans or summary self-assessment	Facilitator
		Number of employees who return for follow-up session	Number of calls or emails regarding self-improvement	Education office
		Request for programs to improve self-mastery		Education office
		Number of employees participants told	Number of email messages or number of return cards	Facilitator
4	Collective learning initiative	Number of employees participants told	Number of email messages or number of cards returned	Facilitator
	Realization of "how I can help" (commitment to the organization)	How can I help sheet	Follow-up session—self-report	Facilitator, supervisors, and participants
	Better planning of education and resources (i.e., nonformal)	Increase use of self-study Self-motivated workforce	Number of participants who return personal opportunity plan	Facilitator, education office

designated as lecture group sessions, and the maps groups returned with others in maps sessions. At the beginning of all sessions, Marcial explained that the information was critical and she was trying two different methods of delivering the same information. In order to appreciate any differences in the methodologies, it was important for the groups to return for follow-up sessions and to do so within their groups.

To further isolate the effects of the Learning Map, Marcial asked the participants to estimate the impact of the program. Any time a participant of the follow-up session made a contribution or submitted a suggestion or idea, all the participants estimated the percent to which the program inspired it. This was accomplished at the time of the follow-up sessions.

The ROI Analysis Plan
Converting Data to Monetary Values

Marcial and Bothell used the participants' applications of what they learned or thought of in the Learning Map sessions to convert data to a monetary value. After participants implemented their planned actions, their implementations were converted to a monetary value using existing regulations and the following methods:

• Monetary values were assigned to what participants did differently using regulations and methods found within the Department of Veterans Affairs.

• *Employee time:* A database was readily available from human resources.

> Fully loaded to include yearly salary + 28% benefits divided by 2,080
> (260 workdays a year × 8 hours a day) gives hourly rate for each employee.

• *Office of Workers' Compensation Program Specialist (internal expert):* This includes the cost of medical care for injury using the billing codes and allowances paid to providers for treatment of an open wound.

Intangible Benefits

Due to the nature of the Learning Map, which was to master the HPDM, most of the anticipated results were difficult to quantify and attach a monetary value to—employee satisfaction, improved communication, increased organizational commitment, and the generation of ideas about how to improve the organization.

Cost

It was important to include all of the cost. Marcial considered the main categories, time and supplies, and a few additional cost items.

The preparation time for the instructor was estimated to be two hours for every one hour of instruction. The cost of materials included the cost of copying. Administration time included taking registration and setting up the room and equipment. The cost of the room was considered nominal. Marcial's time doing the ROI was not included because it was anticipated that she would spend a certain amount of time actually doing an ROI project as part of her recent training in the ROI process. Also the cost associated with the development and distribution of the HPDM map was excluded because the maps are available at no charge to VA medical centers. The VA National Employee Education System absorbs their cost.

ROI Calculations

The ROI calculation compares net financial improvements with the cost of a program. It determines the cost-effectiveness of implementing the Learning Map. It was important to include only financial benefits that occurred to the organization because of the Learning Map. Participants' planned applications and the outcomes of those applications were the only results used in the ROI calculation. See Table 2 for the ROI analysis plan.

The Day the Lights Went Out in Miami

The initial sessions began in February 2000. After the first class, Marcial had to establish a waiting list due to an overwhelming response for both methodologies. Employees were pleased to hear that different formats were being tried and that their time was considered valuable. And they were having fun! By mid-March, the follow-up sessions were under way, and more of the two-hour programs were being scheduled.

Then the unexpected happened. In late March, an explosion in an electrical transformer destroyed the facility's electrical system and caused the entire medical center to be evacuated. The blackout continued for six weeks. During that time employees found themselves working in surrounding local hospitals and other VAs across the state, wherever their patients had been transferred.

This catastrophe made some of Marcial's data collection impossible or unusable. Electricity was available at certain times and in certain locations in the facility. Employees were willing to use flashlights, if necessary, to attend make-up sessions of the follow-ups. Macial's original concerns that employees would resist attending sessions were now replaced with concerns of trying to meet their demand for them. The bottom line for her was to continue the ROI study even under these

Table 2. ROI analysis plan.

Data Items	Method of Isolating Effects of Program	Methods of Converting Data	Cost Categories	Intangible Benefits	Other Influences and Issues	Communication Targets
Collective learning initiative	Analysis of worksheets from Learning Map group	Time savings	Participants' salaries Instructor's salary	Just-in-time training Employees communicating Adds purpose to work Sharing can equal innovation	Director's performance measures could improve	Program participants Employees Executive staff Education council
Better education plan	Analysis of worksheets from Learning Map group	Time savings	Participants' salaries Instructor's salary	Goodwill for participants and others who compete for the classroom space	Better motivated, self-reliant workforce	Employees
How I can help (contribute to the organization)	Confidence level for those who contributed	Use of employee suggestion guidelines—VA				

extraordinary conditions. She would collect whatever data was available and then decide if she could convert it.

There were a total of 96 participants, 43 in the Learning Map group and 53 in the control group. There were 57 participants for the follow-up sessions (21 from the Learning Map group and 36 from the control group). Some participants were clearly unable to return for the follow-up. The usable data resulted from the 96 participants, 57 of whom returned for the follow-up.

Results
Level 4 Measures

The following list represents the organizational results that were influenced by the participants' involvement in the Learning Map and in the classroom group:

BETTER PLANNING OF EDUCATIONAL RESOURCES. Two development approach sheets listed unique ideas for how the specific competencies could be developed. Both came from Learning Map groups.

In a discussion in a follow-up session in a Learning Map group, an employee volunteered to co-develop a presentation with Marcial. She had some expertise in a particular self-development model and had drafted an outline of the program on her own time. She was 100 percent confident that her inspiration to do this was directly due to the program.

REALIZATION OF "HOW I COULD HELP." Two significant employee suggestions resulted completely from the program. They would not have been thought of, or, in one case, acted upon if not for the program. These were also from Learning Map follow-up groups.

A discussion on how to help others enhance personal mastery led to a group idea that the employees wrote in a suggestion. They felt the lobby looked like it could be in any other hospital or building and that decorating it to appear military would acknowledge the patients and their contributions to the country. A military decor would also remind everyone of why the facility exists. By creating this milieu, they felt they were psychologically creating an environment of respect.

The second suggestion represented a safety initiative. The VA had recently approved a policy that let police officers carry firearms on duty. This was a somewhat controversial issue. The suggestion described a change in the procedure for police officers and the storage of firearms when shifts change. The change was to prevent the accidental firing of a bullet. An argument was made that if there had been no change at the very least someone could get shot in the foot. At worst, someone could be killed.

Converting Data to Monetary Values

Following are the calculations of cost savings from the employee suggestions on better planning of educational resources, change in the lobby, and the storage of firearms:

- *Better planning of educational resources.* To place a monetary value on employees' time savings, the education coordinator and the ROI consultant included employees' hourly wages plus the value of employee benefits (.28 of annual wage). The time savings for (A) developing a future program and for (B) an employee willing to help present was estimated to be:

    A. 1-hour savings for development of future program for each of two core competencies =
    2 hours @ $26.22 = $52.44

    B. Time savings for employee being willing to help present the program =
    8 hours prep and 2 hours for presentation = 10 hours @ $26.22 = $260.22
    Total savings = $312.66

- *Change in the lobby decor:* The government estimates the value of the benefit at $500, according to its regulation titled Scale of Awards Based on Intangible Benefits. (This suggestion is in progress. There is a likelihood there will be an improvement in the customer service measure. This could be translated into the cost of keeping a customer, because one of the questions customers are asked that contributes to the overall customer satisfaction score of a hospital concerns the decor and friendliness of the lobby. The score on that question will make a contribution to the overall mean of customer satisfaction. Research and literature show a relationship between customer satisfaction and retaining a customer.)

- *Storage of firearms.* The Office of Workers' Compensation Program (OWCP) specialist (internal expert) explained that the cost for an employee injury could vary. Employees are maintained on the local payroll for two weeks. Then, OWCP pays the employee and bills the cost back to the medical center. The amount paid is 75 percent of the salary (if the person claims dependents) and 66.7 percent (if no dependents). Estimates of the cost of one minor employee accident are as follows:

    3 days of salary at the average rate for that occupation = 32 hours × $20.15 = $644.79.

If the injury were an open gunshot wound to the foot, then including adjustments for geographic factors, an emergency room visit would cost $1,361.92. If the employee had to be admitted for one day, the cost (without salary) would be $2,286.63.

The following equation shows the total cost for medical fees plus lost opportunity cost for salary time away from the job:

$$\$644.79 + \$1,361.92 = \$2,006.71$$

Intangible Benefits

As part of the findings of the ROI study, a number of results were reported that were not used to convert to a monetary value for an ROI calculation. Although not converted to a monetary value, these results are important and help describe the value and benefits of the program. What follows is a description of these intangible benefits:
- generation of ideas
- employee satisfaction—employees wanted to go to the program and felt they were valued
- employee sense of contribution to the medical center—the employees felt they were making a valuable contribution by participating in comparing instructional methodologies
- improved self-mastery for and awareness of the HPDM—employees were actually involved in the essence of the learning content.

ROI Calculation

Following is the program cost for the Learning Map group:

Salaries (participants) = $2415.66
Instructor for 3 sessions x 3 hours + 1 hour prep + 1.5 hours setup and admin = 11.5 hours
@ 26.22 = $301.53. Total salaries = $2,717.19. Copies of handouts = $20.
Total cost = $2,727.19.

Following is the program cost for the comparison group:

Salaries (participants) = $3,818.35
Instructor for 3 sessions $\times$ 3 hours + 6 hours prep + 1.5 hours setup = 16.5 hours @ $26.22 =
$4,250.98. Copies of handouts = $20.00.
Total cost = $4,270.98.

The benefits-to-cost ratio is calculated by dividing the total benefits ($2,819.37) by total costs ($2,737.19) as follows:

$$\$2,819.37 / \$2,737.19 = 1.03$$

The ROI calculation is as follows:

$$ROI = 2,819.19 - 2,737.19 / 2,737.19 = 3\%$$

Communication of the Results

Marcial presented the ROI to Doherty. The calculations were extremely conservative and were presented as a worst case scenario. There were no exaggerations. She used a common-sense approach to do the calculations that made sense to him. As he puts it, "Don't try to sell me any swamp land!" He was willing to rely on the internal experts who supplied the data to her. This saved him the trouble of wondering if her data was credible. It came from his trusted sources. She had set up the best possible situation for herself. But a 3 percent ROI?

Marcial had hoped for a 25 percent ROI at minimum and was disappointed. Doherty was pleased. His expectations were very realistic. Because this was a mandated topic, he had not considered the cost or the benefits of the training. He viewed it as an expected expense. To him, attempting to calculate the cost of mandatory training was valuable. His comment on the 3 percent ROI was, "You did better than break even on a mandatory! Marcial anticipated a loss. Just making the staff happy to go to mandated training is important."

The use of the Learning Map does not appear to be an economical delivery method at first. It now seems evident that its use is worth the time invested and that it has the potential to bring about significant ROIs. An added value is that most medical center directors have heard that employees enjoy Learning Map sessions but now had evidence that they were cost-effective. Directors may now realize they can allow, and even encourage, staff to participate in these sessions and generate improvement ideas.

Doherty presented his own report to his management staff and this information has been provided to the Employee Education System.

Lessons Learned

This type of ROI study was not a common experience in this organization. Since this was the first time this type of study was implemented, much was learned. These lessons learned can help improve the implementation of ROI studies within the organization in the future and can help others in any organization who desire to perform this type of study. What follows is a short description of key lessons learned.

- You can get Level 4 data when Level 3 measures aren't perfect.
- There are always fires or floods or other things that get in the way.

- You can attach higher level evaluation measures to an existing product.
- Employees were pleased to know we were doing a ROI study. They want to know the clear expectations of courses and the impact the courses will have on their jobs and the organization.
- Employees liked the follow-up. They said it reinforced the information and held them accountable.
- It is important to put the ROI results in perspective. Sometimes just breaking even is important. It can lead to better things down the road.
- Use the data of internal experts, whenever possible, even if you think there are better measures.

Questions for Discussion

1. Was it valid to use the argument from the firearm suggestion of prevention of an accident as a potential benefit for the ROI calculation?
2. Should an acceptable ROI be determined? If so, by whom?
3. Was a bias created when groups were told they were participating in a study?
4. Could the methodology for the case be repeated throughout the organization on another Learning Map?
5. What can you do when a crisis destroys your data collection plans?
6. What would you have done differently in this study?

The Authors

Eileen Marcial is the education coordinator at the VA Medical Center in Miami. She began her VA career as a registered respiratory therapist. She became chief of respiratory therapy and earned a B.A in health-care administration from Florida International University. She made the transition from her clinical background and worked for five years as an employee development specialist earning an M.B.A. from the University of Miami. Interested in training and its impact on human resource development, she has been in her present position for 10 years. She is currently defending her dissertation toward her Ed.D. in adult education and human resource development at Florida International University. She is certified in the PRO/FC ROI process. She can be reached at Veterans Affairs Medical Center, 1201 NW 16th Street, Miami, FL 33125; phone: 305.324.4455; email: eileen.marcial@med.va.gov.

Timothy W. Bothell, director of the impact analysis team at Franklin Covey's Center for Research and Assessment, provides consulting services for *Fortune* 500 companies and facilitates measurement workshops at conferences and at public and private locations. Bothell is the co-developer of the Franklin Covey Impact Analysis System.

His expertise in measurement and evaluation is based in more than seven years of experience with educational institutions and three years' experience with corporate clients. Bothell has served as a university instructor prior to working at Franklin Covey. His most recent publication is "Measuring the Impact of Learning and Performance," in *Measuring Learning and Performance,* edited by Jack Phillips. Bothell is currently co-authoring a book about measuring the ROI of project management training with Jack Phillips and Lynne Snead. Bothell has an undergraduate degree in psychology, a master's degree in technology education, and a Ph.D. in instructional psychology from Brigham Young University.

Reference

McMurrer, Daniel P., Mark E. Van Buren, and William H. Woodwell. (2000). *The 2000 ASTD State of the Industry Report.* Alexandria, VA: ASTD.

Measuring Return on Investment on Interactive Selling Skills

Retail Merchandise Company

Patricia Pulliam Phillips and Jack J. Phillips

The case study represents a classic application of the return-on-investment (ROI) process. An interactive selling skills program drives sales increases at a pilot group of retail stores. A control group arrangement isolates the effects of the program. The organization uses the results to make critical decisions.

Background Information
Situation

Retail Merchandise Company (RMC) is a large national chain of 420 stores, located in most major U.S. markets. RMC sells small household items, gifts of all types, electronics, and jewelry as well as personal accessories. It does not sell clothes or major appliances. The executives at RMC were concerned about the slow sales growth and were experimenting with several programs to boost sales. One of their concerns focused on the interaction with customers. Sales associates were not actively involved in the sales process, usually waiting for a customer to make a purchasing decision and then proceeding with processing the sale. Several store managers had analyzed the situation to determine if more communication with the customer would boost sales. The analysis revealed that very simple techniques to probe and guide the customer to a purchase should boost sales in each store.

The senior executives asked the training and development staff to experiment with a simple customer interactive skills program for a small group of sales associates. The training staff would prefer a

This case was prepared to serve as a basis for discussion rather than to illustrate either effective or ineffective administrative and management practices. All names, dates, places, and organizations have been disguised at the request of the authors or organization.

program produced by an external supplier to avoid the cost of development, particularly if the program is not effective. The specific charge from the management team was to implement the program in three stores, monitor the results, and make recommendations.

The sales associates are typical of the retail store employee profile. They are usually not college graduates, and most have a few months, or even years, of retail store experience. Turnover was usually quite high, and formal training has not been a major part of previous sales development efforts.

The Solution

The training and development staff conducted a brief initial needs assessment and identified five simple skills that the program should cover. From the staff's analysis, it appeared that the sales associates did not have these skills or were very uncomfortable with the use of these skills. The training and development staff selected the Interactive Selling Skills program, which makes significant use of skill practices. The program, an existing product from an external training supplier, includes two days of training in which participants have an opportunity to practice each of the skills with a classmate followed by three weeks of on-the-job application. Then, in a final day of training, there is discussion of problems, issues, barriers, and concerns about using the skills. Additional practice and fine-tuning of skills take place in that final one-day session. At RMC, this program was tried in the electronics area of three stores, with 16 people trained in each store. The staff of the training supplier facilitated the program for a predetermined facilitation fee.

The Measurement Challenge

The direction from senior management was very clear: These executives wanted to boost sales and at the same time determine if this program represented a financial payoff, realizing that many of the strategies could be implemented to boost sales. Business impact and ROI were the measurement mandates from the senior team.

In seeking a process to show ROI, the training and development staff turned to a process that Jack Phillips developed. The ROI process generates six types of measures:
- reaction, satisfaction, and planned action
- learning
- application and implementation
- business impact

- ROI
- intangible measures.

It also includes a technique to isolate the effects of the program or solution.

This process involves extensive data collection and analysis. As figure 1 shows, the process includes steps to develop the ROI, beginning with evaluation planning. Four types of data are collected, representing the four levels of evaluation. The analysis develops a fifth level of data as well as the intangible benefits. The process includes a method to isolate the effects of the program and a method to convert data to monetary value. The fully loaded costs are used to develop the actual ROI. This process was already in place at RMC, and training and development selected it as the method to measure the success of this program.

Planning for the ROI

An important part of the success of the ROI evaluation is to properly plan for the impact study early in the training and development cycle. Appropriate up-front attention saves time later when data are actually collected and analyzed, thus improving the accuracy and reducing the cost of the evaluation. This approach also avoids any confusion surrounding what will be accomplished, by whom, and at what time. Two planning documents are key to the up-front planning, and the training staff completed them before the program was implemented.

Following are descriptions of each document.

Data Collection Plan

Figure 2 shows the completed data collection plan for this program. The document provides a space for major elements and issues regarding collecting data for the different levels of evaluation. Broad program objectives are appropriate for planning, as the figure shows.

The objective at Level 1 for this program was a positive reaction to the potential use of the skills on the job. The gauge for this level was a reaction questionnaire that participants completed at the end of the program and facilitators collected. The goal was to achieve four out of five on a composite rating. Also, the questionnaire asked participants to indicate how often and in which situations they would actually use the skills.

The measurement of learning focused on learning how to use five simple skills. The measure of success was a pass or fail on the skill practice that the facilitator observed and for which the observer collected data on the second day of the program.

Figure 1. The ROI process model.

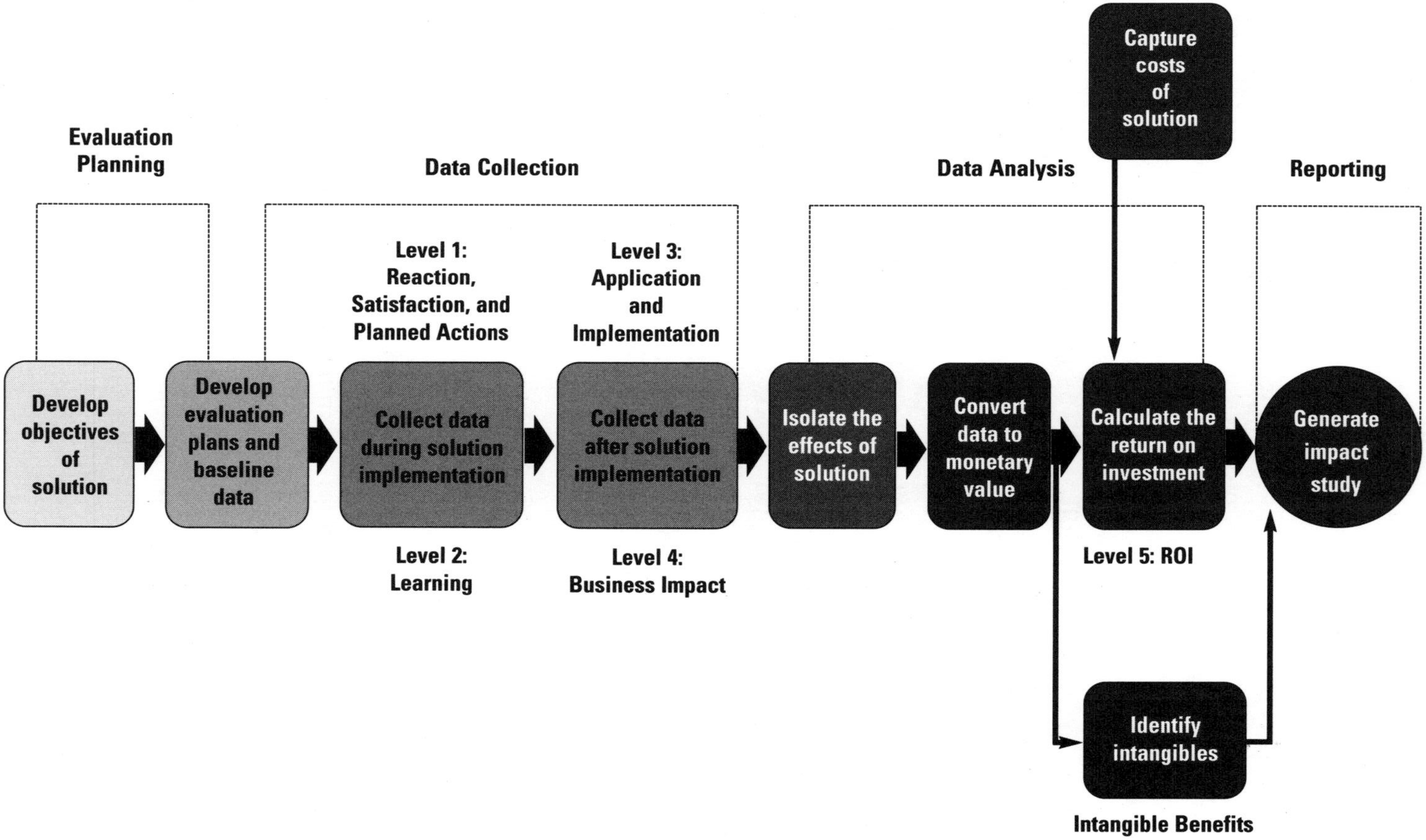

Figure 2. Data collection plan.

Program: _____ Responsibility: _____ Date: _____

Level	Broad Program Objectives	Measures	Data Collection Method and Instruments	Data Sources	Timing	Responsibilities
1	**Reaction and Satisfaction and Planned Actions** • Positive reaction—four out of five • Action items	• Rating on a composite of five measures • Yes or No	• Questionnaire	• Participant	• End of program (Third day)	• Facilitator
2	**Learning** • Learn to use five simple skills	• Pass or Fail on skill practice	• Observation of skill practice by facilitator	• Facilitator	• Second day of program	• Facilitator
3	**Application and Implementation** • Initial use of five simple skills • At least 50% of participants use all skills with every customer	• Verbal feedback • 5th item checked on a 1 to 5 scale	• Follow-up session • Follow-up questionnaire	• Participant • Participant	• Three weeks after second day • Three months after program	• Facilitator • Store training coordinator
4	**Business Impact** • Increase in sales	• Weekly average sales per sales associate	• Business performance monitoring	• Company records	• Three months after program	• Store training coordinator
5	**ROI** • 50%					

Comments:

For application and implementation evaluation, the objectives focused on two major areas. The first was the initial use of the five simple skills. Success was determined from verbal feedback that the facilitator obtained directly from participants in a follow-up session on the third day of training. The second major objective was for at least 50 percent of the participants to be using all of the skills with every customer. This information was obtained on the follow-up questionnaire, scheduled three months after completion of the program, at which the participants rated the frequency of utilization of the skills.

Business impact focused just on increase in sales. The average weekly sales per sales associate was monitored from company records in a three-month follow-up. Finally, a 50 percent ROI target was set, which was much higher than the standard for many other ROI evaluations. Senior executives wanted a significant improvement over the cost of the program to make a decision to move forward with a wide-scale implementation.

The data collection plan was an important part of the evaluation strategy. It provided clear direction on the type of data that would be collected, how it would be collected, when it would be collected, and who would collect it.

Isolating the Effects of the Program

One of the most important parts of this evaluation is isolating the effects of the training program. This is a critical issue in the planning stage. The key question is, "When sales data is collected three months after the program is implemented, how much of the increase in sales, if any, is directly related to the program?" While the improvement in sales may be linked to the training program, other nontraining factors contribute to improvement. The cause-and-effect relationship between training and performance improvement can be very confusing and difficult to prove, but it can be accomplished with an acceptable degree of accuracy. In the planning process the challenge is to develop one or more specific strategies to isolate the effects of training and include it on the ROI analysis plan.

In this case study, the issue was relatively easy to address. Senior executives gave the training and development staff the freedom to select any stores for implementation of the pilot program. The performance of the three stores selected for the program was compared with the performance of three other stores that are identical in every way possible. This approach, control group analysis, represents the most accurate way to isolate the effects of a program. Fortunately, other strategies from the list of 10 approaches in the ROI process, such as trend-line analysis and estimation, would also be feasible. Control group analysis, the best method, was selected given that the situation was appropriate.

The challenge in the control group arrangement is to appropriately select both sets of stores. The control group of three stores does not have the training, whereas the pilot group does. It was important for those stores to be as identical as possible, so the training and development staff developed several criteria that could influence sales. This list became quite extensive and included market data, store level data, management and leadership data, and individual differences. In a conference call with regional managers, this list was pared down to the four most likely influences. The executives selected those influences that would count for at least 80 percent of the differences in weekly store sales per associate. These criteria were as follows:

- *store size,* with the larger stores commanding a higher performance level
- *store location,* using a market variable of median household income in the area where customers live
- *customer traffic levels,* which measures the flow of traffic through the store; this measure, originally developed for security purposes, provides an excellent indication of customer flow through the store
- *previous store performance,* a good predictor of future performance; the training and development staff collected six months of data for weekly sales per associate to identify the two groups.

These four measures were used to select three stores for the pilot program and match them with three other stores. As a fallback position, in case the control group arrangement did not work, participant estimates were planned. In this approach, the individuals would be provided with their performance data and would be asked to indicate the extent to which the training program influenced their contribution. This data, which is an estimate, would be adjusted for the error of the estimate and used in the analysis.

ROI Analysis Plan

Table 1 shows the completed ROI analysis plan, which captures information on several key items necessary to develop the actual ROI calculation. The first column lists the business impact measure. This is in connection with the previous planning document, the data collection plan. The ROI analysis builds from the business impact data by addressing several issues involved in processing the data. The first issue is the method of isolating the effects of the program on that particular business impact measure. The third column focuses on the methods to convert data to monetary value. In this case, sales data would have to be converted to value-added data by adjusting it to the actual profit margin at the store level.

The next column focuses on the key cost categories that would be included in the fully loaded cost profile. Next are the potential intangible benefits, followed by the communication targets. It is important for several groups to receive the information from the impact study. Finally, the last column lists any particular influences or issues that might have an effect on the implementation. The training staff identified three issues, with two being very critical to the evaluation. No communication was planned with the control group so there would not be potential for contamination from the pilot group. Also, because the seasonal fluctuation could affect the control group arrangement, this evaluation was positioned between Father's Day and the winter holiday season, thus taking away huge surges in volume.

The data collection plan together with the ROI analysis plan provided detailed information on calculating the ROI and illustrating how the process will develop and be analyzed. When completed, these two planning documents provide the direction necessary for the ROI evaluation.

Results
Reaction and Learning

The first two levels of evaluation, reaction and learning, were simple and straightforward. The training staff collected five measures of reaction to determine if the objectives had been met. The overall objective was to obtain at least four out of five on a composite of these five measures. As table 2 illustrates, the overall objective was met. Of the specific measures, the relevance of the material and the usefulness of the program were considered to be the two most important measures. In addition, 90 percent of the participants had action items indicating when and how often they would use these skills. Collectively, this Level 1 data gave assurance that sales associates had a very favorable reaction to the program.

The measurement of learning was accomplished with simple skill practice sessions observed by the facilitator. Each associate practiced each of the five skills, and the facilitator inserted a check mark on the questionnaire when the associate successfully practiced. While subjective, it was felt that this approach provided enough evidence that the participants had actually learned these basic skills.

Table 1. ROI analysis plan.

Data Items	Methods of Isolating the Effects of the Program	Methods of Converting Data	Cost Categories	Intangible Benefits	Communication Targets	Other Influences and Issues
Weekly sales per associate	Control group analysis Participant estimate	Direct conversion using profit contribution	Facilitation fees Program materials Meals and refreshments Facilities Participant salaries and benefits Cost of coordination and evaluation	Customer satisfaction Employee satisfaction	Program participants Electronics Department managers at targeted stores Store managers at targeted stores Senior store executives district, region, headquarters Training staff: instructors, coordinators, designers, and managers	Must have job coverage during training No communication with control group Seasonal fluctuations should be avoided

Table 2. Level 1 reaction data on selected data.

Success with objectives	4.3
Relevance of material	4.4
Usefulness of program	4.5
Exercises and skill practices	3.9
Overall instructor rating	4.1
Composite	4.2

Application and Implementation

To measure application and implementation, the training and development staff administered a follow-up questionnaire three months after the end of the program. The questionnaire was comprehensive, spanning 20 questions on three pages, and was collected anonymously to reduce the potential for bias from participants. The questionnaire covered the following topics:

- action plan implementation
- relevance of the program
- use of skills
- changes in work routine
- linkage with department measures
- other benefits
- barriers
- enablers
- management support
- suggestions for improvement
- other comments.

While all of the information was helpful, the information on the use of skills was most critical. Table 3 shows the results from two of the 20 questions on the questionnaire. The first one provides some assurance that the participants are using the skills, as 78 percent strongly agree that they utilize the skills of the program. More important, the next question focused directly on one of the goals of the program. Fifty-two percent indicated that they use the skills with each customer, slightly exceeding the goal of 50 percent.

Because these are simple skills, with the opportunity to use them every day, this three-month follow-up provides some assurance that the associates have internalized the skills. The follow-up session three weeks after the first two days of training provided the first, early indication

Table 3. Level 3 selected application data on two of 20 questions.

	Strongly Agree	Agree	Neither Agree nor Disagree	Disagree	Strongly Disagree
I utilize the skills taught in the program.	78%	22%	0%	0%	0%

	With Each Customer	Every Third Customer	Several Times Each Day	At Least Once Daily	At Least Once Weekly
Frequency of use of skills.	52%	26%	19%	4%	0%

of skill transfer to the job. If the skills are still being used three months after training, it is safe to conclude that the majority of the participants have internalized them.

While many other data collection methods could have been used, it is important to understand the rationale for using the questionnaire. The most accurate, and expensive, method would be observation of the participants on the job by a third party. In that scenario, the "mystery shoppers" must learn the skills and be allowed to rate each of the 48 participants. This approach would provide concrete evidence that the participants had transferred the skills. This approach would be expensive, and it is not necessary under the circumstances. Because the management team is more interested in business impact and ROI, it has less interest in the lower levels of evaluation. Although some data should be collected to have assurance that the skills have transferred, the process does not have to be so comprehensive. This is a resource-saving issue and is consistent with the following guiding principles for the ROI process:

1. When a higher level evaluation is conducted, data must be collected at lower levels.
2. When an evaluation is planned for a higher level, the previous level of evaluation does not have to be comprehensive.
3. When collecting and analyzing data, use only the most credible sources.
4. When analyzing data, choose the most conservative among alternatives.
5. At least one method must be used to isolate the effects of the project or initiative.

6. If no improvement data are available for a population or from a specific source, it is assumed that little or no improvement has occurred.

7. Estimates of improvement should be adjusted for the potential error of the estimate.

8. Extreme data items and unsupported claims should not be used in ROI calculations.

9. Only the first year of benefits (annual) should be used in the ROI analysis of short-term projects or initiatives.

10. Project or program costs should be fully loaded for ROI analysis.

These are macrolevel principles with a conservative approach for collecting and processing data. Guiding principle number two comes into play with this issue. When an evaluation is under way at a higher level than the previous level of evaluation, the earlier evaluation did not have to be comprehensive. This does not mean that Level 3 data cannot be collected or that it should not be collected. With limited resources, shortcuts must be developed and this principle allows us to use a less expensive approach. If the management team had asked for more evidence of customer interaction or wanted to know the quality and thoroughness of the actual exchange of information, then a more comprehensive Level 3 evaluation would be required and perhaps the evaluation would have even stopped at Level 3.

Business Impact

Weekly sales data were collected for three months after the program for both groups. Table 4 shows the data for the first three weeks after training, along with the last three weeks during the evaluation period. An average for the last three weeks is more appropriate than data for a single week because that could have a spike effect that could affect the results. As the data shows, there is a significant difference between the two groups, indicating that the training program is improving sales. The percent increase, directly attributable to the sales training, is approximately 15 percent. If only a business impact evaluation is needed, this data would provide the information needed to show that the program has improved sales. However, if the ROI is needed, two more steps are necessary.

Converting Data to a Monetary Value

To convert the business data to a monetary value, the training and development staff had to address several issues. First, it is necessary to convert the actual sales differences to a value-added data—in this

Table 4. Level 4 data on average weekly sales.

Weeks After Training	Trained Groups ($)	Control Groups ($)
1	9,723	9,698
2	9,978	9,720
3	10,424	9,812
13	13,690	11,572
14	11,491	9,683
15	11,044	10,092
Average for Weeks 13, 14, 15	$12,075	$10,449

case, profits. The store level profit margin of 2 percent is multiplied by the difference or increase in sales. Table 5 shows the calculation, as the weekly sales per associate of $1,626 become a value-added amount of $32.50. Because 46 participants were still on the job in three months, the value-added amount gets multiplied by 46, for a weekly total of $1,495.

Mention of 46 participants brings another guiding principle—number six—into focus. That principle says, "If no improvement data are available for a population or from a specific source, it is assumed that little or no improvement has occurred." This is a conservative approach because the missing data is assumed to have no value. Two of the participants are no longer on the job and instead of tracking what happened to them, this rule is used to exclude any contribution from that group of two. However, the cost to train them would be included, although their values are not included for contribution.

Table 5. Annualized program benefits for 46 participants.

Average weekly sales per employee trained groups	$12,075
Average weekly sales per employee untrained groups	10,449
Increase	1,626
Profit contribution (2% of store sales)	32.50
Total weekly improvement (× 46)	1,495
Total annual benefits (× 48 weeks)	**$71,760**

Finally, annual benefits are used to develop a total benefit for the program. The ROI concept is an annual value, and only the first-year benefits are used for short-term training programs. This is guiding principle number nine. Although this approach may slightly overstate the benefits for the first year, it is considered conservative because it does not capture any improvements or benefits in the second, third, or future years. This operating standard is also conservative and thus is a guiding principle. In summary, the total annualized program benefit of $71,760 is developed in a very conservative way using the guiding principles.

Program Cost

The program costs, shown in table 6, are fully loaded and represent all the major categories outlined earlier. This is a conservative approach, as described in guiding principle number 10. In this case, the costs for the development are included in the facilitation fee since the external supplier produced the program. The cost of the participants' time away from the job is the largest of the cost items and can be included, or the lost opportunity can be included, but not both. To be consistent, this is usually developed as the total time away from work (three days) is multiplied by the daily compensation rate including a 35 percent benefits factor. Finally, the estimated cost for the evaluation and the coordination of data collection is included. Since the company had an internal evaluation staff certified in the ROI process, the overall cost for this project was quite low and represents direct time involved in developing the impact study. The total fully loaded cost for the program was $32,984.

ROI Calculation

Two ROI calculations are possible with use of the total monetary benefits and total cost of the program. The first is the benefit-cost ratio (BCR), which is the ratio of the monetary benefits divided by the costs:

$$BCR = \frac{\$71,760}{\$32,984} = 2.18$$

In essence, this suggests that for every dollar invested, 2.18 dollars are returned. When using the actual ROI formula, this value becomes:

$$ROI\,(\%) = \frac{\$71,760 - \$32,984}{\$32,984} \times 100 = 118\%$$

Table 6. Cost summary for 48 participants in three courses.

Item	Cost ($)
Facilitation fees, three courses @ $3,750	11,250
Program materials, 48 @ $35 per participant	1,680
Meals and refreshments, three days @ $28 per participant	4,032
Facilities, nine days @ $120	1,080
Participants' salaries plus benefits (35% factor)	12,442
Coordination and evaluation	2,500
Total Costs	**32,984**

This ROI calculation is interpreted as follows: For every dollar invested, a dollar is returned and another $1.18 is generated. The ROI formula is consistent with ROI for other types of investment. It is essentially earnings divided by investment. In this case, the ROI exceeds the 50 percent target.

Intangibles

This program generated significant intangible benefits:
- increased job satisfaction
- improved teamwork
- increased confidence
- improved customer service
- improved image with customers
- greater involvement.

Conclusions and Actions
Communication of Results

It was important to communicate the results of this evaluation to the senior executives who requested a program, to the sales associates who were part of it, and to other personnel who were affected by it. First, the senior executives need the information to make a decision. In a face-to-face meeting, lasting approximately one hour, the training and development staff presented all six types of data with the recommendation that the program be implemented throughout the store chain. An executive summary and PowerPoint slides were distributed.

The participants received a two-page summary of the data, showing the results of the questionnaire and the business impact and ROI achieved from the process. There was some debate about whether to include the ROI in the summary, but eventually it was included in an attempt to share more information with the participants.

The electronics department managers, the participants' managers, received the executive summary of the information and participated in a conference call with the training and development staff. This group needed to see the benefits of training since they had to alter and rearrange schedules to cover the jobs while the participants were in training.

Finally, the training staff received a detailed impact study (approximately 100 pages), which was used as a learning document to help them understand more about this type of evaluation. This document became the historical record about the data collection instruments and ROI analysis.

Action

As a result of the communication of the impact study, senior executives decided to implement the program throughout the store chain. For all six types of data, the results were very positive with a very high ROI, significantly exceeding the target. The implementation proceeded with the senior executives' request that the sales data for the three target stores be captured for the remainder of the year to see the actual one-year impact of the program. While the issue of taking one year of data, based on a three-month snapshot, appears to be conservative since the second- and third-year data are not used, this provided some assurance that the data does indeed hold up for the year. At the end of the year, the data actually exceeded the snapshot of performance in three months.

Lessons Learned

This evaluation provides some important insights into the ROI process. In the past, the store chain evaluated pilot programs primarily on Level 1 data (reactions from both the participants and their managers), coupled with the sales presentation from the vendor. The ROI approach provides much more data to indicate the success of training. In essence, companies can use Level 4 and 5 data for making a funding decision instead of making a funding decision on the basis of reaction data, Level 1.

From a statistical significance viewpoint, the small sample size does not allow for making an inference about the other stores at a 95 percent confidence. In essence, due to the small sample size it is impossible to say that the other stores would have the same results as the three in question. A sample size of 200 stores would be needed for statistical soundness. However, the economics of the evaluation and the practicality of the pilot implementation drove the sample size in this case, and in most other cases. No group of senior executives would suggest a sample size of 200 stores to see if the program should be implemented in the other 417 stores. It is important to note in the results that statistical inference cannot be made, but it is also important to remember two points:

- The six types of data represent much more data than previously used to evaluate these types of programs.
- Second, most managers do not make other funding decisions based on data that has been collected, analyzed, and reported at a 95 percent confidence level.

Finally, another lesson was learned about this application of the ROI process. This is a very simple case allowing for a control group arrangement. Many other situations are not this simple, and other methods of isolation have to be undertaken. Other studies, while feasible, are more complex and will require more resources.

Questions for Discussion

1. Are the data and results credible? Explain.
2. How should the results be communicated?
3. With such a small sample, how can the issue of statistical significance be addressed?
4. The use of a control group arrangement is not possible in many situations. How can other potential approaches be utilized? Explain.
5. Would you implement this program in the other 417 stores? Explain.

The Authors

Patricia Pulliam Phillips is chairman and CEO of the Chelsea Group, an international consulting company focused on the implementation of the ROI process. She has provided consulting services and support for the ROI process for several years and has served as co-author on the topic in several publications. She can be reached at thechelseagroup@aol.com.

Jack J. Phillips is with the Jack Phillips Center for Research, a division of the Franklin Covey Company. He developed and pioneered the utilization of the ROI process and has provided consulting services to some of the world's largest organizations. He has written over 10 books on the subject.

About the Editor

Patricia Pulliam Phillips is chairman and CEO of the Chelsea Group, a consulting and research company focused on accountability issues in training, HR, and performance improvement. Formerly vice president of business development with Performance Resources Organization, she was responsible for the development of international and domestic strategic alliances, client relations, and sales and marketing initiatives. She was also director of ROI certification and served as executive director of the ROI Network. In her new capacity, Phillips conducts research on accountability issues and works with clients to build accountability systems and processes in their organizations. She works closely with the ROI certification process and helps to promote accountability practices through publications. Through her organization, Pulliam manages the ASTD *In Action* series and the Gulf Publishing *Improving Human Performance* series, and she works to launch new publications with authors and publishers around the globe.

Pulliam has over 13 years' experience in the electrical utility industry. As manager of market planning and research, she was responsible for the development of marketing programs for residential, commercial, and industrial customers. These programs included such initiatives as the residential load control program, the energy services program, and the district sales initiative. In her capacity as manager of market planning and research, she also played an integral role in establishing Marketing University, a learning environment that supported the needs of new sales and marketing representatives.

As manager in the Corporate Services organization, Phillips initiated and implemented the operation evaluation process. This evaluation process included the development and analysis of surveys, interviews with line management and employees, and participation in line operation activities. The results of this evaluation process served as a planning tool for establishing purchasing procedures for line equipment and tools, an internal process-planning tool to support line operations, and a model for future operation evaluation initiatives. She was also responsible for the development and analysis of customer and employee surveys.

Phillips has an M.A. degree in public and private management from Birmingham-Southern College. She is certified in ROI evaluation and serves as co-author on the subject in publications including *Corporate University Review, The Journal of Lending and Credit Risk Management, Training Journal,* and *Evaluating Training Programs,* 2d edition, by Donald L. Kirkpatrick (San Francisco: Berrett-Koehler Publishers, 1998). She is contributing author to *HRD Trends Worldwide,* by Jack J. Phillips (Houston: Gulf Publishing, 1999). She has authored and co-authored several issues of the ASTD *Info-line* series including *Mastering ROI* (1998), *ROI on a Shoestring* (2001), and *Planning Evaluation* (2001). She served as issue editor for the ASTD *In Action* casebook *Measuring Return on Investment,* volume 3. Phillips is also co-author of *The Human Resources Scorecard: Measuring Return on Investment* (Woburn, MA: Butterworth-Heinemann, 2001).

Phillips can be reached at The Chelsea Group, 350 Crossbrook Drive, Chelsea, AL 35043; phone: 205.678.0176; fax: 205.678.0177; email: thechelseagroup@aol.com.

About the Series Editor

J ack J. Phillips is a world-renowned expert on measurement and evaluation and developer of the ROI process, a revolutionary process that provides bottom-line figures and accountability for all types of training, performance improvement, human resources, and technology programs.

He is the author or editor of more than 20 books—eight focused on measurement and evaluation—and more than 100 articles.

His expertise in measurement and evaluation is based on more than 27 years of corporate experience in five industries (aerospace, textiles, metals, construction materials, and banking). Phillips has served as training and development manager at two *Fortune* 500 firms, senior HR officer at two firms, president of a regional federal savings bank, and management professor at a major state university.

In 1992, Phillips founded Performance Resources Organization (PRO), an international consulting firm that provides comprehensive assessment, measurement, and evaluation services for organizations. In 1999, the Franklin Covey Company purchased PRO, and it is now known as the Jack Phillips Center for Research. Today it is an independent, leading provider of measurement and evaluation services to the global business community. Phillips consults with clients in manufacturing, service, and government organizations in the United States, Canada, Sweden, England, Belgium, Germany, Italy, Holland, South Africa, Mexico, Venezuela, Malaysia, Indonesia, Hong Kong, Australia, New Zealand, and Singapore. He leads the Phillips Center in research and publishing efforts that support the knowledge and development of assessment, measurement, and evaluation.

Phillips's most recent books include *The Human Resources Scorecard: Measuring the Return on Investment* (Houston: Gulf Publishing, 2001); *The Consultant's Scorecard* (New York: McGraw-Hill, 2000); *HRD Trends Worldwide: Shared Solutions to Compete in a Global Economy* (Houston: Gulf Publishing, 1999); *Return on Investment in Training and Performance Improvement Programs* (Houston: Gulf Publishing, 1997);

Handbook of Training Evaluation and Measurement Methods, 3d edition (Houston: Gulf Publishing, 1997); and *Accountability in Human Resource Management,* (Houston, Gulf Publishing, 1996).

Phillips has undergraduate degrees in electrical engineering, physics, and mathematics from Southern Polytechnic State University and Oglethorpe University, a master's degree in decision sciences from Georgia State University, and a Ph.D. in human resource management from the University of Alabama. In 1987 he won the Yoder-Heneman Personnel Creative Application Award from the Society for Human Resource Management.

Phillips can be reached at The Jack Phillips Center for Research, P.O. Box 380637, Birmingham, AL 35238-0637; phone: 205.678.8038; fax: 205.678.0177; email: serieseditor@aol.com.